but it is you

Can

Pat

CARDINAL WISEMAN

CARDINAL WISEMAN

CARDINAL WISEMAN

BY

DENIS GWYNN

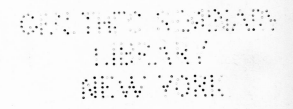

LONDON

BURNS OATES & WASHBOURNE LTD.

PUBLISHERS TO THE HOLY SEE

1929

MADE AND PRINTED IN GREAT BRITAIN

CONTENTS

LIST OF ILLUSTRATIONS

INTRODUCTION

D R. NICHOLAS WISEMAN was in his thirty-eighth year when he left the Rectorship of the English College in Rome in 1840 and returned to England, having been appointed President of Oscott College, and having been consecrated titular Bishop of Melipotamus as coadjutor to the Vicar Apostolic of the Midland District. Ten years later, having been the principal Catholic agent in encouraging the Oxford converts, he was appointed Cardinal Archbishop of Westminster, as the head of the restored English Hierarchy, when the Catholic population of England had been enormously increased by the influx of Irish Catholic immigrants after three years of famine in Ireland. He was himself mainly responsible for the restoration of the Hierarchy ; and the subsequent fusion of the various component factors of the Catholic Church in England—the small old Catholic remnant ; the new converts ; and the immense number of poor Irish Catholic immigrants— was already in process of completion, under his inspiring and vigorous leadership, when he died in February, 1865.

But his life's work, and even his name, was little more than a memory when his successor Cardinal Manning died in 1892, after ruling over the English Hierarchy for twenty-seven years. And when Edmund Purcell, with a reckless conviction of the necessity of making known the whole truth, published his famous biography of Cardinal Manning in 1896, no attempt at a Life of Cardinal Wiseman had yet been made. ' Who and what was Wiseman, it might not unfairly be asked in our generation ? ' wrote Purcell,[1] even so long ago as 1896. ' Wiseman, the story of whose eventful life has never been told ; whose name, since the day of his funeral, when England, it is not too much to say, followed him with sympathetic regret and admiration to the grave, had never been uttered in public, at least within Catholic hearing, until Cardinal Vaughan, on his accession to the See of Westminster, made glad the hearts of English Catholics, by paying a noble tribute—an act of justice— to the more illustrious of his two predecessors. *Magni nominis umbra* is all that Wiseman apparently is to the present generation. And yet which of the Oxford converts, with exception always of the illustrious John Henry Newman, can be compared with Wiseman for breadth of intellect ; for profound Biblical scholarship, for varied learning ; and for intimate knowledge of ecclesiastical history from the earliest period down to his own day ? If the universities of their own land were closed against them, English Catholics, laymen as well as ecclesiastics, few indeed in number as must needs be the case, frequented seats of learning in Rome, in France, in Germany, in Spain and Portugal ; Alban Butler, Bishop Challoner, and Dr. Milner, products of Saint-Omer

[1] Purcell, I, 659.

or Douai, were succeeded by Dr. Wiseman, who ampli-
fied their traditions and enlarged by his learning the
range of their intellectual vision. He had himself enjoyed
to the full all the advantages of higher education in Rome.
He was not only a learned theologian, but was everywhere
recognised as one of the foremost Oriental scholars of
his day.'

Thirty years had passed since Cardinal Wiseman's
death without any attempt to publish a full record of his
life's work, apart from the short biographical introduction to his *Essays on Various Subjects* which an Irish
priest in County Cork, Fr. Jeremiah Murphy, had com-
piled for publication in 1888. The omission had not,
however, been due to indifference to his memory on the
part of his successor at Westminster. Cardinal Manning
had been the most intimate confidant and ally of his later
years, had collected the materials for his Life, but had
postponed any decisive steps towards its publication,
in view of many acute controversies, until the Jesuit
Father Morris had undertaken it seriously in 1893,
immediately after Manning's death. But Father Morris
died soon after the work had been entrusted to him, and
Manning's successor, Cardinal Vaughan—who had himself in his own youth been one of the few intimates of
Wiseman's last years, when he was isolated by so many
unexpected controversies with his own old friends—
handed over all the available documents, as well as the
uncompleted work of Father Morris, to Wilfrid Ward, to
exercise his own discretion as to what should be published.

If Purcell had not scandalised all English Catholics,

and many besides, by his reckless publication of the entire intimate correspondence of Cardinal Manning, Wilfrid Ward's official biography, which was thus belatedly published in 1897, might well have been a more complete presentation of the story of his life. But Purcell's blatant indiscretion, in publishing every letter without regard to public scandal or to the feelings of Manning's colleagues who still survived, inevitably imposed upon Wilfrid Ward a degree of discretion which a biographer, writing a whole generation after the death of his subject, might reasonably have thought unnecessary. The result was a formal biography, incorporating an enormous amount of documents and correspondence which ought, by modern standards, to have been drastically abridged, and the avoidance of any balanced appreciation of the controversies which marked the first years of the English Hierarchy.

Over thirty years more have passed since the publication of Wilfrid Ward's official biography, and the modern reader of biographies may well be excused for regarding with dismay the two compact volumes, amounting to more than 1,200 pages—of which nearly half are printed in close small type—in which Ward, as an extremely able and exceptionally equipped biographer, saw fit to chronicle the life's work of one of the most vital and most distinguished of the great figures of the Victorian age. An immense number of letters are printed in full without the slightest abbreviation, or editing. And even long extracts from sermons and theological writings are reproduced *in extenso*, adding to the length required for Wilfrid Ward's own scholarly and illuminating dissertations upon various phases in the relations of the Papacy with the changing conditions of the nineteenth century. Wilfrid Ward's massive biography naturally remains the principal source to which modern students of Catholic history in England must turn for an account or appreciation of Wiseman's extraordinarily dramatic and influential life. And in the present attempt to retell that life in a form more adaptable to modern requirements, I desire to pay full tribute to the extent and thoroughness and the sound judgement of Ward's masterly use of the documents placed at his disposal.

Later investigations, however, have added to a surprising extent to the essential materials available concerning Wiseman's life. The scandal caused by the publication of Purcell's *Life of Manning* prevented Ward from making full use of the immense number of intimate letters it provided, even though almost every person engaged in Wiseman's own controversies was by that time already dead. But both Wilfrid Ward and Purcell were to add greatly, by other biographies which they wrote afterwards, to the materials available for a true appreciation of Wiseman. Their methods were very different, and Ward must have been horrified by the indiscreet publication of many letters contained in Purcell's *Life and Letters of Ambrose Phillips de Lisle*, which was published in 1900. It revealed for the first time, with Purcell's conscientious disregard of reticence in the use of confidential correspondence, the full story of Wiseman's efforts, as the young President of Oscott, to establish friendly relations with the Tractarians at Oxford. Wiseman's own part in those relations with Newman and his friends before their submission to Rome, was thus revealed to the full light of day ; and the documents dispose once and for all of any suggestion of unorthodox compromise on his part. They show most clearly what a compelling influence was exercised by Wiseman's intellectual powers upon the wavering minds of the Oxford leaders, when they were striving desperately to reconcile their own position as Anglicans with a conviction that Rome alone could claim unbroken Apostolic succession. And they prove conclusively that Wiseman did not at any time agree with de Lisle's notion that the Tractarians could do more for the conversion of England as Anglicans than by becoming Catholics individually ; even though de Lisle's son, in his preface[1] to the biography (which was completed after Purcell's death), was apparently still convinced that Wiseman shared with his father the belief that the best hope of converting England lay in trying to reconcile England to Catholicism by encouraging the High Church Party.

In his *Life of Ambrose Phillips de Lisle*, scarcely less than in his *Life of Manning*, Purcell has unquestionably left for posterity an indispensable record of Catholic history in England, which would never have been made known if he had exercised ordinary prudence and discretion in publishing confidential letters and documents. Manning does certainly stand revealed, by the letters which Purcell made public, as having been on various

[1] Phillips de Lisle, I, viii.

occasions a narrow and suspicious ecclesiastic who was certain to provoke quarrels ; even though Purcell's picture of him as an ambitious and unscrupulous wire-puller has been proved by subsequent revelations to be a gross caricature. Phillips de Lisle has been similarly exposed, by Purcell's indiscreet methods, as a zealous convert whose enthusiasm for the conversion of England led him, through lack of judgement, to urge wholly unorthodox policies. But a later generation, which is far enough removed from the period to review its controversies without heat and with sympathy, may well forgive Purcell such indiscretions in gratitude for the full materials that he made available. And although Wilfrid Ward, as a strictly unorthodox though very human biographer, was deterred from making full use of the materials provided by Purcell's recklessness, his own classic biography of Cardinal Newman, published in 1910, has also added very considerably to the picture of Cardinal Wiseman which he himself had published thirteen years earlier.

Not until after the Great War, however, were the most intimate letters of Cardinal Wiseman himself in regard to the bitter controversies which clouded the closing years of his life, made public for the first time. Purcell's biography of Manning, which claimed to be based upon his entire private correspondence, was in fact far from complete ; and Mr. Shane Leslie's biography, published in 1922, included a mass of important correspondence to which Purcell never had access. Still more revealing were the unpublished letters of Wiseman made public by the late Cardinal Gasquet in the *Dublin Review* of 1919 and 1921 ; and by Mr. Leslie when he was engaged upon the preparation of his *Life of Cardinal Manning*. But the most comprehensive and balanced account of the later controversies of Wiseman with the English bishops in the first years of the new Hierarchy, is to be found in a still more recent book, published in 1927. In his *Life of Bishop Ullathorne*, Abbot Butler, O.S.B., was able to include particularly a full statement of Archbishop Errington's case, in the conflict with Wiseman which resulted in his own dismissal from the position of coadjutor to the Archbishop of Westminster. For a full and impartial presentment of that famous controversy the modern student must be referred to Chapters 8, 9, and 10 of Volume I of Abbot Butler's book, which conveys for the first time a clear picture of the conflict of policies and of men, and does full justice both to Wiseman in his zeal for the conversion of England ; to the old Catholics in England who saw that Wiseman was assuming excessive powers and was antagonising English sentiment ; and to Rome, which decided between them with complete fairness, with inspiration, and with decisive authority. As a corrective particularly to the ludicrous and ill-informed caricature of Mr. Lytton Strachey's essay on Cardinal Manning, in his very popular *Eminent Victorians*, it is a conclusive and overwhelming answer conveyed without any deliberate effort to dispose of his flippant attacks.

The present account of Wiseman's life is intended as a biography for modern readers who cannot be expected to wade through the massive volumes of older biographies on the large scale, and as an attempt to describe the life of one of the most remarkable Churchmen of his time, who was incidentally one of the most picturesque and most vital figures in the earlier part of Queen Victoria's reign. It will be published when the Catholic Church in England is celebrating the centenary of the Catholic Emancipation Act ; and when the extraordinary progress made during the past hundred years has been brought vividly before the notice of Catholics. No popular biography of Cardinal Wiseman is available, yet no student of modern Catholic history can ignore his most remarkable life's work. The son of Irish parents who had settled in Spain as merchants to escape the penal laws, his early years were characteristic of the period, in that his family fled from the revolutionary wars on the Continent to find refuge, first in an Ireland where the penal laws had been abolished, and then in England, where the Continental schools had been forced, and permitted, to return. He left Ushaw as a schoolboy to join the group of young English seminarists who were to resuscitate the English College in Rome which had been sacked and suppressed during the Napoleonic wars. As a young priest he was appointed Rector of the English College, and he was soon inspired with enthusiasm by the general Catholic revival in Europe after the revolutionary period. He became the intimate friend of Lacordaire and Montalembert and Ozanam in France, of Döllinger and Moehler in Germany, of Daniel O'Connell in Ireland.

Through their enthusiasm he was inspired to devote his own life to the revival of Catholicism in England,

B

where the Catholics were only an insignificant and timid remnant, deprecating any attempt to undertake religious propaganda in a hostile country. His dreams of the conversion of England coincided with the Oxford Movement, and when he came in direct contact with its leaders he felt that his own mission in life was to encourage them in their efforts, and later, to find scope for their unbounded apostolic zeal, as members of a Catholic community which still regarded them with intense suspicion. The conversion of Newman, in which he himself played a very considerable part, and the subsequent influx of ' intellectual ' converts, coincided also with the sudden immigration of swarms of destitute refugees from the three years of famine in Ireland ; and the rapid expansion of the Catholic body in England made the restoration of the English Hierarchy an urgent necessity. Wiseman himself was the chief author of the new Hierarchy. He became its first head, as Cardinal Archbishop of Westminster ; and the remaining fifteen years of his life, in failing health and surrounded by hostile influences and by many misunderstandings, were spent in the consolidation of the three elements—old Catholics, converts, and Irish immigrants—which were, under his successor, the convert Cardinal Manning, whom he had welcomed so enthusiastically into the Catholic Church, to become a coherent and powerful body who have since become the most active and most vital religious denomination in England.

A fanatical ' No Popery ' outburst, such as had not been witnessed in England since the Lord George Gordon riots of 1780, greeted his return from Rome in 1850 as the first Cardinal Archbishop of Westminster ; though he had undertaken his journey believing, in his generous impulsive way, that he would be received with scenes of popular jubilation that would herald the return of England to the Catholic Church. His Roman training had left him incapable of understanding the antipathies even of English Catholics towards Rome and towards the claims of a Cardinal to exercise unchallenged jurisdiction among them. The closing years of his life were clouded by estrangements and recurrent appeals to Rome, which drove him to despondency when his health and his prodigious energy were tragically undermined by incurable disease. But within fifteen years of having been burned in effigy in almost every town in England on Guy Fawkes' Day, because of his jubilant pastoral letter announcing the restoration of the Hierarchy, he had won, by sheer personal goodness and attraction and by his great intellectual gifts, such a prestige among the English people that his funeral took place amid demonstrations of popular mourning such as had not been witnessed since the death of the Duke of Wellington. And, in his relation to the other outstanding Catholic leaders, in an age of great national figures, the last words have been said concerning him by Abbot Butler, the biographer of one of his most strenuous opponents on many questions, Bishop Ullathorne of Birmingham. ' From the restoration of the Hierarchy in 1850 until his death in 1865, the dominant figure among the English Catholics was Wiseman. After reading again and again, and maturely pondering over the materials collected for the Lives of the four great Churchmen, Wiseman, Manning, Newman, and Ullathorne,' writes[1] Abbot Butler, ' the impression finally and clearly graven on my mind is that, taken all in all, Wiseman stands out as the greatest. He was not the deep acute thinker that Newman was ; nor the masterful resourceful man of affairs that Manning was ; nor had he the sound practical grip of men and things that Ullathorne had ; but in the combination of a richly endowed nature, and attractive lovable personality, and well-balanced, all-round character, and many-sided intellectual attainments, and successful achievement of a great life-work—in short, as a complete man, he surpassed them all.'

[1] *Life of Ullathorne*, II, 299.

CARDINAL WISEMAN

CHAPTER I

THE END OF AN ERA (1802–25)

IT required the best part of a month for even the most urgent news to reach Rome from England a hundred years ago. And although the announcement that the Catholic Emancipation Act had been placed upon the English Statute Book in April 1829, was a matter that called for public celebrations in the Eternal City, the newly elected Pope Pius VIII did not receive any formal intimation of it until some weeks later. The news was brought to him by the young Rector of the English College in Rome, Dr. Nicholas Wiseman, who had been promoted to the rectorship in the previous year, being then twenty-six years of age.

A contemporary describes him[1] as having been at the time ' tall, slight, apparently long-necked, with features rather pointed and pale, and demeanour very grave.' He was dark, and somewhat foreign-looking, having been born in Seville, where his father was in business as a merchant, an exile from Ireland under the penal laws. He had been at school in England, and had come to Rome as one of a small group of young scholastics sent to revive the English College after its suppression during the

[1] Ward's *Life of Cardinal Wiseman*, I, 88.

Napoleonic wars. He was already famous in Rome as
a young scholar of extraordinary gifts and promise ;
and his boundless enthusiasm for all the traditions of
Papal Rome gave to him in this formal visit to the Pope,
as the bearer of such momentous news, a sense of taking
part in the making of history.

The election of the new Pope was not yet two months
old, and the announcement might well seem to the young
men who inhabited the English College, as one of the
epoch-making events of the new pontificate. But there
were very few English people in Rome at that time, and as
Wiseman himself wrote long afterwards, although to the
Pope, ' who was not only most intelligent but alive to all
that passed throughout Christendom, the full meaning
of this measure was, of course, apparent,'[1] the majority
of people in Rome had very little idea of what had happened. The English constitution was then, even more
than now, ' a puzzle to races accustomed to simple
monarchy for ages, and scarcely possessing experience
of anything between that and bare republicanism. To
tell them that Catholics in Great Britain were excluded
from seats in Parliament bore perhaps with many no more
sense of a hardship than to hear that they were not allowed
a place in the Turkish Divan.' Nevertheless, the English
College decided to celebrate the event in suitable fashion.
Dr. Wiseman, after receiving the fervent and paternal
congratulations of the new Pope, went with his Vice-
Rector to interview the Secretary of State, who expressed
similar gratification. And then they proceeded to celebrate in the Roman way. ' The front of our house was
covered with an elegant architectural design in variegated
lamps, and an orchestra was erected opposite for festive
music. In the morning of the appointed day, a *Te Deum*,

[1] *Recollections of the Last Four Popes*, 248.

attended by the various British colleges, was performed; in the afternoon a banquet on a munificent scale was given at his villa near S. Paul's, by Monsignor Nicolai, the learned illustrator of that Basilica; and in the evening we returned home to see the upturned faces of multitudes reflected in the brilliant " lamps of architecture " that tapestried our venerable walls. But the words " Emancipazione Cattolica," which were emblazoned in lamps along the front, were read by the people with difficulty, and interpreted by conjecture; so that many came and admired, but went away unenlightened by the blaze that had dazzled them into the darkness visible of surrounding streets.'

Wags used to say afterwards that peasants[1] had been heard ejaculating on their way home ' *Santa Emancipazione, ora pro nobis*,' in the belief that the illuminations had been in honour of a newly canonised saint. But to young Dr. Wiseman, even more than to the English scholastics who were his students, the Emancipation Act was the climax of a long struggle for liberation that had intimately affected the fortunes and the movements of his own family. By the year 1802, when he had been born in Spain, the penal code in its old rigours was a thing of the past. But in his own grandfather's time the penal laws in Ireland were still enforced so severely that many of the old Catholic families, who had been deprived of their estates and excluded from every occupation, while being compelled to pay oppressive special taxes for the benefit of the Protestant ascendancy, had taken refuge abroad as soon as they could accumulate money enough to establish themselves. Debarred from the professions, they could find no opportunities to retrieve their fortunes except in trade; but through trade they were able to

[1] *Life of Ambrose Phillips de Lisle*, I, 161.

build up direct connections with Catholic countries where in time they could settle and live in peace. In the seaport towns along the south of Ireland a new class of Catholic merchants gradually came into existence, and carried on a profitable direct trade with France and Spain as well as England.

Waterford was one of the chief centres of their activity, and James Wiseman was a member of the firm of Wiseman Brothers which traded between Waterford and Seville. He had left Ireland in 1771, and established himself in Seville, and there, ten years later,[1] he married the daughter of an Irish family, also settled in Spain, a Miss Dunphy of Kilkenny. She died after eight years, having given him three daughters ; and after a time James Wiseman came to London, where in 1800 he married again, choosing as his second wife another Irish lady of a family with Spanish connections, Miss Xaviera Strange of Aylwardstown Castle, County Kilkenny. On August 2nd, 1802, their second son, Nicholas, was born in Seville, and his mother brought him as a baby to the Cathedral, where he was laid upon the altar and consecrated to the service of the Church. When he was only three years old his father died ; and, soon afterwards, his mother brought him and his brother and sister back to Ireland.

The penal laws in Ireland had been abolished by a succession of measures during the previous twenty years which had been due almost entirely to the courageous and determined efforts of the Catholic merchant-class—

[1] I have followed the more circumstantial account given by Rev. Jeremiah Murphy of Queenstown on page iii of his biographical introduction to the collection of *Essays on Various Subjects* by Cardinal Wiseman, published in 1888. Wilfrid Ward's statement of the Cardinal's parentage is different, but curiously vague. He describes James Wiseman (I, p. 2) as ' a Spanish merchant in Seville,' and says merely that ' he was twice married, first to the daughter of a Spanish General, and next to Miss Xaviera Strange, a member of the family of Strange of Aylwardstown Castle, Co. Kilkenny.'

to which the Wisemans belonged—who composed the great majority of the original Catholic Committee, and provided the funds necessary for its work. The professions had been thrown open to Catholics ten years before Nicholas Wiseman was born ; but in the years that followed upon the Act of Union in 1800, the Catholics were still presenting petitions to Parliament without any prospect of success, claiming their right to be admitted as legislators and to hold positions of importance in the State. For two years, during that period of despondency, Nicholas Wiseman as a small boy was taught in a boarding-school at Waterford. Until their arrival in Ireland he and his brother still spoke Spanish as their natural language ; and when, more than fifty years afterwards, Cardinal Wiseman revisited Waterford during his triumphal tour through Ireland in 1858, he described in a public speech how ' it was there I learned for the first time, as completely as a child could learn it, the language in which I am now speaking.' In the same speech he recalled how he had heard from his mother in his childhood ' histories which remain engraved on my memory, that tell me what my ancestors had to endure to preserve the faith—how they shared in the confiscations and spoliations of property which were the heirlooms of every Catholic in those days. Friends of mine since then have thought it kindness to find in the Record Office in Dublin the original decrees of confiscation and spoliation of the property my ancestors possessed here ; but all this has been nothing compared to the tales she told me of the secret, unseen sacrifices, by which some of her ancestors preserved the faith to themselves and their children.'

After two years in Waterford, when he was eight years old Nicholas Wiseman and his brother were taken from

Waterford by their mother, to begin their schooling in earnest at Ushaw, in the hills of County Durham. By that time they spoke English as a matter of course, but Wiseman's early fluency in Spanish remained with him all his life. Great changes and upheavals had been taking place all over Catholic Europe in the years of their childhood. Spain had already become the scene of the Peninsular Wars. Ushaw itself had come into existence through the French Revolution, which had broken up the famous English College at Douai and driven its teachers as refugees to England, where they founded the two colleges of Ushaw, in the North, and S. Edmund's College at Ware. It had been a drastic change for the Irish child, with his very emotional temperament, to be sent from the soft climates of Spain and of southern Ireland to the bleakness of northern England, and to the austerely ascetic conditions of the school. From countries which were overwhelmingly Catholic in their tradition, he was now brought into the exclusive and almost monastic atmosphere of one of the few schools in England that existed for the education of the old Catholic families, who were so conscious of their own aloofness in a Protestant country. Piety and strict attention to studies were the traditions of the school which had for generations served to keep the Faith alive, among the small and scattered remnant which remained faithful to the Church.

Upon the shy, temperamental Irish boy, the effect of his surroundings was to throw him very much upon his own resources. The great Lingard was Vice-President of the College while he was there, and his personal influence strengthened the child's natural studiousness. And although he was always at the top of his class, he made scarcely any friends at school except among his masters. Before long, he had made up his mind to enter the priesthood, and he was still at the College when an opportunity of which no one had dreamed occurred, by which it became possible for him to go at once as a scholastic to Rome itself.

Cardinal Consalvi had come to England in 1814, in connection with the international settlement after Napoleon's downfall ; and he had been so much encouraged by the unexpected cordiality of his reception that, after his return to Rome, he had investigated the possibilities of reopening the English College. For two centuries the English College in Rome had been the chief training centre for priests in the English mission ; but the French Revolution had wrecked it, as it had wrecked Douai. In 1798 the buildings had been sacked by the French armies which invaded Rome, and for twenty years they had been left untenanted until in 1818 Cardinal Consalvi decided to reopen the College. At Ushaw Nicholas Wiseman had already founded a society for Roman studies with a few other earnest young schoolfriends ; and when an invitation came to enrol as one of the first students in the revived English College in Rome, he accepted it with unbounded enthusiasm. They started on their great voyage at the beginning of October, but it was almost Christmas before the ship in which they sailed from Liverpool arrived at its destination. Even then—three years after Waterloo—it was, as Wiseman himself wrote afterwards,[1] ' long before a single steamer had appeared in the Mediterranean, or even plied between the French and English coasts.' The long sea journey was the only means by which the group of young seminarists could be suitably conveyed with their belongings ; and its duration still depended entirely upon the winds.

---

[1] *Recollections*, 1.

A whole fortnight had been lost in beating up from Savona to Genoa, and another whole week from Genoa to Livorno. Even the last stage of the journey was full of uncertainty, for bandits still infested the roads from the north. And not the least vivid of Wiseman's recollections of the journey to the city where he was to spend the next twenty years of his life, was the sight of ' tall posts on the wayside,' which supported ' ghastly trophies of justice avenged on the spot where crime had been committed— the limbs, still fresh, of executed outlaws.'

But the first glimpse of Rome itself, which had been the centre of his dreams and of his studies for years, was so vivid that he could still recall every detail of it when, as a Cardinal and the head of a restored English hierarchy, he wrote his *Recollections of Rome*, forty years afterwards. Even within that brief interval Rome had undergone great changes since he had first seen it, as a city containing little more than 100,000 people, when he had arrived from his school in Durham at the end of 1818. The road still ran through open country under the overhanging wall of the city, till a narrow gate led into a ' long, close alley.' ' The sculptured terraces of Monte Pincio had as yet no existence ; this was still a green hill, scored by un-shaded roads and chance-tracked paths to its more shapely summit.' He could still remember, after forty years, that slow trundling drive until at last, in a long, narrow street, ' the Pantheon burst full into view.' Then followed ' a labyrinth of tortuous ways, through which a glimpse of a church or palace-front might occasionally be caught askew ; then the small square opened on the eye, which, were it ten times larger, would be oppressed by the majestic, overwhelming mass of the Farnese palace, as completely Michelangelesque in brick as the Moses is in marble ; and another turn and

salutation from the wagging appendage of his grey head to the large silver buckles on his shoes, mumbling toothless welcomes in a yet almost unknown tongue, but full of humble joy and almost patriarchal affection on seeing the haunts of his own youth re-peopled.'

But there were much more striking links between the present and the past than the old toothless porter who had welcomed them in ecstasy. Pius VII was still Pope, and it was only four years since he had returned in triumph to the Eternal City from his long captivity as Napoleon's prisoner at Fontainebleau. The young Englishman—and Wiseman already thought of himself entirely as an Englishman, as he did through all his life, in spite of his Irish parentage and his Spanish birth—still thought of the Sovereign Pontiff as Napoleon's captive ; and the chance of seeing his venerable, sad figure in the ceremonies at S. Peter's was one of the most dramatic prospects of their arrival. But within a few days they were even brought for a personal interview with the Pope himself, who welcomed them to Rome and shook them each by the hand. And a few months later, when Sir Thomas Lawrence had come specially to Rome to paint his famous portrait of Pius VII for the historic group of peacemakers, which is now at Windsor Castle, they saw the picture[1] before it was publicly exhibited, and when the great English artist's masterpiece had become the talk of Rome. With all Rome to explore, with the reconstruction of the English College entrusted to their own industry and zeal, the years that followed passed like a dream of beauty and of achievement. Nicholas Wiseman was the most gifted and the most enthusiastic of the group, and in the new atmosphere, the early gravity

[1] *Ibid.*, 17.

of his character diminished, and the generous affectionate impulsiveness of his Irish temperament responded quickly to the warmth and the splendour of his surroundings.

With a great library in the College itself to reorganise, with the most famous scholars and theologians of all Europe constantly in evidence, in a city small enough 'or everyone of note to be constantly seen, the young seminarist devoted himself to study in every direction. Every week strengthened the sense that he was living in the very centre of the Catholic world. And to the English College there came many of the most important figures in Rome. Monsignor Testa, the Pope's Latin secretary, was a specialist in modern languages, and ' this led to a particular friendship between him and the English College.'[1] ' He was to be found every afternoon taking his walk on Monte Pincio, generally in company with two or three friends.' Among them was the famous Cardinal Mai, and as the Monsignor welcomed the young English students when they went out walking, there were endless occasions for hearing from the highest sources ' the political ecclesiastical chit-chat of the day.' The range of such acquaintances was extended to every part of the world. ' Sometimes a long-bearded Armenian or Syrian, or an American or Chinese missionary, would be in the group, and contribute interesting intelligence from the extremities of the earth.' For in those days, a hundred years ago, the United States were still regarded as being scarcely less remote than China from Rome. And among young Wiseman's contemporaries in the city was the young Irish-American priest, Father McCloskey, who was later to become the first American Cardinal.

The background to all his studies and his religious

[1] *Recollections*, 32.

duties was inexhaustible in its variety and beauty. Forty years afterwards he could still recollect every detail of ceremonies like the Corpus Christi procession, when the venerable Pope would emerge in public from the retirement that old age and the infirmity resulting from his imprisonment had made necessary. He could still see[1] ' the seven-deep lines of spectators, no longer northerners, but the country people mostly, many of whom appear in the almost Oriental costumes of their villages, rich in velvet, embroidery and bullion, pass in succession the religious corporations, as they are called, of the city ; next, the chapters of the many collegiate churches and those of the basilicas, preceded by their peculiar canopy-shaped banners, and their most ancient and precious crosses dating even from Constantine. Then comes that noblest hierarchy that surrounds the first See in the world, partaking, necessarily, of the double function and character of its possessor—prelates of various degrees, holding the great offices of State and of the household, judges, administrators, and councillors. These are followed by bishops of every position of the Church arrayed in the episcopal robes of their various countries, Latins, Greeks, Melchites, Maronites, Armenians, and Copts. To them again succeeds the Sacred College, divided like a chapter, into deacons and priests, but with the addition of the still higher order of bishops. . . . Such were the venerable princes, whose names the stranger asked in a whisper as they passed in that procession before him, and who immediately preceded the final group of its moving picture. Its base was formed by almost a multitude of attendants, such as, could they have been the object at which one could look, would have

---

[1] *Ibid.*, 35.

C

carried one back three centuries at least. The bright steel armour of the Swiss guards upon parti-coloured doublet and hose—the officer's dress being richly damascened in gold—gleamed amid the red damask tunics of bearers walking symmetrically and unflinchingly under a heavy burden ; while the many two-handed swords of the Swiss flamed upwards, parallel with the lofty poles of a rich silver-tissue and embroidered canopy that towered above all, and was carried by persons who deemed it a high honour, and who also wore the quaint costume of days gone by.'

And dominating the whole procession, ' upon a fald-stool richly covered, stands the golden Monstrance,' behind which the Pope himself knelt, borne on a small platform beneath the canopy, with his rich embroidered cape covering the faldstool in front of him. ' Thus he is borne along, so that all may see and join him in his devotion, wherein he is undisturbed even by the motion required to walk in a procession.' So, the first Cardinal Archbishop of Westminster could still recall his own early recollection of the prisoner-Pope—' abstracted from all that sense could perceive, and centred in one thought, in one act of mind, soul, and heart, in one duty of his sublime office, one privilege of his supreme commission. He felt, and was, and you knew him to be, what Moses was on the mountain—face to face, for all the people, with God ; the vicar with *his* Supreme Pontiff ; the chief shepherd, with the Prince of pastors ; the highest and first of living men, with the one living God.'

All this in a city which at the time contained a population no greater than that of many seaside towns in modern England—small enough for every famous person to be known by sight and to be frequently seen, and with its own life so united that few social distinctions could exist.

The splendour and the infinite variety of its monuments and churches was beyond all dreams. Every church was the store-house of some glory or other of the various arts.[1] 'Here is a fresco by Raffaele ; there a chapel or a group by Michelangelo ; in this a dome by Lanfranco, in that a spandrel by Domenichino ; in one a mass of unique marble, a huge flight of steps of materials sold elsewhere by the ounce ; in another a gorgeous altar of precious stones enshrining a silver statue.' Yet all this indescribable wealth of beauty and of treasure was only the remnant that had survived the spoliation by Napoleon's armies. While the young scholastic was revelling with the ecstasies of an artist and the enthusiasm of a born student of antiquities, in the unimaginable profusion of glorious painting and architecture and sculpture in Rome, the older inhabitants of the city were still bewailing the tragedy of all that had been stolen within their own recollection. 'Everything was now poor, compared with what they had seen before the treaty of Tolentino, and the subsequent levies of church treasure during foreign occupation.'

Rome had been the centre of all his boyhood's dreams in Durham ; and now in the unbroken years of study in the resuscitated English College, he became impregnated completely by the atmosphere that contained all the tradition of the Church's history through two thousand years. His ordinary studies in philosophy and theology proceeded steadily until he obtained his degree as Doctor of Divinity, after he had been for nearly six years in Rome. He was not yet twenty-two, but the range and the maturity of his scholarship, extending in many directions, had already won him the confidence

[1] *Recollections*, 55.

of many learned men. In July 1824 the great public
disputation was held in which the young scholastic had
to submit his thesis, and be catechised upon it for his
degree. Only the most brilliant theses were submitted
to such public debate, and it was evidence of the distinction that young Wiseman had brought to the first
efforts in reviving the English College. In the church
where it was held, Cardinal Zurla presided, surrounded
by several bishops, nearly forty prelates, and other professors of the College. Twelve objections, involving
four hundred propositions in all, had been submitted for
the young candidate to deal with, and three eminent
theologians conducted the disputation against him. Wiseman surmounted the ordeal with flying colours, was
awarded his doctorate, and a few days later gave a ' grand
dinner ' to the disputants and to his professors in celebra-
tion of his success. Among the distinguished visitors
who had come in during the disputation to witness the
performance of the young student of the English College
were two ecclesiastics whose names were to figure largely
in Catholic history. One was the great theologian Father
Cappellari, who within six years was to become Pope
Gregory XVI. His unobtrusive arrival, clothed in his
white robes as a Camaldolese monk, had caused a ripple
of excitement when he came in during the disputation,
and a message was sent to him asking that he should take
part as an ' assailant ' ; but he declined to intervene.
And near him, accidentally, there sat the great Frenchman,
Félicité de Lamennais, already famous as one of the
leaders of the Catholic revival since the Revolution,
whose later writings and conduct were to be formally
condemned by the white-robed monk who that day sat
close to him listening to the young Irishman's performance.
' Probably it was the only time that they were ever seated

together,' wrote Wiseman long afterwards,[1] ' when they thus listened to an English youth vindicating the faith, of which one would become the oracle, and the other the bitter foe.'

Some months later, just before Christmas, and exactly six years since the day of his first arrival in Rome, Dr. Wiseman received minor orders as a sub-deacon. In March 1825, when the great celebrations of the Jubilee Year were already well advanced, he was ordained to the priesthood.

[1] *Recollections,* 190.

CHAPTER II

THE ENGLISH COLLEGE IN ROME (1825–31)

SIX years in Rome had transformed the shy, serious-minded schoolboy who made no friends, into a young priest of boundless enthusiasm who already showed a most remarkable gift for inspiring and winning the affections of his contemporaries. The few letters which survive from these earliest years give evidence of his immense capacity for enjoying life, of his enterprise in making the most of his opportunities by winning new friends wherever he went, and of the infectious high spirits which he could communicate to them in correspondence as much as in direct companionship. He had spent some months of vacation at Versailles, with his mother and his sister, before his ordination. There had been too many things to occupy his attention to have any time for letter-writing, except to one or two particular friends. Among them was ' old George ' Errington, who had come with him from Ushaw to the English College, and had already become attached to him in that long and intimate association which was to be tragically ended in the misunderstandings that culminated thirty years later in an appeal against him, as Cardinal Archbishop, to Rome.

But a few glimpses, in an early diary,[1] reveal the exuberant spirits and the keen sense of humour which

---

[1] Ward, I, 52–3.

were to win him friends all over Europe in the following years. On his way back to Rome, in the first year after his ordination, he set down for his own amusement and for his friends various incidents in an absurdly uncomfortable journey. Having prevailed upon a ' saucy young Calabrian ' guide to take him round by a longer route from Ostia, in an unsuccessful attempt to avoid a herd of dangerous buffaloes, he had arrived at Ardea to find a ' miserable pile of dirty hovels ' with no apparent hope of shelter for the night. Finally the blacksmith was induced to provide a room, and a wrangle arose over the price of a hen for their dinner. The hen was killed by the blacksmith throwing a hatchet at it ; and after they had ' climbed up a black ladder to our chamber ' they discovered their own room ' black as a chimney. Door without lock, which we fastened with wooden shovel. Half a window, and that without half its panes. Table two and a half feet high. Pavement half torn up and heaped in one corner, with blocks of marble, etc. Two half-chairs, one of which in chimney. Two hens hatching in baskets, and clucking. Velvet garments, warming-pan, and horsehair in divers parts of room.' Hot water was brought up in a painter's pot, and the dead hen—' in which were found seventeen eggs '—was immediately immersed in it, and then put on the forge until it had been duly boiled.

With such capacity for enjoyment of every sort, life in Rome had become a wonderful combination of study and varied recreations. And within two years of his ordination he was appointed, at the extremely early age of twenty-five, to be Vice-Rector of the College, with every prospect of a permanent residence thenceforward, as well as an official status, in the Eternal City. The two years had been spent in studies which had already gained him a brilliant reputation. The future Cardinal Mai, who had revealed untold possibilities of exploration among old manuscripts, by his discovery of the palimpsests in the Vatican Library, had discerned Wiseman's aptitude for close research and his extraordinary talent for languages. Under Monsignor Mai's personal guidance the young priest had undertaken work on Syrian manuscripts which very few other students were even capable of attempting. Thirty years later, when Monsignor Mai had made a deep mark upon his times as Prefect of Propaganda, Wiseman recalled ' with much tender affection and sweet gratitude ' the quiet hours he used to spend alone in the Vatican Library, surrounded by old Syrian manuscripts, interrupted from time to time by conversations with Mai himself. ' For I was the only person whom he allowed to be there during the midsummer vacation, when the *scriptores* even were absent.'[1] It was a big compliment indeed to the young priest who was already creating a tradition of vigorous and original scholarship in the first years of the restored English College. And his friendship with the learned librarian developed so far that Monsignor Mai would even bring to him for revision his own Syrian treatises.

In Rome even the solemn Library of the Vatican, with its unrivalled collections of priceless old manuscripts, was vivid with bright colours and the brilliance of the Italian sun. Macaulay, after that visit[2] to young Dr. Wiseman at the English College which preceded his famous essay on the history of the Popes, described his own astonishment at what he had seen in the great Library of which he ' used to think with awe as a far darker and

[1] Ward, I, 54.
[2] Trevelyan's *Life and Letters of Lord Macaulay*, I, ch. vii.

sterner Bodleian.' ' All was light and brilliant : nothing
but white and red and gold ; blazing arabesques and
paintings on the wall.' It was in that atmosphere the
young Doctor worked day after day in preparation of the
Horae Syriacae which, as the result of two years' research,
established his reputation all over Europe when he was
still in his twenty-fifth year. Even the ceiling glowed with
colour—' gold and ultramarine as airy and brilliant as
the Zuccari could lay them ' ; while in those long days
of study during the summer vacation[1] ' the half-closed
shutters and drawn curtains impart a drowsy atmosphere
to the delicious coolness which gives no idea of the
broiling sun glaring on the square without.' And as he
sat there day after day poring over the crackling old
parchments, and making new discoveries as he collated
them with the others, the librarian himself—' the dis-
coverer of Cicero and Fronto, of Socrates and Dionysius,'
would come to encourage his young disciple and to compare notes with him.

His first book, when it was published, brought him
not only a reputation among the most eminent Oriental
scholars in many countries, but immediate recognition
in Rome. He was appointed to the professorship of
Oriental Languages in the University of Rome, and the
appointment was a direct act by Pope Leo XII himself.
That austere Pontiff had been elected after the death of
Pius VII in 1823, and Dr. Wiseman had met him on fairly
frequent occasions in the following years. On the day
after receiving his doctorate, he had been presented to
the Pope in person, and soon afterwards he had been
encouraged to present himself as a candidate for the
professorship of Oriental Languages. A Papal Bull

[1] *Recollections,* 187.

had decreed that all professorships were to be open to competition ; but as the vacant chair of Oriental languages affected very few students and was not likely to concern many candidates, it had been announced that the rule would in this case be waived in favour of the direct appointment of a scholar with an established reputation. The announcement had been a blow to the hopes of young Dr. Wiseman, whose professors had encouraged him to compete for the Chair. But once it was made, there was no alternative to acquiescence, unless he were to undertake a direct personal appeal to the Pope. In his *Recollections*, Wiseman described the sequel in terms so elusive that even his official biographer appears to have missed the fact that the story concerned himself. But it reveals the development of determination and self-confidence in his character that, as a very young and newly ordained priest, he should have gone to the Pope for an interview to request his personal intervention in his own favour, against a decision which conflicted with the standing rules concerning university appointments. ' The more youthful aspirant unhesitatingly solicited an audience, at which I was present,' is how Wiseman, as a Cardinal Archbishop thirty years afterwards, described his own appeal to the Pope.[1] ' He told the Pope frankly of his intentions, and of his earnest wish that the recent enactments of His Holiness should be carried out in his favour. Nothing could be more affable, more encouraging, than Leo's reply. He expressed his delight at seeing that his regulation was not a dead letter, and that it had animated his petitioner to exertion. He assured him that he should have a fair chance, " a clear stage and no favour," desiring him to leave the matter in his hands.'

[1] *Recollections,* 195.

excitement that surround the death of one Pope and the election of his successor. As a young student he had been in Rome for the death of Pius VII and the election of Leo XII. He had seen a few years later, the wonderful ceremonies and celebrations of the jubilee year of 1825. Now, Rome was once again made the focus of interest for all Christendom, and he himself had been entrusted with a position which made him definitely a participant. And the excitement over the Pope's election had not yet subsided, when he was called upon to bring to the new Pontiff, in his official capacity, the great news of Catholic Emancipation in his own country.

In ten years of absence from England, he had become steeped in an atmosphere that was utterly different to that of the English Catholics among whom he was, before long, to lead a great revival. But the recollection of that austere, secluded tradition in which he had been brought up at Ushaw was still vivid in his memory, and he could realise the immense change that would result from emancipation. ' We had left our country when young,' he wrote long afterwards in retrospect,[1] ' and hardly conscious of the wrongs that galled our elders ; we should return to it in possession of our rights ; and thus have hardly experienced more sense of injury than they who have been born since that happy era. So some of us could feel ; and had not this its uses ? Whatever may be considered the disadvantages of a foreign education, it possessed, especially at that period, this very great advantage, that it reared the mind, and nursed the affections, beyond the reach of religious contests and their imitation. No " winged words " of anger or scorn, however powerfully fledged for flight, could well sur-

[1] *Recollections*, 250.

mount the Alps ; and if they did, the venom must have dropped from their tip, as this must have lost its pungency, in so long a course. Scarcely any amount of roaring on platforms could have sent even a softened whisper across the sea ; and the continuous attacks of a hostile Press could only reach one in the broken fragments that occasionally tessellated a foreign paper. Thus, one hardly knew of the bitter things said against what was dearest to us.' In the calm, cosmopolitan atmosphere of Rome no bitter insinuations or controversies entered. ' One grows up there in a kinder spirit, and learns to speak of errors in a gentler tone than elsewhere.'

So, just at the time when his own new responsibilities as Rector of the College were compelling him to lead a much more active life, there had taken place in England itself a change which was to create incalculable new opportunities for Catholic expansion. The Church in England had been relieved at last from its ostracism, and under new conditions a great forward movement had become due. In Rome itself, Wiseman was an official channel for communication with the Holy See ; and almost from the outset of his Rectorship the English College became a centre at which an increasing number of English visitors, Protestant as well as Catholic, came to seek introductions. Wiseman himself, both as a young scholar who had made a brilliant reputation, and as a personality who won friends and commanded attention wherever he went, was an ideal President for the College at the time, and his enterprise and his wide enthusiasms quickly made him a very considerable figure in Rome. The Catholic Emancipation Act, and O'Connell's extraordinary success as the author of a new form of popular agitation, had attracted new attention to the Church in England and Ireland ; and Wiseman with his impulsive enthusiasms and his exceptionally wide range of information, was in great demand through the following year. He had been bitterly reluctant to leave his studies among the Oriental manuscripts of the Vatican Library, and to lose the freedom he had enjoyed, with few exacting duties, in the first years after his ordination. But his capacity for administration, and his influence as a personality in Rome developed rapidly, and he could feel how definitely the English College was progressing under his direction. And within two years of his nomination, there occurred yet another sudden change with the death of Pius VIII ; and after a repetition of all the former excitement over the election of a new Pope, he was to find that Pius's successor was a close personal friend of his own.

Barely seven years had passed since as a shy young scholastic, not yet ordained, he had faced the ordeal of a public disputation for his Doctorate. He could recall vividly the alarm that had arisen in his mind when the white-robed Father Capellari had come into the church during the proceedings and had been asked to take part as one of the young student's ' assailants.' The Camaldolese monk had been one of the ' visitors ' of the University then, and in the following year he had been made a Cardinal and Prefect of Propaganda. Now, on the death of Pius VIII, he had been elected Pope, and had taken the title of Gregory XVI ; and the young Rector of the English College, whose career had advanced so swiftly in that short time, had to come with the other notabilities of Rome to present his homage to the new Sovereign Pontiff. They had seen much of each other in the interval, and of late Cardinal Capellari had been taking a special interest in Wiseman's writings. He had not only told Wiseman to expand one of his essays and to have it translated into Italian, but had undertaken to correct the proofs

D

himself, while it was being got ready for official publication by Propaganda. Even during the conclave, when the successor to Pius VIII was being chosen, he had continued to revise the proofs. And now when the young Rector met him, after his election, ' in the narrow passage leading from the private papal apartments,' he was received with an exclamation of delighted recognition such as he had never thought of any Pope showing towards a young priest, and with the amused intimation that from now on he could expect no further assistance in his proof-correcting.[1]

So the year 1831 opened for the young Rector, now only in his twenty-ninth year, but already, within a few years after his ordination, one of the most brilliant young personalities in Rome, a scholar of European reputation, and the personal friend not only of the new Pope himself but of many of the Cardinals. It was no wonder that his rectorship gave a unique distinction to the English College which had been empty and derelict when he had come to it as a schoolboy from Durham only a dozen years before. His gifts as a linguist became known all over Rome. He had the reputation of being able to speak seven languages like a native ; and his talent for Oriental languages added to his prestige when he was confronted with Mezzofanti, on his arrival in 1831 to reside in Rome.[2] His students used to watch, with a certain rivalry, when the two linguists would meet at public receptions or elsewhere and converse, before an amused audience, in Arabic or Persian. Wiseman himself believed that Mezzofanti made a habit of learning just enough words in each new language to make a show in conversation. He used to enjoy these little encounters which enhanced his own reputation. He was even

---

[1] *Recollections*, 263.   [2] Ward, I, 90.

regarded as being somewhat pompous in his erudition. But the simplicity and modesty of his character was undisputed among those who really knew him. His reputation grew with extraordinary rapidity, and Lord Houghton, who saw him constantly in Rome at the time, even records that by 1832—when he was still barely thirty years of age—he was already spoken of as being likely to be made a Cardinal.

CHAPTER III

THE CATHOLIC REVIVAL (1831–35)

THREE Popes had died, and three new Popes had been elected, within the twelve years since Wiseman had been in Rome. At no other time in the century could a young priest have witnessed anything like the same succession of changes at the Vatican. But they were years also in which vital forces were stirring everywhere in Europe ; and in Rome he was at the nerve-centre of the Continent. Revolutions in France and Belgium and Poland had broken out in 1830, and in Italy the spirit of nationalism, which had been active everywhere under the stress of the revolutionary and Napoleonic wars, was already causing a profound restlessness. The Carbonari, as a secret society bent upon altering the existing settlement by revolutionary means, had already spread through the Papal States. Anxiety caused by the discovery of their conspiracies had hastened the death of Pius VIII, which brought Wiseman's friend Cardinal Capellari to the Papal throne.

He had been elected only a few hours in February 1831, when 'in the very square of the Vatican,[1] while receiving the first Papal blessing, the rumour reached us of insurrection in the provinces.' Soon the insurrection did in fact spread and Wiseman described afterwards his

[1] *Recollections*, 270.

vivid recollections of the night of February 22nd. ' It was the carnival time, of the good old days, when later restrictions had not been thought of. On the afternoon of that day, just as the sports were going to begin, an edict peremptorily suspended them; troops patrolled the Corso, and other public places; and citizens were warned to remain at home, as evil-disposed persons machinated mischief. Three days before a plot had been formed for the surprise and seizure of the Fort of S. Angelo; but it had been foiled by the watchfulness of Government.' An armed attack was actually made upon the Post Office, to seize arms and ammunition, but was repulsed. In the English College everyone had to stand by in readiness for any eventuality, as the extent and resources of the revolutionaries were unknown. But the excitement passed away, and an immense response was forthcoming to the appeal for volunteers to reinforce the Civic Guard. To the new Pope, however, this turbulent outburst almost immediately after his election was an ominous warning of the developments that fifteen years later were to compel his successor to escape from Rome itself. Outside the city, the revolution had assumed alarming proportions in Umbria and the Marches. It became necessary to invoke the aid of Austria, and again in the following year; and Gregory XVI's administration soon assumed the character of a stern reaction against the rising tide of nationalism and of popular government.

But with the new generation which regarded democracy and popular government as a necessary change that could no longer be withstood, there had arisen in France especially a group of ardent young Catholics who had been inspired with the mission of reconciling democracy with the Church. In the closing months of Pius VIII's

pontificate, there had arrived in Rome three leaders of
the Catholic revival in France whom Wiseman soon got
to know on intimate terms.　De Lamennais had already
embarked in France upon his campaign to combine the
forces of democracy with a great Catholic crusade, and
his newspaper *L'Avenir* had aroused fierce opposition
among the older royalist clergy in France, to whom
democracy was still identified with militant atheism.
It had aroused a still more vehement enthusiasm on the
part of many young Catholics, of whom Montalembert
and Lacordaire were leaders, and at the end of 1831 they
had accompanied de Lamennais to Rome on a bold mission
to obtain official approval against their opponents in
the French hierarchy.　Their arrival almost coincided
with the death of Pius VIII and the election of his successor, and in the prevailing condition of unrest in the
Papal States their appeal for support in their liberal
tendencies was at a grave disadvantage.　For months
they stayed on in Rome, and after Wiseman had made
their acquaintance they came frequently as guests to the
English College.　In long conversations the young Rector
listened to their fervent plans for a great crusade to revive
Catholicism in all countries.　From Montalembert he
learned at first hand of the young French aristocrat's
visit to O'Connell in Ireland at the height of the Catholic
agitation for the Emancipation Act of two years before.
They spoke to him of England also as a country where
Catholicism must spring into new life ; and when he
asked how did they suggest that such a miracle should be
worked, they implored him to do as they had done in
France, by preparing the men who should become the
leaders of a great revival.

It happened, by a remarkable coincidence, that there
had arrived in the English College in the previous year

a young convert from English Protestantism who was for years afterwards to be the chief prompter of Wiseman's own enthusiasm for the conversion of England. Conversions of Englishmen and women to Catholicism had always occurred from time to time in Rome itself: and Wiseman, as the chief English preacher in Rome, was now naturally the person to whom intending converts should turn for instruction. But George Spencer, the son of an important English peer, was much more than an isolated convert who had sought admission to the English College with a view to entering the Catholic priesthood. He was more even than that most exceptional phenomenon in those days, a convert clergyman from the Anglican Church. For his whole existence was devoted to the dream, which he had formed after his own conversion, of a return of England to her pre-Reformation Catholic faith. He had been ordained as a clergyman in the Church of England in 1823, and had given evidence of a most unusual fervour in his ministry, when he made the acquaintance of a young Englishman, Mr. Ambrose Phillips, who had become a Catholic before going up to Cambridge, where he and another young convert undergraduate, Kenelm Digby, were the only Catholics in the University. The result of his meeting with Phillips was that George Spencer suddenly left the Anglican ministry in 1830, and before long accompanied his young friend to Rome, to enter the College under Wiseman's rectorship. The zeal of his new scholastic was only equalled by that of Ambrose Phillips, whom Wiseman had already met frequently during his repeated visits to Italy after he left Cambridge. And their belief in the imminence of a Catholic revival in England was so intense, although no sign of anything pointing in that direction had yet appeared except for the very small group of conversions in Cambridge, that Phillips was even writing to Spencer in his first year at the English College to say :[1] ' I think in about fifty years England will be Catholic again, though indeed I am disposed to see in the events in Poland so glorious for Catholicity a fulfilment of Sister Antonia Ponte's prediction concerning Pentecost. That something striking will very probably take place in favour of Catholicity before the end of the year '32, I believe and hope, but I cannot anticipate the *total* reconversion of the country in *so short* a period.'

Fantastic though such enthusiasm must now appear, it was still more extravagant at the time ; and Wiseman must have listened with incredulous amusement to similar outpourings of convert zeal from George Spencer in the English College. But Wiseman's own impulsive enthusiasms were to cause similar ridicule in later years ; and the presence in Rome of two young converts of such remarkable intellect and of such social importance as Phillips and Lord Spencer's son, was a portent which appealed at once to his imagination. It coincided with the arrival of de Lamennais and Lacordaire and Montalembert in Rome, and their repeated questionings as to what preparations were being made for a revival of Catholicism in England aroused him to a sense of possibilities that had never been contemplated seriously hitherto. The English Catholics had been content to continue in their tradition of unobtrusive seclusion, even after the passing of the Emancipation Act ; and the idea of undertaking any sort of crusade for the extension of Catholicism in a Protestant country had to be presented from outside. In England itself, the ancient fears and the old habits of retirement had produced not only inertia but a sense that missionary activity among English Protestants would

[1] *Life and Letters of Ambrose Phillips de Lisle*, I, 51.

inevitably recoil upon the very small remnant of the Church that had barely survived the centuries of persecution. But to Wiseman, who had been educated in Rome, and who had been inspired with so much enthusiasm by his own intimate relations with the Popes and the rulers of the Church, such fears were scarcely even comprehensible. His acquaintance with the leading Catholics of so many countries was continually extending ; and he had come to feel it as a reproach that no active preparations had yet been undertaken for the conversion of England ; while his young friends in Rome were now continually giving him reports of the growth of a new Catholic spirit within the Church of England which, they were convinced, would inevitably transform its whole character and expurgate its Protestant prejudices. He became more and more impressed by the fervour and energy of Spencer, and was soon even perturbed when Spencer told him plainly[1] that his own talents were being diverted to idle employment : ' that he should apply his mind to something more practical than Syrian manuscripts or treatises on geology, and that he would rather see him take up with what suited a priest on the English mission as it then was.'

And then, in the early spring of 1833, an unexpected event occurred which was to open Wiseman's eyes very definitely to the possibilities which Ambrose Phillips and Father Spencer had vaguely suggested, without any apparent authority for their personal expectations. There arrived on a visit to Rome two young English clergymen from Oxford, who had already been developing a remarkable interest in Catholic traditions among their friends in the old University, and whose personal ascendancy

[1] Ward, I, 101.

over their contemporaries was to affect the whole course of religious development in England. John Henry Newman and his friend Hurrell Froude had set out together on a voyage to Rome, with a decided interest already in the relations between Anglicanism and the Catholic Church ; having come to the conclusion that the ranks of Christendom must be closed against the attacks of infidelity, but being still fortified, at any rate on Newman's part, by an intense repugnance towards the Papacy and towards Catholicism itself. They obtained an introduction, like most English visitors to Rome, to young Monsignor Wiseman, as Rector of the English College ; and, being immediately attracted by his character, they embarked upon a discussion with him concerning the respective positions of the Churches. ' We got introduced to him,' Hurrell Froude wrote afterwards,[1] ' to find out whether they would take us in on any terms to which we could twist our consciences, and we found, to our dismay, that not one step could be gained without swallowing the Council of Trent as a whole.'

' We made our approaches to the subject as delicately as we could,' Froude explains. ' Our first notion was that terms of communion were within certain limits under the control of the Pope, or that in case he could not dispense solely, yet at any rate the acts of one council might be rescinded by another.' They had ' found to their horror,' however, that ' the doctrine of the infallibility of the Church made the Acts of each successive Council obligatory for ever, that what had been once decided could never be meddled with again—in fact, that they were committed finally and irrevocably, and

[1] Ward, I, 117.

could not advance one step to meet us, even though the Church of England should again become what it was in Laud's time.' So, in that first early meeting between the leaders of the Oxford Movement and the future leader of the Catholic revival in England, it was made plain by Wiseman that there could be no question of compromise. To Froude it was a greater blow than to Newman, who was enormously impressed by the grandeur and the beauty of Rome, but could still write home[1] ' is it possible that so severe and lofty a place is the cage of unclean creatures ? ' He could declare scornfully that it is ' a city still under a curse.' ' Oh that Rome was not Rome ! But I seem to see as clear as day that union with her is impossible,' was his verdict in his last letter before he returned.

Wiseman had apparently made little impression upon him at their first meeting ; and it was Froude who wrote that ' we mean to make as much as we can out of our acquaintance with Monsignor Wiseman, who is really too nice a person to talk nonsense about.' Yet even so late as 1900—nearly twenty years after Newman's death at a patriarchal age—an important London publisher could still produce a book[2] in which it was solemnly suggested that ' Dr. Newman was at this interview with Dr. Wiseman, in company with Froude, formally ordained a priest of the Roman Church, being then, in fact, a member of that communion,' and that he ' was actually a priest while officiating in the Anglican Church.' The truth is that Newman and Froude returned from Rome profoundly disappointed in their hopes of negotiating some sort of compromise between the Catholic Church

---

[1] Ward's *Life of Newman*, I, 53.

[2] *The History of the Romeward Movement in the Church of England*, 1833–64. By Walter Walsh, 261.

and the High Church party in England. But to Wiseman, who had himself dashed their hopes, his conversation with these two earnest but suspicious messengers from Oxford was a revelation which altered the whole direction of his life. Fifteen years later he wrote, in the preface to his essays, that their visit had turned his attention ' to the wonderful movement then commenced in England.' ' From that moment,' he declared, ' it took the uppermost place in my thoughts and became the object of their intensest interest.' And in the same book he alludes to it again as ' what remains marked with gratitude in my mind, as an epoch in my life—the visit which Mr. Froude unexpectedly paid me, in company with one (Newman) who never afterwards departed from my thoughts, and whose eloquent pleadings for the faith have endeared him to every Catholic heart. For many years it had been a promise of my affection to S. Philip that I would endeavour, should opportunity be afforded to me, to introduce his beautiful Institute into England. But little could I foresee, that when I received that most welcome visit, I was in company with its future founder. From that hour, however, I watched with intense interest and love the Movement of which I then caught this first glimpse. My studies changed their course, the bent of my mind was altered, in the strong desire to co-operate with the new mercies of Providence.'

The time had not come yet, however, when Wiseman was to be diverted from his academic career to the main task which lay ahead of him. Not long after the visit of Newman and Froude, George Spencer returned to England as a young priest ; and throughout the year 1833 Wiseman, during many months of serious illness in his chest, was thrown very much on his own resources, as an invalid. His chest trouble made it impossible for him even to preach his usual course of sermons during the winter. And the year was devoted largely to a renewed concentration upon Oriental studies. But his solitude and restricted activities had produced a notable result in consolidating the effect of a succession of crowded years in Rome. For a time he had even lost his first enthusiasm for the spiritual magnificence of the Eternal City. Devoting himself with unrelenting energy to so many forms of work, he had found his ardour deadened, and even his spiritual life had lost its inspiration. As Rector of the English College he had been acting for some years as agent for most of the English Vicars Apostolic ; and he was also entrusted with similar duties in regard to the Primates of the Church in America. A selection of his correspondence with them, published some years ago in the *Dublin Review*, shows how the American Archbishops thus received, through him, their authentic news from Rome. One letter[1] particularly, addressed to Archbishop Whitfield of Baltimore in 1833, reveals the frankness with which Wiseman had already come to regard the shortcomings of the administration of the Holy See in some of its departments. ' The Cardinals of the Congregation,' he wrote, ' place the most complete confidence in Cardinal Weld for all business regarding England and America, though necessarily his previous choice of life [Cardinal Weld was a widower with grown-up children when he entered the priesthood] can in no ways have qualified him for the slightest acquaintance with the ecclesiastical affairs of either. His Eminence somehow or other imagined that Dr. England, whom he had consulted, was opposed to the new limitation, and accordingly voted against it and drew the

[1] *Dublin Review*, October, 1918, 157.

majority after him. Upon conferring afterwards with the Bishop, he was quite dismayed to find that he had gone exactly contrary to his opinion and wishes ; and he expressed himself to a friend of mine in terms of great regret at having by his mistake caused such a decision.' These facts of secret history should, Wiseman told his correspondent, be made known to him for his guidance, 'though it may not be very fit for profane ears.' A 'still more extraordinary blunder' had contributed also to the same decision, which, in the absence of any properly organised relations with the Church in America, had caused profound disappointment. 'The map used upon the occasion not having room for the prolonged tract of Florida without enlarging the size of the sheet, this province was detached and represented separately in a small frame in some vacant corner of the map. Now your Grace must know that Geography is not a branch of education in Italy, and in consequence their Eminences, considering *that* the real place of Florida, decided that the proposed demarcation could not be adopted, as it united Florida in jurisdiction with Louisiana, I think, from which it was separated by such a vast tract of ocean. This will hardly appear credible, but I give it from undoubted authority.'

But a year's enforced rest, after so many crowded experiences, had given time for his energies to recuperate, and had enabled him to obtain a clearer perspective of what life held in store for him. 'I feel as though the freshness of childhood's thoughts had once more returned to me,' he wrote in the early spring of 1834. And with an always increasing sense of interest in the future of Catholicism in England, which was constantly stimulated by news from his convert friend George Spencer, he began to foresee a career of his own in England for which his experience at the College in Rome would have been an immediate preparation.

To found a Catholic University and a scholarly Catholic review in England became objects which he felt it his duty to propound at once. One of the Vicars Apostolic in England, Dr. Baines, adopted his idea for a Catholic University with enthusiasm ; and arrangements for obtaining a Papal charter had actually been made, with a proposal that Wiseman should be appointed as coadjutor bishop to Dr. Baines. In a letter to Archbishop Whitfield of Baltimore in August 1834, Wiseman spoke of the arrangement as having been virtually decided.[1] ' At present the business stands as follows,' he wrote : ' I go to England in Spring to undertake the establishment of a new Catholic University under sanction of His Holiness, who has been pleased to express his approbation, with a kind reserve that I give up none of my situations in Rome till I see, after a year or two, whether I shall continue them. In the meantime a Pro-Rector will fill my situation, one every way qualified for the office, formerly Vice-Rector. Should the establishment flourish, and my presence be of service to it, it is the declared intention of the Bishop, Dr. Baines, to propose me for his coadjutor. Indeed he has done so already, but a delay has been proposed till some other affairs of his diocese are satisfactorily arranged. The probabilities are strong that I shall return no more to Rome to reside. At any rate, my absence will be prolonged.' Wiseman decided, however, that the first step to be taken must be a personal mission of investigation among the English Catholics. All preparations would have to wait until that had been undertaken, and it was agreed that Wiseman should set out on his journey in the summer of

[1] *Dublin Review*, October, 1918, 160.

1835. He already had premonitions that the journey would be the end of his life in Rome ; and with feelings of mingled excitement and regret he prepared to set his affairs in order.

Before his departure on so important a mission, it was arranged that he should deliver in Cardinal Weld's rooms, at the Palazzo Odescalchi, a series of lectures during the Lent of 1835 which would enable him to summarise the results of a dozen years of original research in Oriental and scientific studies. They attracted widespread attention, and were published as *Lectures on the Connexion between Science and Revealed Religion.* Not until twenty years later did the discoveries of Darwin make the subject a matter of immense popular interest ; but already Wiseman had anticipated the necessity of a full and candid discussion as to how far recent researches in anthropology and geology, and especially in Oriental studies, had made it necessary to question the exact meaning of Catholic teaching in regard to the Creation and to the texts of scripture. The immense subsequent development of such studies has made a great deal of Wiseman's lectures out of date. But writing almost a hundred years afterwards, the late Sir Bertram Windle has pointed out[1] that, although Wiseman could have no notion of how important the evolutionary controversy was to become, yet he did ' actually get hold of the great factors on which the evolutionary theory and controversy came to be built ' ; and the evidence which he brought forward in favour of the evolutionary theory was ' plain proof that he possessed a highly scientific mind.' As always when Wiseman lectured, there were many Protestants among his audience. One of these

[1] *Catholic Emancipation,* 1829–1929 (Introduction by H.E. Cardinal Bourne), p. 108.

BISHOP WISEMAN
(*Reproduced by kind permission of Longmans, Green & Co. Ltd.*)

was a young schoolboy who fifteen years afterwards was to become a Catholic, and in due time a bishop, Dr. Patterson. But he was still young enough to share the feeling of his family that attendance at a lecture in Cardinal Weld's Palazzo involved a certain amount of risk even to their personal safety. Long afterwards he could still remember his first view of the lecturer[1] as ' a tall, thin priest, with a stoop and a rather frowning brow and black hair and gold spectacles ' : and he had found the lecture so interesting even as a small boy, that he could still recall a good deal of its subject-matter.

He was not yet thirty-three years of age, though he had been Rector of the English College for seven years, when the publication of these famous lectures added still further to his prestige in Rome, and brought him into still closer contact with many of the leading Catholic scholars and leaders in different countries. But since the visit of Montalembert and Lacordaire with Lamennais to Rome, and since the arrival of George Spencer as one of his students at the English College, his mind had been more and more directed towards the Catholic revival which was actually in progress in France and Germany, and which he gradually felt it to be his own mission in life to assist in England. The revival in France especially was enlisting all the zeal and enthusiasm of brilliant lay Catholics like Montalembert or that astonishing University student in Paris, Frederic Ozanam, whose foundation of the S. Vincent de Paul Society was before long to spread all over the world. In Germany, the movement was rather a philosophic revolt against Protestantism ; but both as a scholar and as a priest Wiseman was equally attracted to the different manifestations of the revival. He had developed a real genius for friendship,

[1] Ward, II, 76.

E

and from Rome he conducted a continual correspondence with zealous French Catholics like Lacordaire and Ozanam, and with a large group of German scholars and thinkers, particularly with Döllinger. At the end of 1833 he was already writing to a friend[1] that ' really the exertions of such men as Schlegel, Novalis, Görres, Manzoni, Lamennais, Lamartine, and even the less pure efforts of Victor Hugo or Janin do show a longing after the revival of Christian principle as the soul and centre of thought, and taste and feeling.' Little more than a year later Lacordaire in Paris was to give an immense impetus to the Catholic revival by his conferences in the Cathedral of Notre Dame. They were delivered as a lenten course in 1835, in the very same weeks when Wiseman's own lectures in the rooms of Cardinal Weld's Palace were causing a similar sensation, though on a less remarkable scale, in Rome itself. And in the same weeks he was exchanging an enthusiastic correspondence with Döllinger in Munich. The German leader had just published the second volume of his History of the Church, and in a letter sending Wiseman a complimentary copy of the book, he expressed his ' fullest approbation ' of Wiseman's suggestions for ' a closer connection between the Catholic clergy of England and Germany.' In the same letter Döllinger states that he has heard that Wiseman would soon return to England and join Bishop Baines at Prior Park. His plans for his English tour were already complete, and in the summer he started on his journey. Passing through Munich and Paris on his way, he renewed his personal contact with the leaders of the Catholic revival in both countries, and, as a further aid to his own intentions, he brought about an introduction between Döllinger and his

[1] Ward, I, 136.

own old master, Dr. Lingard, who had been Vice-President at Ushaw when he had left there as a small schoolboy nearly twenty years before.

He had left England when Catholic Emancipation still seemed quite unattainable, and when the Catholic agitation had subsided into such complete apathy, even in Ireland, that O'Connell still despaired of bringing it back to life. In Rome he had been distant from all the tumultuous agitations and controversies of those exciting years. But it was he who, as a very young priest, newly appointed to the Rectorship of the English College, had to deliver the great news of Catholic Emancipation personally to the Pope. He had seen the gradual disappearance in Rome itself of great figures in the story of Napoleon. New Popes had come and gone, and now the See of Peter was ruled over by one who had even insisted on correcting Wiseman's own proof-sheets on the eve of his election as Pope. For eight years he had himself been a notable and influential person in the Eternal City. He had become as familiar with all the inner workings of the government of the Church as he was with the history and the external life of Rome. At an age when most of his schoolfellows at Ushaw were still only at the beginning of their careers, he was already one of the notabilities of Rome, and a scholar whose name commanded respect among learned men all over Europe. He was the intimate friend of practically every leader of the Catholic revival on the Continent, and they looked to him, as one of themselves, to inaugurate in his own country a movement similar to what they had created. But the one country he could not claim to know, and in which conditions had inevitably changed so much since the days of his own boyish recollections, was the country to which he had determined to devote his labours. He had now set out to visit it as a stranger returning to an almost unknown land, unused to its exceptional conditions, speaking its language only as one of many languages in which he was equally fluent, and so deeply immersed in the cosmopolitan and ecclesiastical atmosphere of Rome that even his ways of speech gave evidence of his foreign education, and expressed the entirely different outlook with which he was to view the religious condition of England.

CHAPTER IV

WISEMAN'S TOUR IN ENGLAND (1835-36)

ARRIVING in London in September, 1835, after a journey which included visits to his friends and sympathisers in Germany and France, Monsignor Wiseman made his way to the house in Golden Square, at the back of Piccadilly Circus, where he was to be the guest for some days of Bishop Bramston, the Vicar Apostolic of the London District. The Bishop's very title was an immediate reminder that he had come to a country where the Catholics were still no more than a small and scattered sect, whose ecclesiastical affairs were managed by four Vicars Apostolic, bishops endowed with titular Sees, who conducted their administration with an authority so vaguely defined in practice that many complications constantly arose. Wiseman was familiar with their special difficulties, for he was agent for most of them in Rome, in his capacity as Rector of the English College. But only actual contact with the lives of the English Catholics could give him any idea of the extraordinary conditions that had resulted from the prolonged era of persecution.

Already the immigration of poor Irish labourers in search of employment had begun ; and in London and Liverpool and the ports, as well as in the mining and manufacturing districts, a considerable element of immigrant Catholic labourers from Ireland and from continental countries had begun to increase the small Catholic population that had survived the penal laws. But apart from them, the Catholics in almost all parts of England were still for the most part grouped around the scattered families of the Catholic aristocracy and gentry who had led their own secluded lives for generations, and could scarcely yet realise that, as the result of O'Connell's popular agitation in Ireland, they at last enjoyed full equality of civil and social rights with the rest of the population. Apart from the gradual immigration of Catholic labourers, which had been gathering in numbers in the past twenty years, there were certainly fewer English Catholics in the whole length and breadth of the country than would equal the population of the small city of Rome where Wiseman had been living since before the passing of the Emancipation Act. And their outlook upon the world, and even upon the Church itself, was profoundly affected by the consciousness of their own numerical weakness, and of their direct dependence upon the leading families who had preserved the Faith among them, through the generations of persecution, and had provided them with priests in the chaplains attached to their own households.

Wiseman had been convinced that he could only understand their conditions by living entirely among them; and in a letter[1] to a friend from Bishop Bramston's house in London he explained whimsically that for his tour through England, he had ' made a resolution never to sleep in an inn or hostelry the whole way; but I intend to quarter myself upon such of the nobility or gentry of these realms as can sufficiently appreciate such an honour. My first station will be in the neighbourhood

[1] Ward, I, 215.

of Birmingham, and other Midland Cyclopean towns, where I have several short calls to make. Thence I proceed to the princely towers and enchanted gardens of Alton, and, so forward to Sir E. Vavasour's.' So, patiently and conscientiously, he proceeded to make the acquaintance of the most representative Catholic families all over England. His own early recollections of Ushaw were a link with many of his contemporaries, and he was no stranger to the traditions of the penal laws which were still vividly present to the minds of most of the gentry. But the mentality which persecution had produced was in such contrast to the enthusiasm and the dignity to which he had been accustomed in Rome, that it required a sustained effort to understand or sympathise with the prevailing attitude in England. Among the younger generation he found some who were already eager to take part in the public life to which Catholics had at last been admitted, and who were much more concerned with the future than the past. But in general he found that the old Catholic families had, as he described it, 'just emerged from the Catacombs.' And it astonished him to find that among the older Catholics were[1] ' many who regret even bitterly the good old days of exclusion, which amounted to monopoly for them and theirs,' while there were others ' whose shackles were removed, but not the numbness and cramp which they had produced.' He still found that the outlook of the Catholics as a whole was dominated by ' the remembrance of a condition of things where one portion of the same community was a suppliant to the other for common rights, and with it the pride of having refused or of having granted, and the humiliation of having long been spurned.'

[1] *Recollections,* 251.

A more discouraging atmosphere for any attempt to bring about a religious revival could scarcely have been imagined. But it was outside the Catholic body, and in unexpected quarters among the educated classes of the Church of England, that Wiseman discovered possibilities which the old Catholics, with their tradition of seclusion and of self-effacement, had never considered. To most Catholics in England this young Rector of the College in Rome who spoke so many languages that his own English was affected and his manner of speech expressed an extremely foreign upbringing, was a curious visitor from a strange world of which they knew almost nothing. To some of them, indeed, his Roman enthusiasms were even a source of suspicion, for the desire of the older generation to repudiate the associations of the word ' Papist ' had not died with the termination of the Cisalpine Club. But among many Protestants who had grown up in an atmosphere of wider toleration, and who had been inspired by the recent romantic revival that Sir Walter Scott and Byron had made popular, the presence in England of this brilliant and enthusiastic young Monsignor, who knew Rome so intimately and who was the friend of so many famous continental figures, aroused feelings of curiosity and real interest. He had returned to London in the late autumn, and agreed to take charge of the Sardinian Chapel in Lincoln's Inn Fields when its Italian priest had to go on a journey to Italy ; and every Sunday the young Monsignor was to be heard preaching in Italian, to a mainly foreign congregation in London—performing a very similar task to the duties which he had undertaken so timorously ten years earlier, as the first preacher to address the small English congregation in Rome in their own language.

For many years afterwards the mere title of a Monsignor

was to have a romantic and unfamiliar sound to English people ; and the reputation of this gifted young priest with his international prestige, and his fluent command of so many languages, spread gradually through London. His appearance in his Monsignor's purple was extremely impressive ; for he was most unusually tall—fully six feet two inches in height. He had begun to grow portly of late ; but his restless, active figure gave evidence of tireless energy ; and his high spirits and enjoyment of life made him a most companionable addition to Catholic society. By December he had been invited to deliver a series of lectures for mixed audiences of Catholics and Protestants ; and, with a sense that he might somehow assist in a work similar to that of Lacordaire in Paris, he undertook a course of two lectures every week. Their effect was almost instantaneous, and they attracted audiences such as had never attended to hear any Catholic preacher before. They ' produced an immense sensation,' wrote one who had been present at them. ' I date from their delivery the beginning of a serious revival of Catholicism in England.' He had never expected such a reception as they met, and the excitement of his success was so great that he recalled long afterwards[1] how he used to ' shed tears in the sacristy of the Sardinian Chapel, fearing that whatever good the lectures were doing to others, they were filling me with vainglory.' But the simplicity and humility of his character remained unaffected ; and in spite of a success which, as he told an old fellow-student, was ' a thousand times beyond my expectations,' he considered himself as no more than an inadequate pioneer attempting to carry into England some echo of the work that his French and German friends were already accomplishing in their own countries.

[1] Ward, I, 233.

In London a letter reached him from Dr. Döllinger in Munich which, after regretting that even Dr. Lingard was unable to read German, asked him[1] sadly ' are there no persons of literary pursuits among your clergy who are capable and inclined to study our theological literature of the last years ? There seems now to be a sort of literary apathy and inactivity on the side of the English Catholics, and yet you are continually attacked, and if I mistake not, your numerous adversaries take too much advantage of your silence. Your Milners, Butlers, and others are gone, without having left successors, and meanwhile the attacks of heresy are becoming daily more various and virulent.' And while such suggestions were being thrust upon him from leaders on the Continent who had inspired his mission, his own startling success as a popular preacher in London had already produced many appeals that he should leave Rome and devote himself entirely to Catholic propaganda in England. At every one of his lectures in the Sardinian chapel he now found that the church was ' crowded to suffocation,' every seat being already filled half an hour before Compline, which preceded his actual address. ' Were it three times as large it would be full,' Wiseman confided in a college friend.[2] He had found on every occasion that even when his lectures extended beyond an hour and a half, the attention of his audience never flagged. ' The common people say they can follow every word and that I make them quite sensible,' he told the same confidant ; ' the priests come in shoals, and they and all the congregation tell me that the whole system and the form of treatment throughout is quite new to them all. Indeed, they wish that I should stay till Lent, and give a fuller course, but this is out of the question.

[1] Ward, I, 140.
[2] *Ibid.*, I, 234.

Nay, *entre nous*—for I write to you as a friend—they say I ought not to go back at all. But I am thus vainly full with you, because it will convince you of what I have often said, that the method I have followed in school was as applicable to a congregation, if simplified and reduced to a popular form, and in this I always thought I could succeed. Everyone agrees that a most successful experiment has been made and that proof has been given of the interest which may be thrown round the Catholic doctrines by a little exertion.'

His success had been beyond all expectations, and it had confirmed to a degree which he had never anticipated, his own subconscious feeling that he possessed the gifts of a great popular preacher and leader of men. He had arrived unexpectedly at a turning-point, where he must decide once and for all whether his life should be spent in a continuation of his academic and administrative work in Rome, or whether he should turn his back for ever upon the studies, and the life, that had given him so many years of unclouded happiness, and throw all his energies henceforward into the work of a popular preacher. For the time being, he was beset with urgent appeals for further lectures which he was unable to refuse. Bishop Bramston requested him urgently not to return to Rome before he had given a second course of lectures at Moorfields in Lent. His reputation had by now increased so rapidly that the second series was even more successful. They attracted a great number of educated and distinguished non-Catholics who had never thought of entering a Catholic church in England before. Lord Brougham was only one of the many celebrities of London's political and social life whose constant attendance at the lectures brought Wiseman an extraordinary prestige. Even in the much more spacious church at Moorfields the crowds were too numerous to allow of everyone finding a seat ; and the young Monsignor, surveying a congregation such as had never assembled in a Catholic church since the penal times, was confronted with packed aisles, where men stood listening without the slightest impatience for over two hours.

Nothing like this had ever been attempted in London since the end of the penal laws ; and it was not only the astonishing intellectual equipment and the persuasive eloquence of the young Monsignor from Rome that produced so deep an impression. Bishop Milner, in a previous generation, had made a similar effort to counter-act Protestant prejudices against the Catholic Church by his controversial writings. But Milner's effectiveness depended chiefly upon his vigorous common sense and his power of stating an argument with lucidity. He could make no claim to the wide and profound culture of Wise-man, and his appeals to reason were too often marred by the intemperate vehemence of his language. But Wise-man not only amazed his mixed audience by the extra-ordinary range of his knowledge, varying his illustrations or his arguments by encyclopædic references to the history or the religions of China or Syria or India, or of the most primitive races of Africa, or discussing with the familiarity of perfect intimacy the prevalent tendencies of recent thought or research in France or Italy or Germany. He appealed with an urbane persuasive style that was entirely new in English controversy—deploring the very name of controversy because it ' supposes that we con-sider ourselves as in a state of warfare with others ; that we adopted the principle which I reprobated of establish-ing the truth of our doctrines by overthrowing others.' And in this quiet cultured style, of a scholar who is concerned only with the truth and who assumes that his audience is equally far from prejudice, he had undertaken to discuss publicly the most fundamental of all controversies for a Catholic leader in England : ' the essential ground of Separation between our Church and those friends and fellow-countrymen whom we would gladly see cemented with us in religious unity.' He was inquiring in his persuasive cultured way—not what were the reasons why Catholics were unpopular or suspected in England, but why the majority of the English people were not Catholics. He was asking boldly, not why Catholics should have adhered to an unpopular religion, but why Protestants should profess the creed in which they had been born. It was the first time that a mixed audience in London had been addressed directly by a Catholic priest upon the hitherto strange and almost incredible phenomenon of recent conversions to the Catholic Church. In England itself, he told them, conversions had been becoming increasingly frequent, but their frequency was ' as nothing to what goes forward elsewhere.' And alluding particularly to Germany, he gave definite instances of professors in Protestant Universities and of other learned men who by different roads, each in the experience of his own field of study, had become convinced—whether by a study of history or of philosophy or of economics or of revolutionary politics—that only in the Catholic Church could truth be found.[1]

It was no wonder that the lectures aroused interest and surprise, and above all among the Catholic body in England who had for so long been accustomed to preserving a strict reticence about their own religion, and who had never dreamed of proclaiming its truth publicly to a

[1] *Lectures on the Catholic Church*, 1886, p. 15.

hostile and incredulous world. Soon after the series had concluded, Wiseman was invited by the editor of a popular encyclopædia to contribute an article on the Catholic Church. His lectures had been widely reported and discussed, and now even his engagements and activities began to appear as matters of interest in the news. And before he had even delivered his second course of lectures at Moorfields, he had been approached by two Catholic laymen, of whom the Liberator Daniel O'Connell was one, with an invitation to assist them in founding the *Dublin Review*, as a quarterly devoted to serious discussion of Catholic doctrine and affairs. The table around which that decision was taken is still preserved in the presbytery of S. Patrick's, Soho Square. It meant more than the foundation of an ambitious and scholarly Catholic review, for it was intended in great measure to counteract the Cisalpine tendencies of the existing *Catholic Magazine*. Wiseman became one of its associate editors and upon him fell responsibility for the religious side of its contributions. It was the ideal organ for an enthusiastic scholar with his immense variety of equipment, who wished to popularise the results of modern Catholic research and to make known the rapid progress of the Catholic revival on the Continent. Wiseman devoted his enthusiasm and his great learning with lavish energy to the success of the new publication. Its first issue appeared in the spring of 1836, and as he was delayed by preparing the proofs of his Moorfields lectures for publication, he prolonged his stay in England until the second issue of the *Dublin Review* had appeared. Then at last he took his departure, and by the beginning of October he was back at his old work as Rector of the College in Rome, after an absence of nearly a year and a half.

He had been growing restless already before he left Rome in the summer of 1835 ; but his experiences in England had made him more than unsettled in regard to his own retention of the Rectorship in Rome. He had discovered his own capacity for leadership, and for inspiring others with his own enthusiasms. Now that his own gifts as a popular lecturer had been so strikingly proved, the idea of returning to England as a pioneer of the Catholic revival became definitely attractive ; and his unique qualifications for the task, with his intimate personal relations with the French and German Catholic leaders, and with the Pope himself and the most influential personages in Rome, made it impossible that he should resume the purely academic life which had been the dream of his youth. There could be no compromise between the two courses. Either scholarship or Catholic propaganda must be treated as a complete life's work. His prolonged absence from Rome had weakened the powerful ties that still attached him to the surroundings in which he had found an entire absorption of his energies and an inexhaustible scope for his enthusiasm and for his talents as linguist, archæologist and scientific investigator. To leave Rome must mean an irrevocable departure from the splendours and the beauties of the incomparable city in which he had attained a distinguished position already, which in time was certain to develop into real eminence in the councils of the Catholic Church. It must mean a final abandonment of the studies and researches in which he had attained an international reputation as one of the most promising and already one of the most accomplished scholars of his age.

But his heart was now fixed in England ; and the sacrifice of all the familiar and dear surroundings, and of all the promise they had offered, already seemed inevitable.

His year's absence had made him a changed man, and he was no longer the shy, grave scholar who had left Rome in the previous year. He had gained new confidence in aspects of his own character which had scarcely been developed hitherto. He had experienced the intoxication of discovering his own capacity as a leader of men; and while month after month had brought forth news of astounding progress being made by Lacordaire and Ozanam and Montalembert and his own contemporaries in France, and of similar developments steadily ripening in Germany, he could not ignore that he had himself broken new ground in the apparently unfavourable soil of England, and that his own immediate success demanded that he should return to carry much further the work which he had only just begun. He had made new friends in England, and not least with the great Irish leader, Daniel O'Connell, whose name was a symbol of Catholic revival all over Europe. With O'Connell he had even become associated directly as one of the founders of a new Catholic review. And even after his return to Rome he continued, through its publication, to inspire and to direct the trend of his own sympathisers and supporters in England. As its principal religious contributor he enlisted the collaboration of some of the most notable Catholic thinkers in Germany and in France; and the new journal became an organ of international discussion.

He had co-operated eagerly in its creation in the conviction[1] that it should 'belong to the present day,' and should 'treat of living questions, and grapple with real antagonists.' Through it he hoped to make at least a modest beginning in making known the Catholic religion

[1] Ward, I, 252.

' as she is in the fulness of her growth, with the grandeur of her ritual, the beauty of her devotions, the variety of her institutions.' But a special interest had prompted him particularly in his desire for a serious organ of educated Catholic thought. In his long visit to England he had made much closer acquaintance with the tendencies and the expressions of the Oxford Movement ; and, free from the inevitable prejudices of English Catholics who regarded Newman and his friends as equivocators who were seeking to make the best of both worlds, and who might quite possibly keep potential converts from breaking with English Protestantism, he watched the evolution of the Tractarian party with a generous sympathy that excluded any suspicion of their good faith.

He had scarcely settled down again to the routine of his duties at the English College, when an article by Newman appeared in the *British Critic* at the end of 1836, which revealed the interest which Wiseman's own lectures in London had aroused among the Oxford Anglicans. ' Romanism has great truths in it,' declared Newman, ' which we of this day have almost forgotten, and its preachers will recall numbers of Churchmen and Dissenters to an acknowledgement of them.' He was satisfied that by such activities on the part of Catholic preachers, ' Romanism will spread among Dissenters and irregulars ' ; and he welcomed Wiseman's success as a substantial contribution towards the revival of Catholic tendencies within the Church of England. Nor for years yet was Newman to become seriously alarmed at the possibility of secessions to the Church of Rome itself. And it was Wiseman himself who before long was to deliver, in an article in the *Dublin Review*, the first decisive shock to Newman's contented contem-

plation of his own efforts. But his praise of Wiseman in
the *British Critic* caused bitter heart-burnings among his
own followers ; and the editor of the *Critic* let Newman
know through a mutual friend[1] that he was ' immensely
disgusted with your Wiseman article, and declares that
if another of the same kind is sent, he will throw up
the editorship.' ' They say you make Wiseman a peg
to hang your attacks upon Protestantism on,' was the
message conveyed to Newman. And some months
later the general indignation found expression in a
fierce tirade against Wiseman's lectures on the
Eucharist.

By that time the first symptoms of the Catholic revival
which Wiseman had initiated were already apparent.
Conversions to Catholicism were becoming more frequent,
and a sensation was caused by the announcement that
among them was so celebrated a person as the architect
Augustus Welby Pugin. In London, where the success
of Wiseman's lectures had been most felt, the Catholics
began to realise that extraordinary developments might
already be at hand ; and that Wiseman's vivid and inspiring accounts of the Catholic revival on the Continent,
with its long stream of conversions from Protestantism
or from irreligion, might indeed have some direct bearing
upon the possibilities of the future in their own country.
Before he left London they had presented him with a
large gold medal, bearing a reproduction of his own portrait bust, in commemoration of his courageous vindication of their faith during his sojourn among them. He
had gone back to Rome encouraged and filled with an
enthusiasm which made him long to return to England.
But he was still almost alone, apart from his former pupil,
Father George Spencer, in thinking that the Oxford

[1] Ward, I, 243.

The plain truth was that he had abandoned his old studious habits, and henceforward he was drawing upon the immense fund of varied scholarship which he had accumulated in nearly twenty years since he had arrived in Rome. His English tour had shown him what enormous advantages he possessed in his natural versatility as well as in his varied learning. He had discovered that in all sorts of fields he could figure as an accomplished expert. His gifts as a lecturer made him in demand everywhere among learned societies ; and his own intellectual equip ment, once he emerged from the intensely academic atmosphere of Rome, enabled him to address popular audiences with complete confidence on all manner of subjects, whether they wished to hear theological discussions or lectures on Church history or archæology, on modern science or on Oriental research. He who had been the most fastidious of scholars now set himself deliberately to exploit his own versatility in instructing and interesting popular audiences.

To his students at the English College the change in his attitude brought a notable increase in his contact with their lives. He was ready to undertake almost anything. He had long been recognised as a connoisseur of music and of the arts. Now he ventured boldly as a performer himself. He frequently acted as organist for the College ceremonies. He showed his high spirits by painting part of the scenery for the first College theatricals. He even wrote a play himself for the students to perform, having pledged to secrecy as to his authorship the very few who were allowed to know that he had written it. He devoted all the time he could spare to social relaxation with his students. He would bring them all out for picnics to some place of historical interest outside Rome, and explain everything to them in his own attractive popular style. He would take them to explore the catacombs, or the old churches, or the picture galleries in Rome, usually bringing with him some distinguished Catholic visitor who was famous as an expert on whatever they were taken to see or to hear. He lectured constantly, but in a more fluent and popular style, though on his own special subjects his lectures were still among the most remarkable and original to be heard in Rome. It was no wonder, as his student Father Kyan wrote[1] afterwards, that ' what with his daily lectures at the University, his weekly sermons, his duties as agent to the bishops in England, his multifarious correspondence, his visitors and his visits, he was too busy to be able to read much.'

But through all the activity and industry of this brief period, in which he was developing his self-confidence, and becoming more expert in the arts of popular instruction and leadership, his thoughts were still centred in England. Before he had left Rome for his English tour, Lacordaire and de Lamennais had impressed upon him that he held great responsibilities in regard to training the young men who should lead the Catholic revival in England ; and since his return, he had concentrated especially upon that object. To impart his own knowledge and experience to his students was the immediate concern of his life ; and he had come back convinced of the need to provide as full a general education to his students as they could obtain in their short years of training in the Eternal City. His enthusiasm and zeal for the Catholic revival had altered the whole trend of his life, and in consequence he was already becoming the victim of persistent misrepresentation. His new methods were criticised at once, and it was generally said that he had

[1] Ward, I, 257.

lost his balance as the result of his success in London. He was accused of vanity and of ambition ; and his abandonment of profound scholarship for the more facile activities which won applause apparently lent sufficient confirmation to the charge. Before long he realised how much he was being misunderstood, and his sensitive temperament was wounded deeply. ' My motives are misrepresented,' Father Kyan heard him say once, even in his own student days. ' Everywhere I encounter a well of reserve. I have my faults, I often do wrong, and if anyone would speak to me like a friend, I should be thankful to have my errors pointed out and be glad to correct them.' But jealousy asserts itself even in Rome, and he could only persevere in his new way of life in spite of the discouragements which hurt him most intimately, and which no amount of applause and increasing prestige could obliterate. For he was essentially most humble, and although he had the ambition to succeed and to achieve all that he was capable of performing, his sole desire was to serve the Church that at once supplied and commanded the whole inspiration of his life. And among the intimate papers revealed by his official biographer there survive the resolutions[1] set down at the end of a retreat given by a Jesuit preacher, a year after his return from England, which he re-read and commented upon regularly for long afterwards. They disclose his own concern at the possibility of becoming unduly elated by his own success ; and the resolutions concerning his duty towards himself are particularly revealing. ' To humiliate pride always, particularly when it arises under the form of good and tempts me with the pretext of doing something for the cause of God,'

---

[1] *Ibid.*, I, 261–4.

is one of them. ' To crush vainglory, particularly when it comes in the practice of good works and in the exercise of my ministry,' is the next ; ' and to try not only to embrace but also to love humiliations and to rejoice in them.'

All through his life, his impulsive and sensitive temperament was to leave him subject to alternating moods of elation and of despair. And the humiliations which he strove so hard to welcome as penances inflicted directly for his soul's salvation, were the cause of infinite grief and distress to his spirit. But his own students loved him, and in his Vice-President, the ' old George ' Errington of former days, he had an ally who, with an entirely different temperament, loved and served him with unqualified devotion. Errington was a well-bred English Catholic of the older type, intensely English in his outlook upon life, and by nature unsympathetic even to the enthusiasms of the Catholic revivalists in France who had exercised such a profound influence upon Wiseman himself. He felt even less sympathy towards the Catholicising movement in the Church of England which, with the blunt and straightforward attitude of an old Catholic, he regarded as worse than insincere. He had learned from the personal experience of his own family and of their friends, that the old Catholics in England had endured persecution and, in more recent generations, a galling ostracism, for their fidelity to the Catholic traditions which the Established Church had succeeded in extirpating from the country. And now, when Newman and a group of ' intellectual ' theologians at Oxford were striving to prove that the Church of England had never really severed its connection with Catholicism, and that it could resume its Catholic tradition by a gradual process of expurgating the later importations of evangelicalism, Errington, like most of the old Catholics, regarded them with a contempt which frequently found expression in furious explosions. And when Wiseman, as the descendant of Irish Catholic refugees in Spain, insisted that every individual Protestant who groped towards Catholicism as the result of historical or theological argument, must be treated with infinite sympathy and must on no account be discouraged or told that he should choose at once between Luther and the Pope, Errington's vehement outbursts at the English College in Rome were a constant and salutary reminder to Wiseman that his own attitude was utterly different to that of the Catholic body in England.

But Errington loved Wiseman devotedly as a personal friend and colleague, and they were entirely united in the desire to raise the standard of education of the English Catholics. One result of the penal laws had been that all the Catholic families in England who could afford to educate their children had been obliged to send them to schools on the Continent until quite recent times. They returned from the colleges in France or Belgium with a foreign outlook upon life, and even with foreign ways of speech—frequently even to the extent of dropping their aitches, as a Frenchman or Italian would. The recent foundation of English Catholic schools at Stony-hurst, Ushaw, Prior Park, and a few other places, had obviated this difficulty to some extent. But the majority of the clergy, and even of the masters in the recently founded English schools, were still men who had been educated on the Continent. To produce a completely English clergy, exempt from such disadvantages, and still more, to raise the standard of their education to a level which could compare with that of the Anglican clergy or school-teachers, was one of the biggest tasks awaiting its solution in the years that followed Catholic Emancipation. And so far as the clergy were concerned, it rested very largely with Wiseman and his Vice-Rector, George Errington, to determine whether the English College in Rome should become the training ground for the *élite* of the English clergy, and, in time, of the English bishops.

To promote that improvement particularly became the immediate object of Wiseman, in the brief period of his return to Rome after his long visit to England; and on that ground he and Errington worked together with un-qualified unity of thought and ambition. For several years they laboured devotedly to that end; while Erring-ton shared completely Wiseman's own conviction that their future lay in England, and that in a short time they must both expect to go back to their own country. Two years after his return to Rome, he was writing[1] to his old master, Dr. Newsham at Ushaw, ' I think it cannot be long before England is my residence. I assure you it will break my heart to separate myself from the students here, for I do not think it possible for greater friendship to exist between superiors and students than unites us to-gether, and I shall deeply lament Rome, but I am ready to make any sacrifice for the great work that has to be undertaken.' Already he was discussing methods of action to be adopted as soon as his hopes materialised. ' What I am most anxious to accomplish,' he wrote from Rome, ' is to establish a small community of missioners, who, living in a common home, should go *bini* (two and two) from place to place giving lectures, retreats, etc., in different dioceses, so as to be out several months at a time, and then repose, so that those at home would be engaged in conducting at certain intervals retreats for laymen or clergy in the house. It would do to begin with six or eight, but they must be truly filled with the spirit of devotion and piety, as well as learned and fluent, not to say eloquent. This idea of mine is well known to most of the young men here, and I would engage out of my small number to find two or three (two Northerns) who would devote themselves to the work. It only requires someone to lead and show the way, and I am sure others would rise up or come forward.'

To form a nucleus of trained and zealous young men eager to undertake such work had been his constant thought since his return to Rome. But the whole education of the English clergy, even apart from such plans, was involved in his work at the English College. Dr. Newsham and others confided in him freely, and he replied with equal candour, that he regarded the existing state of the clergy as ' truly deplorable,' and he acknowledged that he ' had seen much more than he had been prepared for, and than he had intimated ' before he left England. ' The emendation must be radical,' he wrote now, ' and the foundation of future good must be laid at College.' Meanwhile he noted with encouragement the marked improvement that was evident at Ushaw and at Oscott.

He had virtually abandoned his own studies and devoted his whole energies and time, in a life which was never idle, and in which every opportunity for recreation was always turned to some useful purpose, to preparation of himself and of his students for the great mission upon which his heart was already set. And while his preoccupation with the Church in England intensified, the number of his English visitors increased continually. Newman and his friends gave many of their disciples introductions to the Rector of the English College when they proposed to visit Rome ; and through them Wiseman was able to obtain frequent glimpses of the progress of the Oxford Movement. But there were other visitors with a profound interest in Catholicism though they were apart from the Oxford Movement ; and their attitude encouraged Wiseman all the more because they appeared to be more widely representative. Among others the young Macaulay arrived in 1838, introduced by an English Catholic who lived in Rome. In his case, there was no question of Catholicising sympathies, and his reputation was already made as one of the brilliant young Whigs who displayed their talents in the *Edinburgh Review*. Macaulay had come simply as a tourist, steeped in classical literature and history, and prepared to see Rome chiefly as a city of immortal monuments. On his first visit to S. Peter's, immediately after his arrival in Rome, he recorded in his diary[1] how he had been ' for a minute fairly stunned by the magnificence and harmony of the interior. I never in my life saw, and never, I suppose, shall again see anything so astonishingly beautiful. I really could have cried with pleasure.' But until he had met Wiseman at the English College, the Eternal City was still, to his mind, the city of Cicero and Cæsar and Horace and Virgil. ' What would they have said,' he wrote in his diary, ' if they had seen the Pantheon stuck all over with " Invito Sacro " and " Indulgenza perpetua " ? '

But a whole new perspective opened when his friend Colyar brought him to the English College with an introduction to its Rector. ' Interesting cloisters to an Englishman,' Macaulay found there, containing ' several of our native dignitaries who died at Rome before the Reformation. There lie, too, the bones of many Jacobites, honest

---

[1] Trevelyan's *Life of Macaulay*, I, ch. vii.

martyrs to a worthless cause. We looked into the refectory, much like the halls of the small colleges at Cambridge, in my time—that of Peterhouse, for example —and smelling strongly of yesterday's supper, which strengthened the resemblance. We found the principal, Dr. Wiseman, a young ecclesiastic full of health and vigour —much such a ruddy, strapping divine as I remember Whewell, eighteen years ago—in purple vestment standing in the cloister.' Lord Clifford was there also, wearing his uniform as a Deputy Lieutenant of Devonshire, and highly elated at returning from a private interview with the Pope. To Macaulay the whole scene was a revelation. Even Lord Clifford was entirely different to his expectations. He had always imagined a ' great Catholic Peer of old family ' as someone who would be ' proud and stately, with the air of a man of rank, but not of fashion.' But Lord Clifford was ' all quicksilver,' full of conversation about the interview which he had just had with the Pope. Even to meet a Catholic peer was a new experience ; to meet Catholics who spoke intimately of the Pope as a human being was one of the most unexpected surprises even in Rome itself.

Wiseman, in his purple vestments, had conducted his visitors up to his own rooms, and Macaulay found them ' snugly furnished in the English style, and altogether very like the rooms of a senior Fellow of Trinity.' After leaving the College, his visit to the library of the Vatican had astonished him still more by its brilliant colouring and its decorations—the place which he ' used to think of with awe as a far sterner and darker Bodleian.' It filled him with dismay at the neglect of artistic possibilities in Protestant England, and he left the Vatican Museum wishing that he could see ' the walls of S. Paul's encrusted with porphyry and verde antique, and the ceiling and dome

glittering with mosaics and gold.' His staunch Protestant prejudices, however, still comforted him as he
contemplated the civil administration of the Papal
States—where ' there is no avenue of distinction for any
but priests. Every office of importance, diplomatic,
financial and judicial, is held by the clergy.' He did not
stay long enough in Rome, or have any opportunities,
for making acquaintance with the realities of the Papal
government ; and the contrast between his verdict upon
what Wiseman showed to him and what he saw only from
the outside, through the clouded eyes of an early Victorian
Whig, was amusingly evident in his diary. What sort
of administration, he asked a friend in a long letter from
Rome, could anyone expect from a system which entrusted all its responsible offices to bishops and priests ?
They were even more dehumanised than the clergy of the
Church of England, inasmuch as ' our clergy can marry ;
but here every man who takes a wife cuts himself for
ever from all dignity and power, and puts himself into
the same position as a Catholic in England before the
Emancipation Bill.'

Had he consulted Wiseman on the matter, he might
have been even more amazed at the absurdity of his own
preconceived ideas about the Papal government than he
had been at his previous imagination of the murkiness of
the Vatican Library. As it was, he dismissed the whole
system in an epigram : ' old women above, liars and
cheats below—that is the Papal administration.' Yet
even his brief contact with Wiseman had opened his eyes
to a dim perception that not all prelates were necessarily
' old women,' and that the Eternal City was not really
a worm-eaten museum. He had been reading the recently
published *History of the Papacy since the Reformation*
by von Ranke, and it had prepared him to some extent to

believe that the Catholic Church was not yet extinct. But Rome itself had surpassed every expectation, and in a letter to Lord Lansdowne at the very end of 1838, he declared frankly that ' I hardly know whether I am more interested by the old Rome or by the new Rome—by the monuments of the extraordinary empire which has perished, or by the institutions of the still more extraordinary empire which, after all the shocks which it has sustained, is still full of life and of perverted energy. If there were not a single ruin, fine building, picture, or statue in Rome, I should think myself repaid for my journey by having seen the headquarters of Catholicism, and learned something of the nature and effect of the strange Brahminical government, established in the Ecclesiastical State.'

For Wiseman, the opportunity of meeting this very typical young Whig politician and pamphleteer had been an occasion of extraordinary interest. He had already been convinced of the possibilities of finding sympathies towards Catholicism among the contributors to the *Edinburgh Review*, in which Sydney Smith and Francis Jeffrey had for so many years conducted their ardent propaganda on behalf of Catholic emancipation. Before long the same *Review* was to publish Macaulay's great essay on the history of the Papacy, in which Wiseman could trace clearly the influence of his own guidance in various passages. But Macaulay was only one of many distinguished English visitors who came in increasing numbers to Rome. Macaulay had indeed found Rome so full of his own acquaintances that he had difficulty in avoiding them when he wished to see Rome for himself. On the eve of Christmas, he had told Lord Lansdowne, there were ' at present twice as many coroneted carriages in the Piazza di Spagna as in S. James's parish.' And in the throng that crowded to see the great Christmas ceremonies at S. Peter's he had found Gladstone, to whom he introduced himself, as they had never met before. Gladstone also had come to call upon Wiseman at the English College, having attended some of his lectures during his stay in England, and having followed with intense admiration other controversies in which Wiseman had demolished his critics. He had himself begun to make his reputation in the House of Commons, and he had become profoundly interested in the Tractarian Movement at Oxford. With him, too, there had arrived in Rome this December one of his most intimate friends since they had been at Oxford together, the Rev. Henry Manning, who, although still in his early thirties, had made his mark already in the Church of England by his energetic and zealous work as rector of Lavington. Both Manning and Gladstone were still so young that, though they came with glowing letters of introduction when they called, Wiseman had deputed a student[1]—afterwards Dr. Grant, the first Bishop of Southwark—to bring them to the chapel. A few weeks later, when Manning called again, Wiseman had brought him out to see the lambs blessed on S. Agnes's day at S. Agnese fuori le Mura. ' He was not even a bishop,' Manning wrote long afterwards. ' How little we thought that he and I should have the two first palliums in a new hierarchy of England.' It was a remote prospect indeed ; for even after Newman had surrendered to Rome and had brought a train of his disciples with him, Manning was still to stand steadfast against the encroachments of Rome, the chief tower of strength still remaining to the High Church party who had withstood the avalanche of 1845.

So, the winter of 1838 had brought to Wiseman more

[1] Purcell's *Life of Manning*, I, 156.

points of contact with the new tendencies of educated opinion in England. In the interval since his last visit he had also been contributing constantly to the *Dublin Review*, recording in it the continual progress of the Catholic revival on the Continent, and adapting to his English audience the results of his own vigilant observation of many movements in different countries. Now it had become possible to arrange for another visit to England in the coming summer. His connection with the *Dublin Review* had extended the range of his English and Irish acquaintances, and it enabled him to keep in constant touch with the group of English Catholics who shared his own enthusiasms and his desire that the Church in England should be brought into more intimate and cordial relations with Rome. But of all his English correspondents none appealed to his personal affections more strongly than Father George Spencer, who was now co-operating with Ambrose Phillips in an endeavour to organise an international crusade of prayer for the conversion of England. They were consulting Wiseman and urging him to use his own influence with Catholics on the Continent to join with them. Wiseman responded with all his enthusiasm, and it was significant that in suggesting that they should fix upon a different day for the prayers by each congregation—' so that each day the powerful intercession of the Blessed Virgin might be invoked upon us and upon our labours, and reparation be made to her for the outrages committed against her '—he deliberately advised the adoption of the rosary, in the knowledge that there would be prejudice against it among many of the English Catholics. It was not only a continental form of devotion, but especially it was the prayer of the ' poor and ignorant ' : and for that reason he wished that, as a corrective to possible pride, the devotion should be

G

encouraged everywhere. He even offered to write a little treatise on the rosary, for popular distribution in England. 'We are too insular in England in religion as in social ideas,' he wrote[1] to Father Spencer before he set out on his journey, knowing that Spencer, with his own training in Rome, would share his views. To enlarge and Catholicise 'our feelings as much as our faith' was to be a definite part of his programme, now that he felt the time for his own life's mission to be drawing near.

By the summer he had arrived in England again, and he was making the utmost use of every opportunity. In long letters[2] to his mother, written with an intimacy which he would show towards no one else, he confided the success that he was meeting. From Oscott he wrote to say that he was now giving his second retreat, and that his congregation ranged from 'the bishop down to some little boys not much more than children, all equally attentive, equally interested and moved.' On all sides he had met with cordial welcomes and hospitality ; and to his mother he confided that 'wherever I have gone I have had the pleasure of meeting converts who came to me to acknowledge their obligations to my performances such as they are, and I assure you nothing could possibly delight me more than this.' From Oscott he went on to Derby, where he was invited to preach at the opening of the new church. Two bishops attended, and there was 'a great show of vestments' ; while the whole scene, including the church and its decorations, 'would not have done dishonour to Rome.' By the end of October he reckoned that he would have 'preached about ninety times in six weeks, averaging an hour each time' and

[1] Ward, I, 309.
[2] *Ibid.*, I, 309–14.

travelled some 1600 miles in England. He had been in demand everywhere, and had responded to every invitation he could accept. In Yorkshire especially he had been delighted with the progress that he noticed since his earlier recollections. ' In the West Riding they can do what they please ; bigotry is at an end, and processions may walk the streets with no more fear of molestation than in Rome, and the priests all wear the Roman collar and an ecclesiastical costume.' He had been the chosen preacher at the opening of several churches. At one he had been delighted at being accosted afterwards by an old Irish merchant from Seville, who remembered his own family there well, and who had now settled in England after nearly thirty years abroad. Everywhere great audiences came to hear him when he lectured. At Derby he noticed the presence of ' the leading Dissenting minister of the place and crowds of Protestants, including the most respectable inhabitants.'

When the time came for him to return to Rome there could be no longer any question of hesitation about his own future. He had decided to ask definitely for permission to reside in England. ' Even if Rome should refuse to consent to this, my visits must be very frequent. In fact, Dr. Griffiths wants me to be in London for next Lent to preach in London, etc., but this would, indeed, be too soon, and I should hardly have had rest enough after this year's campaign.' But it was taken for granted already that he would be in England in the following year, and most probably for good. Neither the bishops nor the clergy, however, who were so eager to secure his services as a preacher and a lecturer, had any sympathy as yet for the consideration which excited Wiseman's ardour most intensely in the autumn of 1839, when the time was already approaching for him to return to Rome. In

Oxford a tremendous stir had been made by one of his recent contributions to the *Dublin Review ;* and before he had left England again, though he was not yet aware of the full extent of his own achievement, his article on ' The Donatist Schism ' had done more than anything else to upset the balance of the Tractarian leaders and to accelerate the conversion of John Henry Newman and his ablest disciples.

CHAPTER VI

PRESIDENT OF OSCOTT (1839–41)

IN a letter written on board ship, on his way back by Antwerp in the middle of November, expressing his thanks for much kindness and hospitality, Wiseman conveyed to his friend Bagshawe the consciousness of his own success which he felt in contemplating the crowded months of his visit. 'When I look back at what I have got through in England,' he wrote,[1] 'it appears to me like a dream. I feel completely at a loss to discover what can have gained me the influence I have been able to exercise upon others, or what I have done to make my presence desirable. For everything I have done has fallen wonderfully short of my desires, and everything I have acquired or effected has gone wonderfully beyond my expectations. I can only attribute it to the usual course of Providence of selecting the poorest instruments for its ends.'

Reports of his successful mission had preceded him to Rome, and in the English College it was obvious already that his permanent departure for England could not be much longer delayed. The English bishops had sent word to the Pope expressing their earnest desire for his release from the Rectorship so that he might assist them ; and very soon after Easter the fateful decision was made known. It was now nearly twenty years since Gregory XVI, in the year before he had himself become a Cardinal,

---

[1] Ward, I, 335.

had listened to the public disputation in which Wiseman, before his ordination, had won his degree as a Doctor of Divinity. Their subsequent friendship had been continued ever since, and the Pope, grown old now, could only wish well to the brilliant young Rector of the English College, whose reputation had spread all over Europe and whose services were being so urgently requested by the Vicars Apostolic in England. Wiseman himself had been one of the Pope's principal informants in regard to the gradual expansion of the Church in England— through continual immigration from Catholic countries and through the remarkable series of conversions which seemed to promise such results on a much larger scale, if Wiseman's own anticipations concerning the Oxford Movement should be fulfilled. The Catholic Emancipation Act had obviously introduced a new era, in which the old provisional arrangement of Church government through Vicars Apostolic—as though England, once Catholic, were now no more than a pagan country with scattered missions—would have to be replaced sooner or later by a restored hierarchy. And year after year had brought encouraging signs that the Catholic population was increasing much faster than by the natural rate of growth. New churches were being built all over the country, and new congregations were forming.

The time had plainly come when some distinct development must take place ; and Gregory XVI was already disposed, by what he had heard from Wiseman on many occasions, to make new provisions which would not only keep pace with the recent continual expansion but would allow scope for possible developments on a larger scale. Only four Vicars Apostolic hitherto had divided between them the entire direction of the Catholic body ; and their work had increased beyond the capacity of four bishops. So the Pope now decided to augment their number to eight ; and, as one of the four was already advanced in years, he appointed Dr. Wiseman to become coadjutor to Dr. Walsh, whose jurisdiction covered the Midland District. There was a special reason also for appointing Wiseman to the Midlands, with limited episcopal duties. For Oscott was close to Birmingham, and as coadjutor to Bishop Walsh, he could combine his work as an assistant bishop with the Presidency of one of the most important Catholic Colleges in England. The appointment was made known in May, and Wiseman, now aged 38, and having been Rector of the English College for twelve years and a resident in Rome since he had left Durham as a schoolboy, was duly consecrated bishop in the College chapel early in June. He was able to choose the titular See by which he would be known, and he elected to be Bishop of Melipotamus, in honour of a former Vicar Apostolic of that See who had been martyred in the exercise of his ministry. The time for parting for ever from Rome had come at last, and his emotional temperament was sorely tried by the mingled feelings of elation at the thought of his new mission in England, and of affectionate regret for the surroundings to which he had become so deeply attached, in a residence of over twenty years. ' Affection clung to every stone there, like the moss which grew with it,' he wrote long afterwards, and ' when this slender but strong tie was cut, most of the future happiness had to be invested in the mournful recollections of the past.'

In the first week of September, 1840, he arrived at last in England, consecrated a bishop now, and authorised to begin in earnest that great mission for which he had so long prepared. On September 16th, he reached Oscott, to be met with a triumphal welcome. The schoolboys had assembled at the lodge gates and drew his carriage up to the entrance of the College. The whole staff had donned their clerical vestments and formed in a procession to conduct him at once to the College chapel, while they all intoned the anthem *Ecce Sacerdos Magnus*. He was greeted with a solemn address of welcome to which he had to reply. His arrival had been awaited with tremendous excitement, for his reputation in England had been immensely enhanced by the success of his tour during the previous year ; and on the Continent he had become so widely known that the French Catholic organ the *Univers* proclaimed his appointment by announcing that he was ' going to take his place among the new Augustines whom a new Gregory sends forth to achieve a second time the conquest of England.' And at Oscott the interest in his arrival had been stimulated with unbounded enthusiasm by his friend, Father Spencer, who was a member of the College staff. Spencer could now feel that at long last the years of preparation were at an end, and the great work of the conversion of England was about to begin. Wiseman had scarcely had time before his arrival to exercise his new episcopal functions ; but on the first day after his consecration in Rome he had ordained two priests for the English mission, and he had given confirmation to the wife of a Belgian diplomat whom he had received into the Church shortly before.

To continue in England itself the work of education which he had been conducting with such conspicuous success in Rome for years, was the task that lay before him as President of Oscott. But he had come to England with a distinct sense of his own personal mission as a propagandist and as a leader of the Catholic revival. And the fact that he had been appointed coadjutor to the Midland District gave him immediate responsibilities and scope in regard to the Oxford Movement, which was developing within the district allotted to him. Before he had left Rome, he had already become aware of the sensation which had been caused at Oxford by his article on the Donatists in the previous summer. He had not written it with any sensational intention, and it was only one of several articles in which he had examined closely the theological and historical claims of the Catholicising party in the Church of England. Their general object, in so far as they desired to eliminate hostility to Catholic doctrines, and to create a more Catholic atmosphere within the Church of England, had commanded his sympathy ever since he had met Newman and Hurrell Froude in Rome seven years earlier. But he was continually discussing their attitude in public lectures or in the *Dublin Review*, and his article on the Donatists had been an extremely sympathetic attempt to consider how the Church of England would stand in relation to the Catholic Church even if all that the Tractarians claimed could be proved true, in regard to the continuity of Anglican orders and the continuity of Catholic doctrines.

To many Catholics of the old school, who regarded the whole Oxford Movement as an insincere and hypocritical attempt by dissatisfied Anglicans to call themselves Catholics without leaving the Church of England and forfeiting their ecclesiastical positions, Wiseman's sympathy with Newman and the other Tractarians seemed almost indecent. His article on the Donatists, in one sense, carried this sympathy to greater lengths than before. But its argument had precisely the opposite effect upon the Tractarians themselves. Instead of growing furious at the mere suggestion that Protestants should claim an unbroken continuity from the days before the Reformation, Wiseman had brushed aside the abstruse historical points of dispute, and boldly asked the Tractarians to consider how they would stand even if they could establish their claim. He had remembered that an almost precisely similar claim had been made in the fifth century, when the Donatists, who had no difficulty in proving the validity and continuity of their orders, had been confronted with the same problem. S. Augustine had dealt with their position at the time, and Wiseman now recalled that old controversy in its bearing upon the Tractarians. The controversy which had hitherto exasperated and bewildered most Catholics, and many Anglicans, by the highly technical manner in which it had been conducted, was suddenly simplified and made as plain as daylight by Wiseman's new approach to it. Leaving all historical investigation aside for the moment, he pointed out that S. Augustine's answer to the Donatists would be inevitable in regard to the Tractarians also. Their claim to be part of the Catholic Church could never survive so long as they refused to accept the supremacy of the Holy See. S. Augustine had dismissed the whole controversy with the Donatists by merely asking one of the Donatist bishops whether he could exercise his faculties in any part of the Catholic Church—as any orthodox Catholic bishop could. And when the Donatist bishop had been forced to admit that his faculties were thus limited, Augustine had simply pointed out that the whole is greater than any part which may claim equality with the whole, and that those who separated themselves from the whole Church thereby placed themselves in a state of schism.

The argument seems nowadays so simple that it is difficult to imagine how it had been overlooked. But Wiseman stated it with his brilliant powers of lucid argument, and he showed such an extraordinary closeness of analogy in detail between the claims of the Donatists and almost every claim that was then being put forward by the Tractarians, that his article compelled immediate attention. Its effect was all the greater both because Wiseman had entered the lists against the learned theologians of Oxford with a training and range of knowledge fully equal to their own, and because Newman in particular had been in recent years appealing more and more to the authority of the early Fathers of the Church. Now, Wiseman, in his persuasive and sincerely sympathetic way, was able to invoke a final decision by S. Augustine himself against them.

The article had been published for some time before Newman's attention had been called to it, but Robert Wilberforce showed it to him in September and its effect was instantaneous. Newman had recently been making a close study of the Monophysite schism, and its lessons had raised uncomfortable doubts in his mind. Now Wiseman's article was to attack him at the sorest point again. Wilberforce had pointed particularly to the words of S. Augustine ' *securus judicat orbis terrarum* '; and Newman himself has described[1] the immense shock it had given to his previous sense of security. ' He repeated these words again and again and, when he was gone, they kept ringing in my ears. " *Securus judicat orbis terrarum* "; they were words which went beyond the occasion of the Donatists ; they applied to that of the Monophysites. They gave a cogency to the article which had escaped me at first. They decided ecclesiastical questions on a simpler rule than that of Antiquity ; nay, S. Augustine was one of the prime oracles of Antiquity ; here, then, Antiquity was deciding against itself.' But long before Newman had ever contemplated writing his *Apologia*,

[1] *Apologia pro Vita Sua*, 116.

the disturbing effect of Wiseman's intervention had been made known to all Newman's friends. ' I must confess it has given me a stomach-ache,' he wrote[1] after reading it, to Rogers. ' You see, the whole history of the Mono-physites has been a sort of alterative. And now comes this dose at the end of it. It does certainly come upon one that we are not at the bottom of things. At this moment we have sprung a leak ; and the worst of it is that those sharp fellows, Ward, Stanley and Co., will not let one go to sleep upon it. I seriously think this a most uncomfortable article on every account, though, of course, it is " *ex parte*." '

Wiseman had in fact dropped a bombshell among the earnest Tractarians in Oxford on the eve of his departure to Rome during the previous autumn ; and through the winter Newman's fears had been amply fulfilled. He had been continually bombarded with urgent questions as to how Wiseman's argument could be circumvented. Newman had been forced to admit that this was their ' Achilles heel,' though ' a man must be a good shot to hit it.' And it had affected his whole attitude towards Rome during the last months before Wiseman left the Eternal City, to establish himself, so disconcertingly near at hand, in Oscott. Henceforward the Tractarians abandoned completely their assertion that Rome and not Canterbury was schismatic. And even so early as in October Newman had made the appalling confession to Henry Wilberforce that he might quite conceivably be driven ultimately to a complete submission to Rome.[2] The crisis passed, but it had left a subdued temper among the Tractarian leaders in Oxford ; and while they viewed Rome now with awe instead of the old hostility, the less adventurous spirits

[1] *Newman's Letters*, II, 286.
[2] *Life of Newman*, I, 68.

among them had grown apprehensive at the thought of Wiseman's coming to live in person within such easy reach of Oxford. They were unaware of the enormous difficulties that surrounded Wiseman himself in his new appointment. Father George Spencer, the convert parson was there, and the Oxford leaders attributed to the Catholic leaders a concern for their own conversion which made them regard Spencer with suspicion as the agent of Machiavellian plans. The Vice-President of Oscott, Dr. Logan, was also a convert ; so they had reason enough, on the face of things, for believing that Wiseman's arrival as President would be followed by an intensive bombardment of their own position. But in truth neither Logan nor Spencer had any great influence in the College, although Wiseman derived immense encouragement from their presence at Oscott. He was to find very soon how little sympathy was felt among his staff for his own ambitious and visionary programme. The convert architect Pugin was constantly there also ; but even he, as the pioneer of the Gothic revival, found more points of disagreement than of agreement with Wiseman's Roman outlook ; and only their common enthusiasm for the conversion of England made it possible for them to work together in the great architectural schemes which Pugin had planned.

But Wiseman had consecrated his whole being before his arrival at Oscott to the work of converting England ; and against innumerable and continual disillusionments and discouragements he strove valiantly to persevere in his own unwavering faith. His own staff, the clergy of the Midland District, the old Catholic families, all considered it their duty before long to endeavour to give him a more reasonable outlook upon the true conditions of the Church in England, and to open his eyes to what they regarded as the dishonesty and the insincerity of the Oxford party upon whose aspirations he had built such hopes, in his remoteness from the realities of English life. They impressed upon him the importance of his work in the College itself, and of the scope for so brilliant and versatile a scholar in educating the English Catholic body, without allowing his attention to be diverted to the fantastic eccentricities of the Tractarians at Oxford. But Wiseman fought valiantly against all their efforts to destroy his chivalrous enthusiasm. It was not to preside over a school in England that he had asked the Pope to relieve him of his great responsibilities at the English College, in Rome, and to sacrifice his own career and reputation in original scholarship. He still clung to his conviction that ' among the providential agencies that seemed justly timed, and even necessary ' for the great purpose of his own life, was ' the erection of this noble College, in the very heart of England.' ' Often in my darkest days and hours,' he wrote in a memorandum[1] afterwards, ' feeling as if alone in my hopes, have I walked in front of it, and casting my eyes towards it, exclaimed to myself, " No, it was not to educate a few boys that this was erected, but to be the rallying point of the yet silent but vast movement towards the Catholic Church, which has commenced and must prosper." I felt as assured of this as if the word of prophecy had spoken it.'

It had been assumed naturally enough that, with a coadjutor bishop as its new President, and one who enjoyed such immense prestige throughout England as well as in Rome, the College would have to be content with a limited claim upon Wiseman's time and energies. They were proud of his reputation, and dazzled by the

[1] Ward, I, 348.

ARCHBISHOP ERRINGTON

extraordinary versatility and learning which enabled him to speak with authority, and apparently with expert knowledge, upon almost every subject, when he brought an unending succession of celebrities to visit the College. And they felt fewer misgivings when he himself succeeded in getting his old colleague George Errington brought back from Rome to collaborate with him once more— Errington who inherited all the best traditions of the Catholic gentry, who was determined to raise the standard of education among the Catholic clergy, who was so sound as an administrator, so devotedly loyal to his superior, and who alone seemed capable of impressing upon him the necessity of avoiding romantic adventures in search of ambiguous converts, and of concentrating upon the solid work of reconstruction and organisation among the existing Catholic body. But always Wiseman seemed to be susceptible to the sentimental appeals of the convert Father Spencer ; and his preoccupation with the Oxford Movement became the subject of continual reproach. His friendship with the convert Pugin was one of the most picturesque and paradoxical features of the new regime. Pugin had, with Spencer and Phillips, looked forward with restless impatience to the arrival of Wiseman, as the one English Catholic of high standing who shared their own belief in the seriousness of the Oxford Movement. With his own great popular prestige as the reviver of Gothic architecture, he had been welcomed with open arms by old Dr. Walsh, the Vicar Apostolic in Birmingham, and he had built several beautiful churches in the district, besides the Cathedral church of S. Chad's, which was the first Catholic Cathedral to be built in England since the Reformation. But Pugin's impetuous enthusiasms had led him into acute con- troversies. His efforts to reintroduce the old English

vestments in the churches had resulted, in the year before
Wiseman's arrival, in a formal discouragement of his
plans from Rome itself, at the instigation of the older
school who distrusted him as a convert innovator, with
complete indifference to the fact that he was really trying
to revive pre-Reformation practices. The rebuke from
Rome had contained references to ' an architect converted
from heresy ' which pained Ambrose Phillips bitterly.
He had been the chief encourager of Pugin's efforts, and
in a letter to Lord Shrewsbury he had complained[1]
mournfully that ' they suspect our sincerity.' ' It is not
Propaganda that I complain of,' wrote Phillips, ' it is a
set of nominal heartless Catholics here at home, who have
misrepresented and calumniated us to Propaganda.
Men, who have no scruple themselves of violating rubrics
every day of their lives, who hesitate not to wear chasubles
of worsted in defiance of the Church, and who only cry
out against the restorers of the ancient glories of Religion,
because they know they do nothing themselves to restore
her long-lost influence, and because they hate those who
devote themselves zealously to the blessed work of re-
converting England. . . . I can tell you it is the same
party who are endeavouring to crush the restorers of
Christian art, who have vowed that Dr. Wiseman shall
never be bishop in England.'

Pugin's own protests[2] on the same subject to Phillips
were characteristically explosive. ' This is the result of
some diabolical falsehoods and misrepresentations made
at Rome by our adversaries. . . . Dr. Walsh found the
churches in his District worse than Barns ; he will leave
them sumptuous erections. The greater part of the
vestments were filthy rags, and he has replaced them with

[1] *Phillips de Lisle*, II, 220–1.
[2] *Ibid.*, II, 222.

silk and gold. For this he has been censured ! ! ! I am sick at heart. The apathy of the Catholic body on these things is alarming. I had formed dreams of returning glory ; but if this censure of the Propaganda is persisted in after the remonstrance which has been sent, I shall abandon all my hopes. I see everything that we had hoped dashed to pieces. Do not deceive yourself. My dear friend, do not deceive yourself ; the Catholics will cut their own throats, the clergy will put down religion. These are hard sayings, but they are twice mad fools : straining at gnats and swallowing camels, the very men who do not hesitate to violate rubrics every day to suit their own convenience or their pockets, now swelling with indignation and horror at the idea of an ample surplice or flowing chasuble such as almost every saint in the calendar wore. Administer baptism out of an old physic phial ; reserve the Blessed Sacrament in *dirty cupboard ;* say Mass in vestment made out of an old gown ; burn gas on the altar ; have everything as *mean*, as *pitiful*, as *shabby* as you please : hire Protestant performers to sing. *Leave out every ceremony in the ritual :* do all this and you will be right. But if you venture to speak of antient glory and ecclesiastical dignity, oh, you are a man of extravagant opinions, an enthusiast, a visionary—and *ecclesiastical censure* awaits you. Again I say I am disgusted.'

In such a mood did the great architect and his ardent friends await the arrival of Wiseman in Birmingham as a man after their own heart and as their own future champion at Rome. But the arrival of Wiseman, with his flamboyant Roman ideas and his love of brilliant colours and Italian atmosphere, soon produced wholly unexpected complications. Their taste in art was almost incompatible, and Wiseman's expert knowledge of Roman architecture and painting and sculpture were not the least of his varied

H

accomplishments. But Pugin, with his dark cloak and strange-looking trousers, his long hair and his irrepressible flow of explosive conversation about Gothic art, was the most intolerant of critics ; and he believed in his own mission to lead a Catholic revival in the arts as firmly as Wiseman believed in his own mission to lead a religious revival. If Pugin disapproved of a church steeple he would declare that the architect ought to be hanged from it. On a visit to S. Edmund's College he once[1] found Dr. Cox vested in an old French cope and preparing to say public prayers for the conversion of England. ' What is the use, my dear sir, of praying for the conversion of England in that cope ? ' was Pugin's agonised protest. If anyone introduced operatic music into church ritual, he would leave the building in an uncontrollable outburst of rage against such desecration. But Wiseman was a considerable expert on Italian music as well as the plastic arts, and he too had had dreams of introducing new and vigorous, though very different, ideas into the artistic expression of the Church in England.

Pugin had not only built S. Chad's Cathedral in Birmingham but was persevering vigorously in schemes for its development. Within a few months the conflict between his own austere ideas and what he regarded as the pagan influences of the former Rector of the English College in Rome had produced threats of his immediate resignation from the position of architect to the Cathedral. A frantic letter[2] from Pugin reached Ambrose Phillips in December, announcing that ' an affair has happened at Birmingham which has gone through me like a stab. We have had a tremendous blow aimed at us, and that from the centre of our camp. Dr. Wiseman has at last

[1] W. G. Ward and the Catholic Revival, p. 386.
[2] Phillips de Lisle, II, 213.

shown his real sentiments by attempting to abolish the great Rood Screen, after Mr. Hardman has given £600 for its execution. I say attempted, because I immediately wrote to John Hardman to this effect, that if the screen was suppressed, I should not remain architect to the church *one day* longer. . . . Yesterday I was informed the screen was not to be allowed ; but what a miserable state of things, the grand division between sacrifice and the worshippers, between priest and people, to be attempted to be abolished by those who *should* be foremost in their restoration. My dear Phillips, we nearly *stand alone*, if we except the Oxford men, for among them I find full sympathy of feeling. But the real truth is the churches I build do little or no good for want of men who know how to use them.' Nor were rood screens and medieval vestments the only matters over which conflict arose with Wiseman, when Pugin and Phillips had counted upon his fullest sympathy. Pugin was uncompromising in all things ; and in the same letter of protest to his ally he asserted with tragic emphasis that ' till the old Gregorian Music is restored nothing can be done.' His views on the prevalent Church music were almost inexpressible. ' Keighley was opened the other day,' he wrote concerning another of his churches, ' with a most horrible scene. Not only was all decorum violated but a regular row took place between the musicians, who quarrelled about their parts in the church.' ' Every building I erect is profaned,' he protested, ' and instead of assisting in conversions, only serves to disgust people. The church at Dudley is a complete facsimile of one of the old English parish churches, and nobody seems to know how to use it. The present state of things is quite lamentable and were it not for the Oxford men I should quite despair.'

It was evidence of Wiseman's personal humility and

desire to be adaptable that the crisis was surmounted in
a way which made him and Pugin close allies afterwards.
W. G. Ward in his old age used to tell the story[1] of an
occasion when their views clashed dreadfully in a church
which Pugin had built at Nottingham. Pugin had been
showing the mysteries of the building to an Anglican
friend, and had whispered solemnly that no one without
holy orders could enter the Sanctuary, when a priest
appeared there suddenly in company with two ladies.
Pugin summoned the sacristan in a passion of indignation,
and demanded their instant removal, when he was informed in an awed voice that it was Bishop Wiseman
conducting friends over the new church. Pugin, according to W. G. Ward's story, simply burst into tears. Even
on the matter of the Cathedral there were further acute
disagreements. In February 1841, Pugin wrote in
another outburst[2] to Ambrose Phillips : ' You will
be grieved to hear that all the altar fittings that were
made for Birmingham have been condemned by Dr.
Wiseman because they are all in strict conformity with
the antient solemn practices. I have just given up now
all hope of that church coming to anything really good :
it will not be the thing. Poor Hardman is quite disheartened since the attempt on the screen, and Mr.
Moore is thwarted in every way by the endeavour to
thrust Italian novelties into the churches we were raising
in the true old style. The bishop is cutting his most
energetic assistants from under him.'

But they found much common ground in other directions. In a revival of the Church's liturgy they co-operated
with unqualified harmony and enthusiasm ; and in the
great dream of converting England to Catholicism they

[1] *W. G. Ward and the Catholic Revival*, p. 386.
[2] *Phillips de Lisle*, II, 225.

recognised one another as indispensable allies. Pugin's genius was fully acknowledged in Oxford, and his conversion to the Catholic Church had been noted uneasily as a portent which could only with difficulty be explained away by his personal eccentricities. His conversion had, in fact, endeared him to many of Newman's disciples. They had felt all the shock occasioned by Wiseman's bombshell about the Donatists ; and, with intellects less subtle than Newman's, they had been driven much further forward towards acceptance of the Catholic doctrines. In February 1840, before Wiseman had yet been appointed to Oscott, Pugin had visited Oxford and been received enthusiastically by many of the Catholicising party ; and he had repeated his visit in October, a few months after Wiseman's arrival as coadjutor to the Vicar Apostolic in Birmingham. Pugin was an irrepressible talker, and he had enjoyed enormously his protracted conversations with W. G. Ward and Faber and Dalgairns and Bloxam, who was his special friend among the group. And when he returned to Birmingham, Wiseman had been able to gather from him a great many sidelights on the actual state of mind in Oxford. The substance of it was that they resented vigorously any suggestion of individual submissions to Rome, and still hoped for some sort of compromise with the Catholic Church which would give separate recognition as a local branch to at least a section of the Church of England, even if it contained only the more advanced High Church party.

There was as yet no means of knowing how far the influence of the Oxford Movement had extended ; but abundant evidence pointed to the widespread sympathy which it commanded all over England. Newman's personal leadership still exercised an almost hypnotic influence over the younger and the more intellectual elements in the Church of England, and his direct influence in Oxford was phenomenal. Not within living memory had any personality dominated Oxford as he had succeeded in dominating it. A new seriousness and earnestness affected all classes of people in the University, at a time when many of the professorships were still awarded almost without regard to academic qualifications, when dons were required to have scarcely as much ability or learning as an ordinary schoolmaster, and undergraduates passed their years as students in the University in a corresponding indifference to study or serious thought. But the Oxford Movement had somehow inspired the whole life of Oxford with a new interest in philosophy and history and scholarship, even apart from the austere rector of S. Mary's, who attracted to his church every don or undergraduate or studious person in the University town who was of any importance. That fact in itself gave encouragement to Wiseman and a confirmation of the high hopes which, from afar or in hurried visits to England, he had built upon the possibilities of the Oxford Movement. And when he learned that his own articles in the *Dublin Review* had been among the decisive factors in intensifying the Catholic tendencies of the movement which Newman inspired, he became more eager than ever to obtain direct information as to the progress of events in Oxford. In Pugin he had found one of the very few links in England between the Oxford Movement and the Catholic body, and Pugin's visit to Oxford in the early autumn of 1840, soon after his own arrival at Oscott, brought him into closer contact than he had yet found possible with the mentality of the Tractarian leaders.

Before Wiseman had come back to England, Father George Spencer also had gone to Oxford, on a mission to invite the Tractarian leaders to join in a definite crusade of prayer for the reunion of the Christian Churches. For two years now Spencer and Ambrose Phillips had been working to develop their international crusade of prayer among Catholics for the conversion of England, and they had met with a ready response in several countries, where Wiseman's intervention had carried much weight. The idea of asking the Oxford leaders themselves to pray for the reunion of Christendom was a new development, which must involve still closer consideration of their own position in regard to the Catholic Church ; and Spencer's friends in Oxford had no illusions as to his ulterior object. Newman himself had been deliberately rude and had refused to meet him at dinner, on the ground that he was an apostate from the Church of England. But it had cost him much to repudiate such advances from an old friend who still played so large a part in his thoughts, and he had written to him[1] afterwards, complaining half-heartedly that the English Catholics were a political and not a religious party, and telling him not to expect any sympathetic reception before he had broken off his connection ' with Mr. O'Connell and Ireland and the Liberal Party in England.' But a year had passed during which the ferment had been working constantly in Newman's mind, and in February 1841 there appeared the famous Tract 90—the last in fact, though not in intention, of the long series of ' Tracts for the Times,' of which the greater number had been written by Newman himself. Wiseman's article on the Donatists had been the beginning of the end. His arrival at Oscott had only hastened the pace, and now Newman had been impelled to writing a Tract which declared, in more daring and deliberate terms than he had yet adopted, that even the Thirty-nine Articles of

[1] Ward, I, 334.

the Church of England could only be interpreted ' according to the sense of the Catholic Church.'

For years now the Catholicising tendencies of the Tractarian party had been watched with increasing distrust and repugnance by the older theologians ; but Newman's influence and prestige and extraordinary gifts of writing made his critics hesitate before delivering any concerted attack upon him. Tract 90, however, carried the assertion of his Catholic claims to such a pitch that the inevitable explosion came at last. Newman's irrepressible disciple, W. G. Ward, brought a copy of it in great excitement to the rooms of a tutor of Balliol, Mr. Tait, who was afterwards to become Archbishop, and insisted upon his reading it at once. Tait waded through a good many pages without any special sign of being outraged in his feelings, until he came to one passage which awoke him to anger. Going at once to Ward's room, he demanded a clearer explanation of what he believed it to convey : and having been confirmed in his interpretation of it, he proceeded to rouse the other tutors against it. For some days nothing decisive happened, and Newman believed that danger of condemnation was passed. But a protest was soon lodged by Tait and three other tutors, and a few days later the joint protest by the Heads of Colleges released the long suppressed storm of exasperation through the country. One bishop after another came forward to repudiate publicly any association with the Tractarian leaders, and the immediate result was Newman's decision to discontinue publication of the ' Tracts for the Times.' The storm had broken with a vengeance, and within a few months Newman's unchallenged influence upon the Church of England was irretrievably shattered. In Oxford itself, interest in his teaching was increased, even after the heads of colleges had purposely changed their dinner hour so that under-graduates might be discouraged from attending his sermons. But although Oxford watched with growing excitement and curiosity the inevitable progress of New-man towards a complete surrender to Rome, his influence throughout the Church of England was broken, and he and his disciples were henceforward definitely suspected of dishonesty and of cowardice in refusing to abandon their positions.

1841 end of

T.M.

1841

Tract XC the 39 articles
must be interpreted according to
the sense of the C. Ch

CHAPTER VII

RELATIONS WITH THE TRACTARIANS (1841–42)

TO Wiseman the publication of Tract 90 and the commotion which it produced was in one sense the fulfilment of his dearest hopes. Ever since their first interview in Rome in 1833, he had watched the development of Newman's religious views with a tender and affectionate solicitude. Now, at last, his full acceptance of Catholicism seemed to have been brought definitely within sight. But this new phase had none the less surely destroyed most of the dream which had filled Wiseman's mind for so long. Through Newman's influence within the Church of England, he had believed that the Protestant Church would become more and more definitely Catholic, until the time arrived when the conversion of the Catholicising leaders would bring the majority of Anglicans as a body into the Catholic Church. But Tract 90, while it revealed the progress of Newman's own views up to a much more decisive stage, had in fact wrecked his own ascendancy within the Church of England. It had scandalised many of those who had followed him loyally and enthusiastically hitherto ; and it had at last provided the occasion for a general revolt by the traditional Protestant party, who had been impatiently waiting for the first opportunity to raise again the old "No Popery" cry.

Nevertheless, it was more a blow to those who had

encouraged Wiseman in his expectations from the Oxford Movement than to Wiseman himself. His own attention had been concentrated chiefly upon Newman ; and the uproar over the publication of Tract 90 seemed to have certainly forced Newman further along the road to conversion. But Ambrose Phillips, and still more Pugin, had been inspired with the hopes that Newman would undermine the Protestant traditions of the Church of England before he could see his own way to submission to Rome. Pugin had been in direct touch with the Oxford leaders by correspondence through the weeks in which the Tract was being written ; and the letters he received were submitted to Wiseman in the hope that he would withhold any further attempt to accelerate Newman's personal conversion, until his influence upon the Anglicans had extended still further. But when Tract 90 resulted in a violent reaction against Newman and his friends, Wiseman realised that their influence upon English Protestantism had been exploded ; and he was impatient now to extend a helping hand in the belief that they could no longer escape the logical consequences of their own frustrated efforts within the Church of England. Convinced that the time for immediate action had arrived, he wrote a letter at once to Newman, explaining that he had no intention of presuming upon their previous slight acquaintance in Rome, and that he only felt an ' earnest anxiety to convince.'

On that basis he set out to argue with Newman's contention that the Catholic Church had introduced practices and beliefs which conflicted with the decrees of the Council of Trent. Not for years had any Catholic prelate in England been so excellently equipped for replying with full authority to criticisms of the practice of Rome. Wiseman had lived for more than twenty years there, as a student, as a teacher, as Rector of the English College, and even as professor in the University of Rome itself. Other Catholic controversialists with Roman experience, when confronted with similar attacks that were obviously based upon ignorance or prejudice, had almost invariably retorted with scornful or bitter indignation. But Wiseman, with his unrivalled and universally recognised knowledge of the Roman system, besides his prestige as a theologian and historical student, was now patiently and persuasively pleading with Newman to reconsider his opinion. In an elaborate analysis of the objections raised by Newman, Wiseman disposed of each criticism in turn, before concluding with a masterly concentration upon the most vulnerable point. He had been replying to Newman's suggestion that Rome had been unfaithful to the decrees of Trent. But how came Newman to be appealing to the decrees of Trent at all ? Only a few years ago, he pointed out—with a dexterous argument so gently introduced that it could not be resented as a hostile thrust—Hurrell Froude had been alluding scornfully to the Catholics as ' wretched Tridentines.' Since when had the Tractarians changed their attitude in regard to the Council of Trent, to such an extent that instead of denouncing it, they should acclaim its decrees as a fount of authority ?

' I say this in a spirit, not of reproach, but of charitable warning,' Wiseman pleaded : ' you then blamed us for adhesion to them ; you now blame us for departure from them.' If their own judgements varied so, was it not possible that they themselves, rather than Rome, should be suspected of not knowing the real truth ? Then he recalled a long series of vital questions upon which the Oxford school had most unmistakably altered their views. ' When, in fine,' he concluded, ' you were more remote

to drive any plain man into resignation. They were appalled by Wiseman's persistent and increasing encouragement of a group of Anglican divines who at best were muddle-headed theologians still persevering in their attacks upon Catholic doctrines and practices. Conversions to Catholicism had been occurring with greater frequency for a number of years ; and the Tractarian Movement could scarcely fail to deter many probable converts by providing them with some sort of ingenious compromise that would at least postpone the necessity to face the sacrifices involved in a straightforward submission to Rome.

The old Catholics believed that Wiseman completely misunderstood the situation, and that his encouragement of the Tractarians was becoming positively mischievous to the prospects of the Catholic Church in England, within little more than a year of his arrival from Rome. They felt that he understood neither the effects of his own conduct upon the Church in England, nor the mentality of the Anglican divines whom he was encouraging ; and that his quixotic notions of placing a charitable interpretation upon all their actions were entirely misguided. Expostulations began to pour in upon him. His old master at Ushaw, Dr. Lingard—for whom he had exercised his influence, to provide a retreat when blindness overtook him, before he had yet left Rome—now wrote to him[1] earnestly to remind him of movements similar to this in the Reformation times. With his unrivalled learning in the history of the Reformation period, he plied Wiseman with instances of a similarly misplaced confidence on the part of English Catholics in Laud's day. And Bishop Griffiths, the Vicar Apostolic of the London District, where Wiseman had delivered the lectures which made his

[1] Ward, I, 378.

reputation in England, and led to his ultimate recall from Rome, now wrote in a similar strain to Dr. Lingard's, imploring him to be more prudent, and protesting that ' scarcely shall we find in history a body of schismatics returning with sincerity to the obedience of faith.' And before long a pamphlet asking bluntly ' Are the Puseyites sincere ? ' was published by a Catholic priest, Mr. Rathbone, who even asserted in it that ' the embrace of Mr. Newman is the kiss that will betray us.'

To Wiseman's acutely sensitive and emotional temperament such criticisms brought a real agony of distress. He was admittedly new to English conditions, and he was not even a Vicar Apostolic, but the coadjutor of an aged bishop who shared the views of the generation that had grown up in the austere and suspicious habits of seclusion which had been universal in England before the Emancipation Act. Even at Oscott he was constantly being reproached and urged to adapt his outlook to a more reasonable perspective of English conditions. In his distress he turned, with implicit confidence, for guidance to the Pope with whom he had the immense advantage of a long personal friendship. And Gregory XVI, knowing Wiseman intimately, and being inspired by a universal charity towards all the world, reassured him by expressions of confidence in his judgement as well as his good intentions. Even his friendship with O'Connell, and with Catholic Liberals in France like Montalembert and Lacordaire, created complications, both by prejudicing many of the old English Catholics against him, and by giving a new pretext for Newman to resist the prospect of any association with such forces. Newman and his friends declared that they were prepared to meet his cordial advances half way if he would undertake to desist from further attempts to secure individual sub-

missions to Rome, on the understanding that their
own minds should be left open and that in the last resort
they would be able to command a wider influence in the
Church of England if they should ultimately find surrender
inevitable. But Wiseman would make no such promise,
even though Ambrose Phillips and Pugin, who were his
chief source of contact with the Oxford leaders, hoped
strongly that he would. To Phillips he had written within
a month after the publication of Tract 90, to say how much
he wished for an opportunity of direct communication
with the Oxford leaders[1], but he ' had felt that he would
only be embarrassing them by any intercourse, as should it
become known, it would be immediately thrown in their
faces.' ' God knows that I would give my life,' he had
added, ' if it would hasten the reunion of this country,
or of part of it, with the Apostolic See and the Church
Catholic.'

And a few days later, in a memorable letter, after
explaining that Bishop Walsh, as Vicar Apostolic of the
Midland District, shared his own view that they should
neglect no opportunity of exploiting every possibility
that might arise through the Oxford Movement, he
wrote to Ambrose Phillips with absolute candour, of his
own desire to see an infusion of new blood into the
Catholic body which had fallen into a ' low state.' One
thing, he declared,[2] would at once affect the improvement
that everyone must desire. ' Let us have an influx of
new blood ; let us have but even a small number of such
men as write in the Tracts, so imbued with the spirit of
the early Church, so desirous to revive the image of the
ancient Fathers—men who have learnt to teach from
S. Augustine, to preach from S. Christopher, and to feel

---

[1] Ward, I, 382.
[2] *Ibid.*, I, 385.

I

from S. Bernard ; let even a few such men, with the high clerical feeling which I believe them to possess, enter fully into the spirit of the Catholic religion, and we shall be speedily reformed, and England quickly converted. I am ready to acknowledge that, in all things, except the happiness of possessing the truth, and being in communion with God's true Church, and enjoying the advantage and blessings that flow thence, we are their inferiors. It is not to you that I say this for the first time. I have long said it to those about me—that if the Oxford Divines entered the Church, we must be ready to fall into the shade and take up our position in the background. I will gladly say to them " *Me oportet minui.*" I will willingly yield to them place and honour, if God's good service require it. I will be a co-operator under the greater zeal and learning and abilities of a new leader. Depend upon it, they do not know their own strength. It is true that, weak as we are, they cannot prevail against us, because a stronger One than they is with us, and supports us. But let them be with us, and their might, in his, will be irresistible. Abuses would soon give way before our united efforts, and many things which now appear such to them would perhaps be explained.'

With such intense convictions, it was impossible for Wiseman to hold aloof from encouragement of the Oxford Movement, no matter how much criticism he might provoke among the old Catholics. His letter to Phillips, written while the storm over the publication of Tract 90 was in full blast, was forwarded to Pugin at once with a request that he should show it to his Oxford friends. It was no wonder that they sought his sympathy there after, and felt confident that at least one Catholic did not impugn their motives or doubt the sincerity of their religious aims. But Wiseman himself still continued to

receive new converts.   On Good Friday he was writing
again[1] to Phillips to announce that ' Mr. C. Hemans,
son of the poet, a charming young man, with all her
feeling and inspiration, came here on Thursday, a Protestant, and leaves us this evening a Catholic. He is not
the only *straggler* towards Rome that has come in my way :
I have several most singular and interesting corre-
spondences, with persons I have never seen, but who are
most anxious to become Catholics.' ' I believe Mr.
Newman is right,' his letter continued ; ' a fire has been
kindled—not by them, but by God. He can use the chaff
and straw of his barn floor for this purpose as well as
burning brands from his altar—and this fire no man can
extinguish. But its spread may be much checked,' he
noted significantly ' not by Protestants, but by Catholics,
some of whom seem unknowingly bent upon doing it.'

Already he had decided that the Catholic hostility
towards the Tractarian Movement was a problem upon
which Rome itself should decide. He felt that a full
report of the developments and their possibilities should
be made known at once to the Pope personally. His own
familiarity with the leading personages in Rome gave him
an immense advantage for preparing the ground ; and he
had decided accordingly to send ' a full account of all
that is going forward to one of the discreetest members of
the Sacred College, Cardinal Mai, with a request that he
will show what I write to none but the Pope.' If he could
once be certain that he had gained the full approval of
the Pope himself, then ' I shall not care for all the world,
nor allow differences of opinion to check my exertions.'
To Dr. Russell of Maynooth he wrote about the same time[2]
declaring his unqualified conviction that the Tractarians

[1] *Phillips de Lisle*, I, 285.
[2] Ward, I, 388.

' are every day becoming more and more disgusted with Anglicanism, its barrenness, its shallowness, and its " stammering " teaching. Their advance is so steady, regular, and unconscious, that one of two things must follow : either they will bring or push on their Church with them, or they will leave her behind. The first is their great object ; the second may be their gain. If their Church repel them and attempt to damp their efforts, they will abandon her, for their hearts have allowed Catholicism to take too deep root in them for it to be plucked up by . . . Anglo-episcopal authority.' In the meantime, should individuals request advice as to their duty, he was convinced that there could be no alternative to impressing upon them the duty to yield at once to conviction. Hitherto, however, he had found none of them ready for any such decisive step, and in such cases he believed that they must ' push them forward in their view so as to make them diffuse it in every direction,' and ' invite them towards us rather than repulse them.' For his own part he wished that they could become Catholics immediately and one by one, ' but if they will not do that, I should be sorry to check them in their present course.'

It was evidence of the isolation of Wiseman's position at the time that he should have had to turn to Maynooth for allies in the work to which he had determined to devote his life. In Dr. Russell, who was one of the principal contributors to the *Dublin Review*, he had found a real sympathy with his own enthusiasms, and he was overjoyed to learn that direct relations had been opened between the Irish theologian and Newman, as the result of their own correspondence. Dr. Russell also was an isolated figure, but his generous nature succeeded in modifying the attitude of various Irish priests who had been delivering invectives against what they regarded as the hypocrisy and dishonesty of the Tractarians. A more difficult and apparently insuperable problem was to dissociate Catholicism in Ireland from the strongly democratic programme and the violent political methods of Daniel O'Connell, who was identified in the eyes of the world with the views of the whole Irish laity. And even the saintly Archbishop Murray in Dublin, who shared Wiseman's enthusiasm for the Catholic revival on the Continent, and had almost immediately introduced branches of Frederic Ozanam's Vincent de Paul Society to his own diocese, was unable to restrain the Irish hierarchy from an almost unqualified association with O'Connell's public activities. Newman, as a fastidious Conservative, detested O'Connell's politics and methods ; and when O'Connell's defiant claim that Catholicism involved support of popular movements was still a serious stumbling-block even to so intellectual a theologian as Newman, it sufficed by itself to deter many old-fashioned Anglicans from even contemplating a submission to the Catholic Church.

That special aspect of the problem had been impressed upon Wiseman directly by Ambrose Phillips, who had succeeded in drawing Newman into an important confidential correspondence through the intervention of their mutual friend Bloxam. ' While Rome is what she is, union is impossible,' Newman had written.[1] ' Rome must change first of all in her spirit. We must see more sanctity in her than we do at present. Alas ! I see no marks of sanctity, or, if any, they are chiefly confined to converts from us. . . . I say not all this in reproach, but in great sorrow. What Hildebrand did by faith and holiness they do by political intrigue. Their great object

[1] *Phillips de Lisle, I, 205.*

is to pull down the English Church. They have to do with such a man as O'Connell. Never can I think such ways the footsteps of Christ. If they want to convert England, let them go barefooted into our manufacturing towns—let them preach to the people like S. Francis Xavier—let them be pelted and trampled on—and I will own that they can do what we cannot. I will confess that they are our betters far . . . I can feel nothing but distrust and aversion towards those who offer peace yet carry on war.' That letter had been written in the week after Tract 90 had appeared ; and Wiseman, when he was shown it, could forgive its complacency and its ignorant prejudice in his elation at the extraordinary advance which the Tract had made. He could rely upon the inexhaustible patience and eagerness of Ambrose Phillips to reply at suitable length, with evidence that the Catholics were not as devoid of better feelings as Newman, in his ignorance, believed. Ambrose Phillips was in a unique position for answering Newman, not only as a convert himself with infinite sympathy towards the difficulties of Anglicans, but as the zealous pioneer of various monastic foundations in England, in which the ascetic virtues were in fact practised in a degree which the censorious Newman could scarcely conceive. And Phillips had even gone so far,[1] in his desire to be encouraging, as to ' effect a stoppage of the circulation of Dr. Wiseman's Tracts against the High Church claims in this neighbourhood.' ' I have no right to judge a Bishop,' he wrote, ' but I confess I thought the publication of those Tracts ill-timed from the first moment I heard of them, and I was not aware till a few days ago that any had been circulated hereabouts ; for the future it is stopped. I should deem it ungrateful to circulate such things now, after the

[1] *Phillips de Lisle*, I, 208.

glorious vindication of the Pope of Rome from the absurd charge of his being the Anti-Christ which appeared in the last Number but one of the *British Critic*.' He suggested politely, however, that ' the Oxford Men ' should not continue to circulate such tracts as Mr. Percival's *Roman Schism*. ' It is in vain that I call upon our men to conciliate, when they can retort upon me such violations of a conciliatory course on the part of the Anglicans at Oxford.'

It may be doubted whether Wiseman himself, who had already incurred so much disapproval by his leniency towards the Tractarians, would have countenanced the extreme lengths of compromise to which Phillips was prepared to go in order to gain Newman's confidence. But Newman knew that Phillips had the ear of Wiseman, and of Dr. Walsh, the Vicar Apostolic in Birmingham ; and he continued the correspondence even after Phillips had impressed upon him most emphatically that he could claim no official or authoritative status as a negotiator. And Wiseman was so anxious to establish some sort of real contact with Newman that he was prepared to overlook much in the excessive zeal of his convert friend. His allies in the great task he had undertaken were few enough ; and he was glad that Phillips, in his sanguine way, should take the Earl of Shrewsbury also into his confidence. Phillips wrote to Lord Shrewsbury to tell him that a most confidential report was being forwarded by Wiseman to the Pope through Cardinal Mai ; and without entering into particulars, he expressed his own conviction[1] that ' of this you may rest assured that the reunion of the Churches is certain.' His account of his own plans, in which he hinted clearly that Wiseman concurred, was that Newman had ' lately received the adhesion of *several hundreds* of the clergy,' and that,

[1] *Phillips de Lisle*, I, 217.

' as the dissenting party is on the alert,' and as ' they are joined, politically at least, by the Low Church Party,' ' we find it necessary to *blind* them, the more so as we are not ready to act yet, and probably shall not be for the next three years AT EARLIEST.' This, he explained, was the reason why the ' Oxford Men ' were at present placing an exaggerated emphasis upon the practical abuses supposed to exist among Catholics—' for the purpose of throwing dust in the eyes of the Dissenters and the Low Church Men.'

Had Wiseman known what intrigues were being attributed to him in this way by Ambrose Phillips it may well be that he would have felt obliged to publish a formal disclaimer. But Phillips was so convinced by his own expectations from the Oxford Movement, that he was already trying to mobilise influences in Rome against any precipitate action. ' Urge at Rome the necessity of immense prudence and forbearance,' he wrote to Lord Shrewsbury, who was on a visit there, ' to do everything to *encourage*, nothing to *damp* : not to call upon those Men quit their own communion in order to join ours, but to proceed on courageously with their holy and glorious intention of *reconciling* their CHURCH to OURS : remember this involves the reconciliation of the *kingdom*, of the *aristocracy* with all its wealth and power, of the *Nation*. A false step would spoil all, would produce a Protestant reaction, and would defeat the hopes of the Holy See for another century.' He even desired Shrewsbury to show his letter, if it might be helpful, to the General of the Jesuits, to Lacordaire, and to Cardinal Mai.

What Rome would make of this extravagant zeal can easily be imagined. To be urged by the young convert squire in Leicestershire to ' forward matters *gently*, and

not *precipitately*,' was a piece of advice which the Holy
See very seldom needed. And the last paragraph of his
letter, declaring that ' we must have the Whigs out before
we can complete things,' revealed a still more insular point
of view, which might easily have damaged Wiseman's
prestige. But Cardinal Mai and the Pope himself had
known, from long acquaintance with Wiseman, that
he was well able to withstand any invitation to mix a
religious crusade with English party politics, or to relax
his efforts in winning converts because a group of ' Oxford
Men ' required time to make up their minds. Tract 90
had widened the scope of the controversy enormously,
and its effect had certainly been to revive Protestantism
in the Church of England rather than to win fresh adherents to Newman's party. And Wiseman in fact,
though he published a letter in the *Tablet* which gave
great pleasure to Bloxam, still adopted a tone so different
from that of Phillips that Newman hinted broadly, in
his next letter, that only a sense of deference to the
Bishop's position prevented him from making invidious
comparisons. Even Newman felt that the unbridled
enthusiasm of his Catholic correspondent ought to be
damped down. He thanked him in a later letter for kind
messages conveyed from Wiseman, but added[1] with more
than a faint touch of his genius for irony : ' Of course it
cannot but be most deeply interesting to me to know that
any persons are thinking of me at solemn times. May
their prayers be fulfilled in their substance, that is, in
God's way, though not in the way which they think is
God's ! ' And with that sincerity which had already captivated Wiseman, he impressed upon the Catholic intermediary, whose deferential attitude would have been so
flattering to a lesser man, that ' You overrate our exertions,

[1] *Phillips de Lisle*, I, 224-5.

our influence, our tendencies. We are but a few, and we are what we are. Many times before now in the course of the last 300 years has a hope of concord arisen among Christians, but as yet it has ever come to nothing. When was a great schism ever healed? Why should ours cease, if that between the East and West had continued so long? And if a growth in sanctity be a necessary condition of it in both parties, what stipulation can be more costly, more hopeless? No, I feel that both parties must resign themselves to dying in their estrangement; but that is no reason they should not, though they be a few against many, both pray and labour against it.'

Never, in all the immense output of his genius, did Newman surpass the beauty and the poignancy of that letter to the correspondent whom he had not even seen. Never did he give more compelling proof of the utter sincerity and loneliness of his own pilgrimage, than in this passage of intimate self-revelation to a young man of great possessions but of transparent integrity and nobility of character, who was actually imploring Rome itself, with an influence that was by no means inconsiderable, to accept at his own exaggerated valuation the achievements and the intellectual importance of the leader of the Oxford Movement. Had Newman, with his strong prejudices against Rome still obscuring his vision and distorting the direction of his life, retained even the ordinary human instinct to score off his opponents, he had a unique and completely unhoped-for opportunity to entangle the more sentimental among the English Catholics, and to discredit even his most dangerous opponent, Bishop Wiseman at Oscott. As yet, there was not the slightest disposition on Newman's part to acknowledge that he had been defeated in any way. They were still adversaries, contending, albeit with a

most unusual chivalry, on opposite sides ; each seeking
to prove in the presence of the whole English public that
his opponent was in the wrong. And the wildly indiscreet
letters which Newman had been receiving from Ambrose
Phillips were sufficient to cause a devastating explosion,
if Newman had allowed any inkling of them to be made
known. Rome itself would have been compelled to issue
a formal condemnation of this zealous convert who, with
the best intentions, was prepared to appeal to Rome itself
to temporise while its avowed adversaries were playing
with the idea of their own potential submission upon
inconceivable terms.

And behind Ambrose Phillips there was the immense
personal prestige of Wiseman, with his international
reputation and his long experience as Rector of the
English College in Rome. He had compromised himself
to an extent that could never have been explained away,
if the approaches by Ambrose Phillips had been made
public. And if Wiseman's prestige and influence could
have been undermined, the relief to most of Newman's
followers throughout the country—who still regarded
him as an Anglican champion, and not as a weakling preparing to surrender—would have been immense. But
with Newman, personal ambition, or even the desire to
defeat an opponent, had long ceased to have any influence whatsoever. And it was the supreme distinction
of Wiseman in regard to the Oxford controversy that,
in spite of his inexperience of English conditions, in
spite of all the obvious pitfalls against which his most
loyal and devoted friends among the old Catholics were
continually warning him, he discerned the true character
of Newman's religious odyssey, and persisted against
every sort of opposition, in asserting his own conviction
that Newman was no hypocrite or timeserver, but some-

thing very near to be being a saint. 'I feel now quite satisfied,' he had written[1] to Dr. Russell of Maynooth, very soon after the appearance of Tract 90, 'that Mr. Newman is acting with the greatest sincerity, that his whole affairs are directed towards a reunion, not a distant theoretical union, but a practical one, and that as soon as it can be openly agitated without causing too great alarm.'

[1] Ward, I, 388.

CHAPTER VIII

THE SURRENDER OF NEWMAN (1842-45)

NEWMAN'S letter of deliberate discouragement had thrown Ambrose Phillips into a mood bordering upon despair. But Phillips was the only Catholic whom Newman could regard as holding the view that the Oxford Movement should be encouraged to persevere in its endeavour to Catholicise the Church of England without pressure being brought to bear upon individual leaders to abandon their efforts and to surrender at once to Rome. Had Wiseman shared the attitude of Phillips, the submission of Newman might have been delayed for many years. But he was being attacked by a much more persistent critic in his own camp, W. G. Ward, whose insatiably adventurous temperament made him entirely indifferent to consequences so long as the demands of logic were satisfied. Ward never ceased to bombard him with protests against manifestations of the Protestant spirit, which had become much more frequent since the publication of Tract 90 ; and his irrepressible inquiries for answers, either to the Protestant reactionaries or to the sympathetic advances by Wiseman and his friends, left Newman utterly without peace.

A stony silence surrounded the Oxford leaders for some time after Newman had written his deliberately discouraging letter to Ambrose Phillips. Bernard Smith, who had his own sources of information, wrote to Wiseman to say that he also was unable to penetrate the 'mysterious silence.' And Bloxam, the zealous intermediary between Newman and Phillips, wrote despondently that he was 'greatly puzzled to know what could have been in Newman's letter to have dismayed, grieved and annoyed Bishop Wiseman.' Newman on his side professed inability to judge whether it was the manner or the matter of what he had written that could have given offence. And before long Newman was writing again to Phillips to impress[1] upon him again that he 'did not expect the union of Churches in our time,' and that he personally 'most distinctly could not be party to any agitation' for reunion. He intended to 'remain quiet in his own place, and to do all he could to make others take the same course.' 'This I conceive to be my simple duty,' he wrote ; 'but over and above this paramount consideration, I believe it to be the wisest and more expedient course for the eventual union of the Church Catholic. I will not attempt to reap before the sowing ; I will not set my teeth on edge with sour grapes.' But he warned Phillips solemnly that, while he quite expected to see individual instances of secession to Rome, yet 'if such an event were to happen, it would be a greater misfortune to you than a grief to us. If there is any one thing calculated more than another to extinguish all hope of a better understanding between Rome and England, by discrediting us with our own people and rendering us suspicious of yourselves, it would be the conversion by you of some of our members. If your friends wish to put a gulf between themselves and us, let them make converts ; but, not else.'

To Phillips this letter was a still more crushing blow. And after months of reflection, he despatched a long letter

[1] *Phillips de Lisle*, I, 228.

to Cardinal Acton in Rome, in 1842, reviewing in great
detail and with intimate personal knowledge the history
of the Oxford Movement from its beginnings, emphasis-
ing all the influences or signs that seemed to indicate a
desire for reunion of Anglicanism with the Catholic
Church, and repudiating any imputation of insincerity
against the Tractarian leaders. His memorial was written
with extraordinary intensity of feeling, and with real
eloquence ; and it still revealed a spirit of indomitable
hopefulness. ' Oh, yes, England is ripe for the harvest,'
he declared,[1] ' England will again be an island of Saints.
She will be one of the brightest gems in the Church's
diadem, but the hour is not yet quite arrived ; there must
be, my friends tell me, a great scourge first, a storm
must cast to the Earth the last fruits of Protestantism
before the tree shall be in a condition to bear Catholick
fruit. Everything that we see around us gives warning
of the coming storm ; when it shall have passed, the atmosphere will be clearer, and we shall see better in what
way God will restore His Kingdom in England.' For the
present he implored, in all humility, that the Holy See
should take the preliminary step of restoring the Catholic
hierarchy, for ' if this were done Catholick Bishops would
be prepared for the old Sees, ready to take the place of
the Anglican ones as they died off, when once Government should take the Reunion up. If we go on as we are,
we shall never do much. We are so dreadfully disunited
(I mean we English Catholicks) and I attribute it in a great
measure to the small number of Bishops and the absence
of an antient holy hierarchical organisation.' So, even
the exuberant spirits of Ambrose Phillips had been cast
down ; and the nature of his pleading at Rome was

---

[1] *Ibid.*, I, 237

scarcely calculated to enhance the reputation of Wiseman for balanced judgement, when he was already being criticised on all sides for his exaggerated sense of the possibilities of converting England from its deeply rooted Protestant traditions.

Wiseman also had passed through a stage of bitter disillusionment. In May 1841, when the storm was still raging over Tract 90, he had written to Phillips to say[1] that his latest report upon the Oxford Men had ' filled him with consolation and sincere joy.' He intended at once to forward the contents of the letter to the Pope through Cardinal Mai, as before, and he believed that a journey to Rome during the vacation had become imperative, since such matters could not be adequately discussed in writing. He explained his own sense of responsibility if he should become (as he ' earnestly desired to become ') ' the organ of intercourse between the Holy See and their Oxford friends ' ; and he felt that ' clear and direct instructions ' from Rome were now urgently necessary. ' Again, I should like something to emanate from the Pope towards encouraging our views—recommending mildness, prayer, calling on the Bishop for reform, etc., and particularly checking all alliance with Dissenters. All this I could probably get done by going on the spot, but not otherwise. I have entered on this matter to ask you what you think of such a plan—*no one, of course, must hear of it.*' Only his own Bishop, Dr. Walsh, was to be told, apart from ' one most prudent person,' whom he had already consulted under confessional secrecy, in order to have some advice for his own guidance. That such a letter from any Catholic bishop should have encouraged Ambrose Phillips in his own exalted frame of mind was inevitable,

[1] Ward, I, 391.

and all the more when the Bishop was Wiseman, who was well known to command the Pope's special confidence and to be intimately acquainted with the most important Cardinals in Rome.

But before Wiseman's second letter to Cardinal Mai had been dispatched, a blow had fallen which made him refrain from sending it. A letter from Newman had, he told Phillips, not only been ' most distressing ' but had thrown him on his back and fearfully dispirited him, so that he had begun even to fear that he might have been deceiving himself all along—as so many devout and friendly Catholics had implored him to realise—and might even have been ' misguiding the Holy See.' The letter from Newman had arisen out of a defence of O'Connell which Wiseman had undertaken, from his personal experience, upon a certain point. In that Newman had acquiesced ; but he had taken the opportunity to tell Wiseman that he regretted his ' attempt to vindicate the invocations of the B.V. used in the Church.' Newman, he now told[1] Phillips in dismay, ' augurs it as a bad omen that we do not give them up. Now really, if his expectation was that the Church, or we, should give up our tender and confident devotion towards the Holy Mother of God or that the least of her pastors would join (on his private judgement) with Mr. Palmer in condemning expressions sanctioned and approved by her Pontiffs, how high indeed must his demands of condescension be before we can hope for reunion ! ' It had been a tremendous shock to Wiseman's whole confidence in the trend of the Oxford Movement ; and his protest to Phillips was almost a personal reproach. For it was Phillips and George Spencer who had first aroused his sympathy

[1] *Ibid*, I, 393.

K

with the movement when he had been in Rome ten years
before ; and it was upon Phillips he had lately relied
chiefly for a full and candid account of the real feelings
that lay behind their published writings and speeches.

In the following months his letters to Phillips showed
more and more that he was working now for individual
conversions rather than for any corporate reunion with
the Anglicans. ' My own impression,' he wrote,[1]
' still is that the first break-up of Protestantism will be
the secession of a large body of young men who will not
have patience to wait for the more prudent measures of
their leaders. I believe there are many ready for this step,
but none dares to take it first, and I think the enemy of
man will fight hard for preventing the first.' Exciting
possibilities, however, arose when he had to go to Oxford
in the course of his ecclesiastical duties ; and the question
of whether he should meet Newman had to be decided.
Bloxam conveyed to him the general feeling that a meeting
would be imprudent, as it would only lead to rumours
and gossip. But Wiseman expressed an earnest desire
that any of the Tractarians who wished should come and
visit him afterwards at Oscott. He had been profoundly
impressed by a remark of Bernard Smith's, that they regarded Catholic practices and institutions ' as things pas
or possible, not as things actually existing and acting.
And in the summer the first of such visits had taken
place. Before long the ice had been broken, and the
hospitality of Oscott was extended with increasing fre
quency to leaders and to younger disciples of the Move
ment, who would come in a spirit of distrustful curiosity
but were invariably captivated by the human sympathies
the religious enthusiasm and the scholarly culture of it
President.

[1] Ward, I, 393.

Among his own circle in Oscott Bishop Wiseman's connection with the Oxford controversy was naturally the subject of great interest. One of his pupils during these critical years was the future Lord Acton, who gave his personal recollections to Wilfrid Ward long afterwards, when his own contemporaries—Lord Dormer, Archbishop Stonor, Bishops Bagshawe and Knight, and all his other immediate friends—were already dead. ' We were proud of him,' Acton wrote ;[1] ' we were not afraid of him ; he was approachable and gracious, and no great friend of discipline, and I heard him boast that he never assigned punishment. We were conscious that he was a conspicuous, even a celebrated man, and that he had the best of the Oxford controversy. The converts used to appear amongst us, and he seemed to exhibit their scalps.' But even his pupils, or at least, the more discerning, like Acton himself, were aware of the difference of outlook among the various members of the College staff. The ' Roman element,' as he calls it, was chiefly represented by Wiseman's most intimate friend George Errington, whom he had brought from the College in Rome to become his assistant once more. There was a distinct group of early converts who had become Catholics before the Oxford Movement—Father Spencer, Dr. Logan, and Father Heneage. There was an admixture of Irish Catholics on the staff ; and there were the ecclesiastics drawn from the ranks of the clergy in the Midland district. And after a time there were even converts from the Tractarian Movement itself—Renouf, Bernard Smith, and J. B. Morris. To amalgamate and direct all these diverse elements would have been a task beyond the capacity of most Rectors ; and Acton, in

[1] *Ibid.*, I, 348.

retrospect, declared his own belief that Wiseman scarcely even attempted it. ' He was thinking of other things, and looking far afield, and these other things were what characterised him. We used to see him with Lord Shrewsbury, with O'Connell, with Father Mathew, with a Mesopotamian Patriarch, with Newman, with Pugin, and we had a feeling that Oscott, next to Pekin, was a centre of the world.'

To have conveyed such an impression to his pupils was in itself a great achievement, and Acton was not alone in regarding it as ' stimulating and encouraging,' and as a reinforcement of his authority. And a similar impression was given to his biographer by Bernard Smith, who had become one of the College staff in the years immediately preceding Newman's conversion. ' A man with great gifts, great designs, and a truly large heart,' was his description of Wiseman, whom he regarded as ' emphatically a great Bishop rather than a great President.'

From his first appointment to Oscott there had been this inevitable conflict between his dual responsibilities as a College President and as a coadjutor Bishop who felt that he had a special mission to encourage the Oxford Movement. Bernard Smith states quite frankly that he displayed a surprising ignorance even of ordinary matters of College routine and of the methods adopted by his staff. But his public activities reflected his own prestige upon the College ; and his pupils, no less than his professional staff, responded vigorously to his personal example. And the more zealous of his staff shared Smith's own conviction that ' as a Bishop, constantly visiting various parts of the diocese, giving retreats to the clergy, urging them to greater zeal and raising their tone, he was indeed an acquisition to the Church in England ; and still more as a centre of the Catholic Movement.' His direct personal influence was very wide. ' Not only was he in direct communication with leaders of the Oxford Movement, but he was in touch with the world in a way in which no other English Catholic of the time was. He was much away from the College visiting at great houses, Protestant and Catholic. His presence at Oscott, as well as that of Mr. Spencer and Mr. Heneage —an ex-diplomatist, who received Holy Orders—brought there from time to time distinguished men of the world. We had visits from such men as Mr. Gladstone, Lord Lyttleton, the Duc de Bordeaux, Daniel O'Connell, Lord Spencer, Monckton Milnes (afterwards Lord Houghton) and many others.' It was with such figures they always associated him. Alone, he was often uncommunicative and wrapped in his own thoughts. But in a distinguished gathering he was always stimulated to his best form, and there could be no one more interesting. And when O'Connell came, on his occasional visits, to discuss the progress of Catholicism as one of the founders of the *Dublin Review*, and as the leader of the Catholic democracy in Ireland, even the suppressed Irish side of Wiseman's character would suddenly emerge ; and students and pro-fessors would watch with fascination the two big genial Irishmen, walking arm-in-arm and roaring with laughter as they exchanged good stories. It was no wonder that the boys regarded him with hero-worship, which was only in-tensified by his affectionate enjoyment of his occasional relaxations among them, and deepened by his relation with many of them as their confessor and spiritual director. With them, the gravity of his manner would entirely disappear, and he would mingle with them as light-heartedly as any of themselves. His spontaneous enthusiasms and his impulsiveness, however, frequently had its disadvantages for those members of the staff who were responsible for discipline or for finance. Bernard Smith states that ' once he had made friends with Pugin, he gave him *carte blanche* to a great extent. He always seemed to think that the necessary money ought to come somehow. The result was considerable pecuniary embarrassment for the College, and for this among other reasons he was criticised by the professors.'

But Wiseman had brought such an enlargement of interests and of activity to the College since he became its President, that he could not be judged by any ordinary standards. The prospect of his arrival, with all his prestige both in Rome and in England, had been an immense encouragement ; and as a personality he had more than fulfilled expectations. Anxieties and criticism of him for devoting so much attention to the Church of England had followed, but the new phase which opened when he began to have Tractarian visitors at the College was very soon to produce such startling results that criticism was quickly silenced. Bloxam and Ward and Oakeley had boldly ventured to accept his hospitality, besides staying with Ambrose Phillips in Leicestershire ; and in October, 1841, the visit of a Fellow of Magdalen, Ralph Waldo Sibthorpe, resulted in a tremendous sensation. Sibthorpe decided at once to become a Catholic, and there was no denying that Wiseman's persuasiveness had won him over. The first signs of inevitable crash had at last appeared. Newman accepted the news as stoically as he could, considering that his own warnings had been ignored with disastrous results. Ambrose Phillips could only dread the breakdown of all his own efforts to build up friendly relations, and his fears were soon confirmed by the cessation of Bloxam's constant correspondence.

But Pugin's restless enthusiasm was always active,

and his genius as an architect gave him access to many who were prepared to tolerate his proselytising fervour as an eccentricity. Bernard Smith had been presented with a living in his father's disposal in Lincolnshire, and he invited Pugin to stay with him while designing the interior decorations of his church. They conversed freely about religious matters, and Smith's unguarded allusions to Catholic priests officiating in disguise produced a terrific explosion on Pugin's side. Having admitted that he had once heard Catholic doctrines preached in a Wesleyan chapel, and explained reflectively that he thought it must have been 'a Roman priest assuming the rôle of a Wesleyan minister without the Wesleyans being aware of it,' Smith was ferociously reprimanded by Pugin and told that it was his duty to make the acquaintance of English Catholics in order to avoid the repetition of such ignorant accusations of dishonest conduct. Smith felt remorseful and acted upon Pugin's advice. He accepted an introduction to Wiseman, made friends with some of the Catholic clergy in Birmingham and was enormously impressed by his visits in their company to the sick and dying. Smith's earnestness and simplicity had won the confidence of Newman to a degree which many abler men never approached ; and through him Newman also gradually developed doubts as to the ubiquitous machinations of Jesuits, in which he still vaguely believed.

Social intercourse with the English Catholics was producing more effect than all the interminable controversies by correspondence, and not the least factor in Newman's change of attitude was the report of a conversation between Bernard Smith and a simple Catholic priest in a northern parish. Smith had been so much astonished by finding the priest reading a volume of S. Augustine that he felt that the volume must have been taken down solely to create a favourable impression. Refusing to be bluffed, he had left the house and returned several times within an hour in order to test whether the book would have been put back upon the shelf. He confessed afterwards that he had been unable to believe that such interest in the Fathers could possibly be genuine in a Catholic priest ; and the good priest was so astounded that he declared that he would have thrown the book at Smith's head if he had guessed what suspicions were in his mind. It dawned upon him with awful clearness that his own prejudice had been inexcusable ; and while his conscience was still grieving him, he received a visit from his own bishop who told him that Pugin's decoration of his church, which had so delighted himself, was ' unmistakably Roman.' In December he accepted an invitation to hear Wiseman preach at Nottingham, and he was present when, after Mass, Wiseman publicly received a Jew and a Socinian into the Church. His defences could hold fast no longer, and he accompanied Wiseman back to Oscott. A few days later he had become a Catholic, his parish at Leadenham had been left without a rector, and his desertion created such a fury of protest that the Bishop of Lincoln even attempted to have him imprisoned.

Even Newman's imploring appeals to come and talk over matters at Littlemore before taking the final plunge had been unavailing. Wiseman's gentle sympathy had produced a conversion which set all England talking ; and it had a most direct repercussion in Newman's own mind. Smith's bishop had openly accused Newman of having caused Smith's conversion, and even of having told him to continue in his ministry after he had ' turned Romanist '—since only on those grounds could he explain Smith's outrageous acceptance of Pugin's decorations at Leadenham.   And although Newman had in fact done his best to restrain Smith's fatal step, he was now compelled to answer the Bishop of Lincoln's accusations, which involved taking stock of his own position once more.   The result was a decision that, while he still believed that an Anglican who became a Roman Catholic might continue to take part in the Anglican communion, he must at least retire from any ecclesiastical responsibility or position in the Church of England.   And the time had now come when Newman[1] was definitely contemplating ' retirement into lay communion ' himself.

Wiseman's campaign had indeed begun to make startling headway.   In a letter[2] to Cardinal Acton in Rome, Wiseman reported the conversion of Bernard Smith and declared jubilantly that ' during the past twelve months there have been more converts than for ten years previously.   Recently I baptised in the Cathedral at Nottingham a Mr. Richards, a Unitarian.   He is a public lecturer on Astronomy, and expects that some fifteen of his pupils will take the same step.   On the second Sunday of Advent I received the abjuration of thirty-six in the Cathedral before High Mass, and in a few weeks we shall receive fifty more.   On Sunday next I am to go to Wolverhampton to receive twenty into the Church, and in many other places much also is being done.'   Smith's conversion had been the most severe shock Newman had yet received since the publication of Tract 90.   And even his most intimate friends were already feeling that the foundations of their position had been undermined.   The atmosphere of Oscott had begun to exercise an appalling and irresistible fascination.   Wise-

[1] *Apologia pro Vita Sua*, 184.
[2] *Dublin Review*, January, 1919, 5.

man's hospitality and sympathy alone seemed to offer consolation and that sense of secure tranquillity for which they all craved. He had invited one of the Tractarians to spend Christmas at Oscott, and though he had gone to France instead, he had felt there as though he had floated out into the great sea of which Oscott was but the near and inviting harbour. 'Everything seems flat after this,' he had written[1] to Wiseman, in regretting his inability to accept the invitation to Oscott. All reticence had broken down, and he was telling Wiseman already that 'day after day, I feel that the thread which binds me to the English Church is becoming weaker and weaker; and if I may credit my Oxonian friends, my visit to Oscott threatens to be more than temporary.' Bernard Smith's surrender had unnerved them all.

But the following year dragged on without event. Cut off from any direct correspondence with Oxford, where Newman was by this time scarcely ever seen—living instead in the seclusion of his hermitage at Littlemore—Wiseman could only hope and pray. He impressed upon Ambrose Phillips that 'decidedly we must keep very quiet, at the same time that we must back and help our friends, but not attack.' And then in October there fell a blow which reduced Wiseman to the depths of desolation. Sibthorpe, the first of his notable converts from Oxford, reverted to the Church of England, and the news spread like wildfire. The Oxford leaders who had been doubting and hesitating for so long were suddenly stiffened in their resistance, and thanked God that they at least had been spared from acting too precipitately. The Catholics who had suspected the sincerity of Wiseman's converts, even when he appeared to be making most

[1] Ward, I, 414.

CARDINAL NEWMAN

(*portrait by Sir W. Ross—reproduced by kind permission of the Fathers of the Birmingham Oratory*)

headway, were appalled and humiliated, and rushed from all quarters to implore Wiseman to desist from further adventures which produced such scandalous results. He himself was too prostrate even to leave his bed on the first day after hearing what had happened. And even when Seager, who had been attracted as an Orientalist by Wiseman's profound knowledge of the Eastern languages, came to Oscott to be received as a Catholic, the consolation was still overclouded by the suspicions with which the Catholics viewed any others who might follow Sibthorpe's example. In regard to Ambrose Phillips, Wiseman's attitude had undoubtedly undergone a change as the result of his recent bitter disappointment. He would no longer tolerate any question of temporising or of postponing efforts to secure individual conversions. ' Were a Catholic who had the opportunity of bringing any one into unity to neglect it,' he wrote[1] in a much more emphatic tone than marked their previous correspondence, ' on the ground that Providence seemed to work by exceptions in the present state of things here, he would certainly sin ; for he would be violating a clear and positive duty, in favour of his private judgement and views regarding which he had no authority from revelation or tradition.' So, the next year also dragged on, and in the summer of 1844, Wiseman found himself sufficiently free from preoccupations to undertake a visit to Spain, for the first time since he had left it as an infant forty years before. But when he returned, events had developed with a headlong rapidity which seemed to show that the long-expected crisis had at last arrived.

In June, 1844, W. G. Ward, who had remained in close touch with Oscott throughout, but whose restless

[1] *Ibid.*, I, 418.

temperament had made Newman avoid his society and treat him with considerable distrust, published his *Ideal of a Christian Church*. Wiseman had heard from Ward privately[1] that the purpose of the book was no less than ' to show that Rome is the great exemplar to which they must study to approach, and he will not admit the existence of a single practical corruption.' Its publication inevitably produced a terrific explosion in Oxford ; and in February, 1845, Convocation, assembled in the Sheldonian Theatre to pass judgement upon the book, formally deprived Ward of his degree. The whole Tractarian Movement was brought up under review at a tempestuous meeting ; Newman's writings became involved in the general explosion, and only the fact that the Proctors were his personal friends prevented a formal condemnation of Tract 90. A universal panic had seized the sympathisers with the movement, and Pusey publicly dissociated himself from it. Deserted by his former allies, and saved from condemnation only by the kindly intervention of a few friends, Newman in his hermitage at Littlemore had to contemplate the destruction of all that he had striven to accomplish within the Church of England. For months previously definite rumours had been reaching Wiseman that Newman's mind was at last made up ; and after the condemnation of Ward in February, the news of his final surrender was expected from day to day.

The weeks passed in intolerable suspense at Oscott, but even in June no sign had yet been made from Littlemore. At last Wiseman could endure the strain no longer, and he deputed the convert Bernard Smith to go to Oxford and make a direct investigation. For several years New-

---

[1] Ward, I, 423.

man had scarcely stirred from his secluded hermitage, where he lived among the few friends—Dalgairns, Edward Stanton, Bowles and Ambrose St. John—who occupied the group of cottages with him. They had adopted an almost monastic routine of life, restricting themselves to two meals a day, spending half the day in strictest silence, and reading, writing, or praying all the time except during their daily walk. Newman himself was completely engaged in writing his *Essay on Development*, and he wrote standing erect at a high desk for almost incredible periods of uninterrupted work. All this ascetic routine had developed in the interval since Bernard Smith had shaken them all, by his own surrender to Wiseman nearly three years earlier; and he was appalled now to see what ravages had been wrought in Newman's fragile frame and sensitive face by the strain of mental agony which he had undergone. Newman, who had regarded him with such deep affection of old, now greeted him with an austere frigidity, and he was left alone with the others to answer their many questions as to how he had adapted himself to his new surroundings. In that austerely studious atmosphere few rays of human sympathy had penetrated in the recent years; and Newman's friends inquired curiously how their old colleague, who had deserted them, had managed to find any common ground with the English Catholics who cared so little about theology or history. They asked did he not honestly find them ' impossible ' people. They listened incredulously when he told them that Wiseman, with his well-known learning and versatility and wide culture, was by no means the only educated Catholic at Oscott; that the old Catholic Errington was as remarkable a man as one could wish to meet; and that the two converts, George Spencer and Ambrose Phillips,

had been able to provide all the sympathy and understanding which a stranger could desire. So the afternoon
passed, and at dinner-time Newman himself reappeared.
He was more reserved and reticent than ever, but from
the very moment he entered the room Smith realised
that he wished to convey an unmistakable message.
To his amazement and delight, Smith saw that Newman
had deliberately put on a pair of grey trousers. To his
old curate, the action was more eloquent than hours of
speech. It was like the hoisting of a white flag. And it
meant that Smith was to inform Oscott that his old
master no longer regarded himself as being in holy orders.

But if Bernard Smith, who knew Newman's fastidious,
secretive ways, and his extraordinary manner of con-
veying great decisions by unobtrusive signs, returned to
Oscott triumphant at the result of his own mission of
inquiry, it needed all Wiseman's sanguine faith to accept
Smith's statement that the end was now at hand. What
manner of man was this, he might well ask, who was so
timid that he would not even speak one word when he
had reached the conviction that he had sought for years ?
Once again the weeks passed, but by the end of the
month Lord Shrewsbury conveyed the final news that
W. G. Ward was about to take the plunge. And while
August and September passed without a sign, at last the
news arrived that Newman's own disciples in Littlemore
could wait no longer. Dalgairns and Ambrose St. John
departed from Littlemore together, never to return.
At Aston in Staffordshire Dalgairns made his submission
to the Italian Father Dominic Barberi ; and at Prior
Park—where Wiseman had long ago hoped to join Bishop
Baines in founding a Catholic University—St. John also
solemnly proclaimed himself a Catholic. Stanton also
had decided that he must do the same, and in October

he wrote to Newman that he intended to be received into the Church by the Jesuits at Stonyhurst.

The end had in fact come at last. Left alone with Bowles at Littlemore, Newman could hold out no longer. He replied to Stanton at once, begging him to come back, and announcing that Father Dominic Barberi was coming to receive him into the Church. But even Father Dominic had not been told what was the purpose for which he had been summoned. Not until he stepped out of his coach at Oxford, soaked through already by the torrents of rain that had poured all day, did he receive any positive intimation that Newman wished to be received into the Church. They had never even met, and Newman knew of him only as a zealous missionary priest who had dreamed from his boyhood that somehow he would play a part in the conversion of England, and who had written a long and intensely sympathetic reply in French to a letter from one of the Tractarians which had appeared in the *Univers*. But reports of his extraordinary activities among the poor Catholics scattered through the factory towns of the Potteries had reached Newman. He had heard of the indomitable courage and simple faith of this Italian priest, born of the humblest stock, who had been labouring through fierce opposition, against continual physical violence and daily demonstrations of hostility, in his self-imposed attempt to revive Catholicism in a northern city. Four years before, Newman had written,[1] scornfully enough, to Ambrose Phillips, to complain that the Church of Rome gave no evidence of sanctity, and to say ' if they want to convert England, let them go barefooted into our manufacturing towns—let them preach to the people like S. Francis Xavier—let them be pelted

[1] *Phillips de Lisle*, I, 205.

and trampled on—and I will own that they can do what we cannot.' Was it that his own arrogant words of reproach still haunted him ? Or was it merely coincidence that Dalgairns had gone to Father Dominic in Aston, and had now come back to visit Newman, as a Catholic now, who had left his old master to struggle on in deeper loneliness than ever ? At any rate it was to Dalgairns alone Newman murmured, almost in a whisper, as he and Ambrose St. John set out to meet the coach in Oxford on that drenching afternoon, ' When you see your friend, will you tell him that I wish him to receive me into the Church of Christ ? ' And so Father Dominic had gathered the purpose of his mission at the last moment before they met face to face. Stanton had arrived by the same coach, and they were all united again at Littlemore that evening. The Italian priest entered the house and had sat down to dry his sodden clothes before the fire when the door opened, and Newman, coming towards him, threw himself at his feet, and begged him to hear his confession and receive him into the Church. Early on the following morning the ceremony took place, and Newman, Bowles, and Stanton were all received at the same time, while St. John and Dalgairns, already Catholics, assisted in the little oratory.

CHAPTER IX

THE FIRST HARVEST (1845-50)

FOR ten years, since his first prolonged visit to England in 1835, Wiseman had dreamed and hoped that what had now at last happened might yet come true. From the beginning he had felt a direct personal responsibility in regard to encouraging the Tractarian Movement, and his own efforts, his persuasiveness, his appeals for a charitable attitude, his personal hospitality and sympathy, had contributed immensely to bringing about the conclusion which had also been hastened in no small degree by his direct interventions in the controversy. From the very beginning he had fixed his hopes upon the conversion of Newman himself ; and now at long last Newman had not only submitted, but was turning inevitably to Wiseman as his friend and protector in the irrevocable course he had undertaken.

But although Newman had surrendered, those early dreams had shrunk to strangely small dimensions in their fulfilment during the past year. It was not now the triumphant leader of a great movement within the Church of England who came to receive his confirmation at Wiseman's hands. The Tractarian Movement had been shattered to pieces by Ward's exuberance, which had aroused even the whole University of Oxford in revolt. For several years since Newman's resignation of the

rectorship of S. Mary's, and his retirement from
Littlemore, the leadership of the Tractarian remnant had
devolved upon W. G. Ward. And the decision of Convocation to proscribe his book in February, 1845, had
not only thrown Pusey into the opposite camp, but, in
Dean Church's words, resulted in ' a rout in which they
were driven headlong from the field.' Ward, as a defeated
general, had laid down his arms and come to Wiseman
as a solitary convert, whose influence upon the Church
of England was forever at an end. But his reckless onslaught had at least put an end to the prolonged agony
of his old leader, in the hermitage of Littlemore. And
now it was only the five inmates of that secluded hermitage
devoid, to all appearance, of any further power to command allegiance, whose belated and almost forlorn
appearance at the gates of Oscott represented the
diminished fulfilment of Wiseman's earlier dreams.

Their first meeting, after those long years in which
they had contended, with such chivalrous antagonism, as
the leaders of opposing forces, was an ordeal for both
men. Even the presence of George Spencer and Bernard
Smith could not mitigate the tension of the moment
when they met face to face for the first time. Newman's
shy and fastidious reserve left him all but dumb ; and he
and Wiseman sat together almost in silence, having exchanged scarcely a word beyond a few remarks about
the journey, until the strain was broken by a messenger
to announce that a schoolboy wished the Bishop to
hear his confession in the chapel. On November 1st,
next day, the confirmation took place, and Newman
and his friends gradually settled down to their strange
surroundings, cast adrift from all their former moorings
and completely at sea as to how the future years were to
be spent. In deference to Newman's feelings, his arrival

at Oscott had been kept from the newspapers, but the secret leaked out almost immediately ; the excitement of everyone connected with the College could not have been restrained for long.

Wiseman's hopes and his policy had been vindicated so unmistakably that for the time being he could ignore all the criticism that had caused him such bitter unhappiness for years. But already apprehensions were being felt in regard to Newman's future activities, and the awful example of Sibthorpe's conversion and relapse was still recalled upon every possible occasion to restrain Wiseman's tendency to generous impulses. Upon him fell the task of deciding the future plans of his new converts. He offered them almost immediately the old buildings at Oscott, in which the great Bishop Milner had spent so much of his time, to provide a home which should take the place of Littlemore. Newman accepted it eagerly, and renamed it Maryvale ; and before long, when the news of his conversion spread through the country, it also became a focus of extraordinary spiritual influence, which was to extend further even than that which he had exercised at Oxford. Wiseman's joy at having received him went beyond all words. Even the incidents connected with his confirmation had seemed like an omen of extraordinary promise. ' We had *ten* quondam Anglican clergyman in the chapel,' he wrote[1] to Dr. Russell of Maynooth. ' Has this ever happened before since the Reformation ? '

For the present, there was no necessity to make plans for Newman's future, as he had his book to finish. The bulk of it had been written in his last years as an Anglican, but it would present a survey of the development of his views, and a slight addition would make

[1] Ward, I, 433.

everything clear. Wiseman and he had already established relations of complete mutual confidence, and he was entirely satisfied that ' the Church has not received, at any time, a convert who has joined her in more docility and simplicity of faith than Newman.' ' I have often said,' he wrote in conclusion to Dr. Russell, ' I should be ready to sing my *Nunc Dimittis* when Mr. Newman should have joined us ; and I must not draw back from my word.' Nor had he the slightest thought of doing so, now that they had grown to know each other intimately. And Wiseman, with an increasing consciousness of the hostility that his efforts must arouse among the old Catholics, who still regarded Newman with distrust as well as a certain natural jealousy, proceeded deliberately to plan for the fulfilment of his own earlier prediction—that, if the Tractarian leaders could be won over to Catholicism, he himself and the other recognised leaders of the English Catholics must be prepared to stand down and give full scope to their superior abilities and religious fervour.

Had Wiseman not been in England, the path of the Tractarians towards Rome would unquestionably have been very much more laborious. But it was in encouraging and helping them after their conversion, even more than in accelerating and facilitating their surrender, that he contributed most remarkably to the infusion of new blood and the creation of new energies in the Catholic Church in England. What Newman and his friends after their submission, when they were execrated by the English Protestants and still regarded with profound distrust by the English Catholics, would have done if they had not been able to turn to Wiseman, with his boundless sympathy and his congenial tastes, it is hard indeed to imagine. Even as it was, Newman's acutely sensitive

nature was often hurt cruelly by the suspicion that still
surrounded him. And Wiseman, in his determination
to provide the fullest scope to his distinguished neophytes,
and in his confidence that a fusion between converts and
old Catholics would take place within a reasonable time,
was to find that his task as the champion of the Oxford
converts was to involve him also in years of disheartening
opposition.

Even to find homes for the lonely and often destitute
men and women who before long implored his assistance
and encouragement, was a problem that would have
required much preparation in advance. The first small
group who had accompanied Newman in his submission
was before long followed by an influx which gathered
momentum as the year passed. Faber had been among
the first to feel the consequences of their giving way.
He too decided that his position in the Church of England
had become untenable ; and after visits to Newman at
Littlemore and Wiseman at Oscott he had returned to
his parish,[1] to announce from the pulpit to his dumb-
founded flock that the doctrines which he had been teaching seemed to him now incompatible with the Church of
England. He then hurried down from the pulpit, and
throwing off his surplice in a state of great emotion, had
left it lying on the floor. Faber's final step had been
postponed for two considerations which in the following
years were to cause acute anxiety and heart-burning to
many convert clergymen. He felt that he must forsake
a congregation who had grown dependent upon him,
and whom he had been able to help greatly. And he
had also incurred large debts in building almshouses and
in other parochial activities, which he could not hope to

---

[1] *Life of Faber*, 235–7.

repay once he surrendered his living—which was worth
£1400 a year[1]—and cast himself upon a world where no
occupation seemed to await him. In his case, this special
problem was solved by the great generosity of an anonymous friend, who did not share his views but admired
him greatly as a clergyman, and begged to be allowed to
pay off his debts. But for most of the clergymen who now
felt an overwhelming impulse to follow Newman in
becoming Catholics there was no such help available.
Wiseman's letters to Phillips nevertheless chronicle a
continual series of such conversions from month to month;
and before long he was faced with the urgent, and
apparently insoluble, problem of making provision for the
temporal needs of those who became popularly known as
'Mr. Newman's victims.'

Mr. Marshall, for instance, had to confide[2] in Wiseman
that he was 'reduced to great straits' and that he was
'suffering cruel persecution from friends and family.'
Wiseman naturally turned to Phillips for assistance, but
the problem was growing rapidly beyond all manageable
dimensions. The same Mr. Marshall had 'brought over
seventeen of his parishioners, including the district
surgeon, and he has several others under instruction.'
There was less difficulty in providing for those, like
Mr. Coffin, who were not married, and who desired to
study for the priesthood. Faber had already arranged
to form a small community of converts in Birmingham.
But the influx was growing all the time, and in many
cases it meant that whole families were deprived of their
means of livelihood. Scores of others—both men and
women—were immediately disowned by their families
and deprived of all financial support, while a strong

[1] Ward, I, 443.
[2] *Phillips de Lisle*, I, 301.

CHAPTER X

THE PAPAL AGGRESSION (1850)

EVEN though the restoration of the hierarchy was on all sides regarded among Catholics as being imminent, and although Wiseman himself had been most strongly recommended during the negotiations in 1847 as ' the only man for the situation,' it never dawned upon him, even on his arrival in Rome, that his own appointment as a Cardinal might be the first step in that great decision. He had bade farewell to his closest associates with indescribable grief, impressing upon Faber and Newman and the converts who were most dear to him, his own sense of the absolute necessity of obedience, and endeavouring to set an example to them of fortitude amid the wreckage and frustration of all his personal hopes. Setting out in August, he reached Rome in the first week of September, and on September 13th he had his formal interview with Pius IX. Only then did he know that the historic step was about to be taken. The Pope had been so deeply impressed by the many appeals for Wiseman's return to England, that he had decided to send him back there as the head of the new hierarchy.

On the last day of September his nomination as Cardinal was duly made ; and having drafted his first pastoral letter as Archbishop of Westminster, with October 7th as its date, which was to announce the tremendous news to the Catholics of England, he set out for home on October 12th. His pastoral had been sent on ahead, and he proceeded by slow stages on his journey, receiving with suitable dignity and graciousness the extraordinary demonstrations of enthusiasm that his appointment as the first head of the restored English hierarchy had aroused in the Catholic countries through which he had to pass. At Florence, one of his old tutors at Ushaw, Mr. Sloane, was now established in considerable state as a rich man. Staying for several days as his guest, Wiseman received formal congratulations in person from the Archduke of Siena, who even created a decisive precedent in his honour, by accepting a lower status than that of the Cardinal when they dined at his own Court.

At the end of the month he reached Vienna, where he dined in state with the Emperor of Austria. The grandeur with which he was received everywhere added to the new anxiety that he had already felt in Rome, as he contemplated the expenses required of a Cardinal's establishment; and in his letters to friends in England he was already discussing how the problem should be met. But he could not expect to receive any letters on his way home until he reached Bruges. In the meantime, his mind was feverishly busy with plans for the future, and his days were being spent in acknowledging on behalf of the Catholics of England the universal expressions of jubilation which surrounded him.

It was in Vienna, where he had been received with enthusiasm by the Emperor, that the first news reached him of how the great development had been received in England. Looking through the *Times*, his attention was immediately attracted by seeing his own name figuring prominently in its leading article. As he read the article, while he drove through the streets of Vienna in his magnificent carriage, his whole expression changed, and

a dark cloud seemed to descend upon all the world. That
Dr. Wiseman should have been raised to the purple
was no surprise, the *Times* declared, in view of his distinction ' as one of the most learned and able members
of the Roman Catholic priesthood in this country.'
' It is no concern of ours,' said the *Times*, ' whether Dr.
Wiseman chooses in Rome to be ranked with the Mon-
signori of the capital. He is simply at Rome in the
position of an English subject, who has thought fit to
enter the service of a foreign Power and accept its
spurious dignities. But this nomination has been
accompanied by one other circumstance which has a
very different and very peculiar character. We are informed by the " Official Gazette " of Rome that the Pope
having recently been pleased to erect the City of Westminster into an archbishopric, and to appoint Dr. Wiseman to that See, it is on this new-fangled Archbishop
of Westminster, so appointed, that the rank of Cardinal
is so conferred.'

What, the article continued, was this new dignity
and appointment intended to convey ? Did it mean
' no more than if the Pope had been pleased to confer on
the editor of the *Tablet* the rank and title of the Duke of
Smithfield ? ' If so, it might be dismissed as a ' clumsy
joke.' But if not, then ' we confess that we can only
regard it as one of the grossest acts of folly and imper-
tinence which the Court of Rome has ventured to commit
since the Crown and people of England threw off its
yoke.' As an explanation of the Pope's taking ' this
ridiculous and offensive step,' the *Times* mentioned the
suggestion that it was intended as a retaliation on the
English Government for the hostility which had been
imputed to it. But it dismissed that suggestion as being
wholly inadequate to account for ' one of the most

daring assumptions of power it has put forward in this country for three centuries.' Its own verdict was that the Pope had completely mistaken the attitude of the English people, believing their tolerance to imply indifference, and the ' renovated zeal ' of the Church of England to betoken ' a return towards Romish bondage.' It was ' not sorry ' that his indiscretion and that of his advisers had in fact ' led them to show the power which Rome would exercise if she could, by an act which the laws of this country will never recognise and which the public opinion of this country will deride and disavow, whenever His Grace the titular Archbishop of Westminster thinks fit to enter his diocese.'

Here indeed was not only an outburst of extraordinary insult and aggression towards the Pope, but a direct personal threat that Wiseman must expect to face unpleasant consequences as soon as he landed in England. Wiseman might well have qualms at the thought of the pastoral letter which he had already despatched to London, and which would have been published all over England before he could possibly consult with his friends. If the mere announcement that he was to be Cardinal Archbishop of Westminster aroused such a blaze of fury, what sort of reception would the outraged Protestantism of England give to the unrestrained and ecstatic pastoral letter in which he had himself conveyed the official decision ? With a numbing pain at his heart, he sat down that evening to write a personal letter to Lord John Russell as Prime Minister, to counteract the hostility which was luridly reflected in the *Times*, and to clear up certain points upon which misunderstanding was almost certain to arise. Before leaving England he had made a point of having a personal interview with Lord John Russell, on the subject of diplomatic representation

THIS IS THE BOY WHO CHALKED UP "NO POPERY!"—AND THEN RAN AWAY!!

(Reproduced by kind permission of the proprietors of "Punch")

f England at the Vatican Court, and he had then
informed the Prime Minister of his own definite departure
to take up his residence in Rome. What would Lord
John Russell say now at finding him on his way back to
England so very soon afterwards, as the principal agent
of an ecclesiastical constitution which had provoked such
bitter resentment ? ' I spoke to your Lordship,' Wiseman now wrote[1] to him, ' as about to leave England
without intention of returning, and it may possibly be in-
sinuated now that such was not the case. I beg, therefore,
to assure your Lordship that I was most sincere when I
spoke of my departure as final, with no idea that I should
return. I am anxious that no impression should remain
on your Lordship's mind that I had the slightest intention
to deceive you.' Dealing with the misrepresentations
contained in the *Times*, he reminded the Prime Minister
that the new hierarchy had been agreed upon three years
years before, ' and a copy of it was shown to Lord Minto
by the Pope on the occasion of an audience given to
his Lordship by his Holiness.' Its scope, Wiseman
now formally pointed out, ' was purely ecclesiastical,'
without any ' secular or temporal delegation ' ; that his
own duties would still be, as before, ' to promote the
morality of those committed to my charge, especially
the masses of the poor ; and to keep up those feelings
of goodwill and friendly intercommunion between
Catholics and their fellow-countrymen which I flatter
myself I have been the means of somewhat improv-
ing.'

But long before his letter had reached Lord John
Russell, the Protestant fury in England had been inflamed
to fever pitch. Wiseman had been too severely shaken
by what he had already gathered from the *Times*, to be

[1] Ward, I, 535.

capable of enjoying any further the extraordinaril[y]
affectionate greetings which he encountered as his journe[y]
proceeded. He hastened homewards as fast as possibl[e]
At Cologne he had no time to do more than visit th[e]
Cathedral for early Mass, and in the morning to have [a]
cordial meeting with the Archbishop, Cardinal Geisse[l]
who stayed with him until his train left the statio[n]
At Bruges he was able at last to receive letters from h[is]
own people in England ; and their tenor added sti[ll]
more to his distress, and decided him to complete h[is]
journey so quickly that he arrived in the small hours [of]
the morning on November 11th, at Mr. Bagshawe['s]
house in Fitzroy Square, before even his Vicar Gener[al]
had been able to receive news of his coming. By th[e]
time his pastoral had been published all over Englan[d]
Dr. Whitty, his Vicar General, had even hesitated for [a]
short time before deciding to let it be made publi[c]
The storm of indignation to which the *Times* had giv[en]
expression on hearing that the English bishops were [to]
have territorial titles was already rising in intensit[y]
A few days after publishing the article which had stru[ck]
such a blow to Wiseman when he was in Vienna, th[e]
Times had demanded[1] ' is it, then, here in Westminste[r]
among ourselves and by the English throne, that [a]
Italian priest is to parcel out the spiritual dominion [of]
this country—to employ the renegades of our Nation[al]
Church to restore a foreign usurpation over the co[n]
sciences of men, and to sow division in our politic[al]
society by an undisguised and systematic hostility to t[he]
institutions most nearly identified with our national fre[e]
dom and our national faith ? Such an intention mu[st]
either be ludicrous or intolerable—either a delusion [of]
some fanatical brain or treason to the Constitution.'

[1] The *Times*, October 19, 1850.

Wiseman's pastoral, written under the stress of great
emotion in Rome, and expressing the consummation of
all his own hopes for many years, was so provocatively
jubilant in its tone and in its flamboyant eloquence that
it could not fail to intensify the public anger. But there
could be no question of withholding it from publication,
and its effect was even more inflammatory than Dr.
Whitty had feared. Public demonstrations assumed such
a violent form all over the country, and particularly in
London, that a hurried consultation of Wiseman's friends
was held to decide whether he had better be prevented
from landing in England. Only a very small minority were
in favour of his coming ; and some even desired that he
should be requested to return immediately to Rome
to report developments to the Pope. It was not only
fears for his personal safety, but apprehensions as to what
faux pas he might make after his arrival, that reduced
them to the verge of despair, when he had himself
expected so confidently to have a triumphal return. By
October 27th, the Pastoral had been read publicly in all
the churches in the London District. It was headed with
the challenging announcement that it was issued ' from
out the Flaminian Gate of Rome.' And after describing
in highly emotional and coloured language the historical
importance of the new hierarchy and the enormous possibilities it brought for the future, he announced his own
appointment as Archbishop in the following terms :
By a Brief dated the same day, his Holiness was further
pleased to appoint us at the same time the administration
of the Episcopal See of Southwark. So that at present,
and till such time as the Holy See shall think fit otherwise to provide, we govern and shall continue to govern,
the counties of Middlesex, Hertford, and Essex, as
ordinary thereof, and those of Surrey, Sussex, Kent,

Berkshire and Hampshire, with the islands annexe
as Administrator with Ordinary jurisdiction.'

The Pastoral had been composed in Rome, in a moc
of intense spiritual exultation, and in the midst of extr
ordinary congratulations from all the most distinguishe
personages and institutions that Wiseman knew so we
in the Eternal City, to which his thoughts had alway
turned for consolation and for guidance with unque
tioning loyalty and obedience. And in its concludir
passages he gave expression to ideas which in themselv
went far beyond even the attitude of many devo
English Catholics, in language which could scarcely ha
been more calculated to inflame that irritation which ha
been growing among the Protestants of England sin
the Tractarian leaders had challenged their conceptic
of the Anglican Church. 'The great work, then,
complete,' wrote the new Archbishop of Westminste
'what you have long desired and prayed for is grante
Your beloved country has received a place among th
fair Churches, which, normally constituted, form th
splendid aggregate of the Catholic Communion ; Cathol
England has been restored to its orbit in the ecclesiastic
firmament, from which its light had long vanished, an
begins now under its course of regularly adjusted actic
round the centre of unity, the source of jurisdiction,
light, and of vigour.' 'Then truly is this to us a day
joy and exaltation of spirit,' his pastoral went on, 'th
crowning day of long hopes, and the opening day
bright prospects. How must the saints of our countr
whether Roman or British, Saxon or Norman, look dov
from their seats of bliss with beaming glance upon th
new evidence of the Faith and Church which led the
to glory, sympathising with those who have faithful
adhered to them through centuries of ill-repute, for th

truth's sake, and now reap the fruit of their patience
and long-suffering ! And all those blessed martyrs of
these later ages, who have fought the battles of the faith
under such discouragement, who mourned, more than
over their own fetters or their own pain, over the desolate
ways of their own Sion and the departure of England's
religious glory ; oh ! how must they bless God, Who hath
again visited His people.'

It was no wonder that such language stung the traditional Protestants of England to fury ; no wonder that
all Wiseman's critics among the English Catholics were
aghast at his lack of comprehension of the English
mind, and that even his friends were overwhelmed by the
reckless, blundering indiscretions of his first pastoral letter
as the leader of the restored Hierarchy. The *Times*
was already the most important organ of conservative
opinion, and it had somewhat modified the old reckless
habit of vulgar vituperation which had been so outrageous
in its attacks upon O'Connell before his death. But
its language rose to lurid flights as it commented upon
the extraordinary document that the new Cardinal
had thought fit to issue in announcing to England the
momentous decision of the Pope. Wiseman's indiscretions had given a new weapon with which to belabour
the Whig Government, for The *Times* had discovered in
a French Catholic paper what purported to be an account
of Pius IX's own words in regard to the appointment.
The Pope, it appeared, had discussed the matter with
Lord Minto (whose special diplomatic mission to Rome
had been the outcome of Wiseman's own representations
to Lord Palmerston three years before), and the *Times*
now bellowed that, although the plan had apparently
been communicated to Lord Minto at that time, ' yet the
English Government has seen no reason to offer any

adverse expression of opinion to it ; so that while one
of the effects of Lord Minto's unfortunate journey was
to promote the revolution in Italy, the other is to promote
the re-establishment of the Roman Hierarchy in England.
For a Scotch nobleman who is neither a Jacobin nor a
bigot, it must be confessed that these results are strange
instances of diplomatic ability ; and Lord Minto will be
consigned to the judgement of posterity between
Ciceruacchio and the Archbishop of Westminster.
The whole controversy opened up possibilities of making
party capital against the Whigs, which Disraeli was not
slow to utilise. He, like many other M.P.'s, was invited
by his constituents to join in a public protest against the
' Papal Aggression '; and with his customary dexterity he
explained to the electors of Buckinghamshire in a letter
dated November 8th, his own attitude towards ' the recent
assault of the Court of Rome on the prerogatives of our
Sovereign and the liberties of her subjects.' He pointed
out that the Whig Government had already given official
recognition to the ecclesiastical titles of the ' Romish
bishops of Ireland ' and had ' addressed them as nobles,
sought their counsel, and courted their favour,' even to
the extent of ' presenting them as nobles and giving them
precedence over the nobility and dignitaries of the
National Church ' during the visit of Queen Victoria
to Ireland. ' The fact is,' wrote Disraeli, ' that the
whole question has been surrendered and decided in
favour of the Pope, by the present Government ; and
the Ministers who recognised the pseudo Archbishop
of Tuam as a peer and a prelate cannot object to the
appointment of a pseudo Archbishop of Westminster,
even though he be a Cardinal. On the contrary, the
loftier dignity should, according to their table of precedence, rather invest His Eminence with a still higher

thousand people, moved on to Camberwell, with vociferous shouts of ' No Popery,' ' Hurrah for the Queen,' and ' No foreign priesthood,' following it all the way. A still more impressive demonstration took place at Salisbury, where the main street was packed to suffocation long before the torches were lighted and the effigy of His Holiness was brought out. Then the procession formed up ' in the following order : torch-bearers, brass band, torch-bearers, his Holiness in full pontificals, seated in a huge chair ; torch-bearers, bishops, three abreast ; torch-bearers, Cardinal Wiseman, etc., etc. Within the precincts of the Close the National Anthem was played amid deafening cheers.' After a parade of the whole city in this manner, the effigies were all carted on to a huge timber platform erected over tar-barrels. A volley of rockets was the prelude to the playing of the Doxology by the band ; and as the flames rose to the platform and a great quantity of fireworks were set off, ' there followed the Morning Hymn and the National Anthem, in which thousands joined.'

While these stirring scenes were being enacted, Wiseman was still hurrying homeward from Vienna, and he did not reach Cologne until two days later. By the time he arrived in London on November 11th, the campaign against him had developed considerably further. The Bishop of London had denounced the whole Catholic clergy on November 8th as ' emissaries of darkness ' ; and on the day of Wiseman's arrival the Bishop of Manchester was proclaiming that ' Rome clings to her abominations.' These were only the first samples of a series of episcopal attacks upon the Catholic Church during the closing weeks of November, among which the Bishop of Bangor's reference to ' a foreign prince insolent in his degradation,' and the Bishop of Oxford's description of Catholicism as 'subtle and unclean' were fair samples. In December the Bishop of Hereford used still more picturesque language in his allusions to 'the sorcerer's cup' and the 'crafts of Satan,' while the Bishop of Carlisle boldly declared just before the end of the year that her claims were 'profane, blasphemous and anti-Christian.' By that time the excitement was already beginning to subside; but it had reached its climax on the day before Wiseman arrived in London, when the newspapers contained the reports of the Lord Chancellor's astounding speech at the Mansion House dinner, in which he had quoted, amid wild applause, the lines:

" Under our feet we'll stamp thy Cardinal's hat,
    In spite of Pope or dignities of Church."

CHAPTER XI

WISEMAN'S APPEAL TO THE ENGLISH PEOPLE
(1850)

INTO this hectic atmosphere, when threats to his personal safety had been issued by the leading London newspapers, and when even the Lord Chancellor had just delivered what was almost a direct incitement to violence against him, Wiseman now returned without knowing even the events that had filled the previous week. The messages which reached him at Bruges had prepared him for the worst, and he had shown his courage by hurrying back to London without even resting for one night after his long journey from Italy. But his friends were already thoroughly intimidated, and they were terrified lest he might make some effort to retrieve his first error in judgement which would in fact only make matters worse. Seldom indeed has any newly appointed Cardinal in history returned to his own people to meet such a discouraging and unfavourable reception.

Having arrived very early in the morning at Mr. Bagshawe's house, since his own was in the hands of decorators and painters, he sent at once for his Vicar General and for Sir George Bowyer, as one of the leaders of the laity in the new archdiocese. He commissioned Sir George Bowyer to go immediately to interview some member of the Government in order to counteract the misrepresentation of what had occurred. Bowyer obtained an interview with Lord Lansdowne, who was Lord President of the Council ; and he was able to learn that the Prime Minister had published his letter to the Bishop of Durham without any previous consultation with his colleagues. Lansdowne himself declared that he deeply regretted the letter, and after several more interviews, expressed his own view that there had been an ' enormous misunderstanding.' Upon Dr. Whitty, as Vicar General, had fallen the full responsibility of deciding whether Wiseman's pastoral should be published or withheld ; and he was immensely relieved to find that Wiseman did not blame him in the least. But his feelings were more mixed when Wiseman showed him at their first meeting, the page of foolscap upon which he had already begun to write the first paragraph of an ' Appeal to the English People.' Wiseman's style was most uncomfortably flamboyant, and his ' Flaminian Gate ' pastoral had provided awful evidence of his inability to appreciate the extent of Protestant prejudice in England. That he was likely to mend matters by issuing a second public proclamation might well be doubted.

But Wiseman's courage in returning immediately to face the storm had brought new heart to those who knew him best, and on the following day he went openly to visit S. George's Cathedral in Southwark. He had boldly made it known that he would himself officiate at the public Mass, and a huge crowd had assembled before his carriage, drawn by a pair of greys, drew up punctually at eleven, and he emerged with his chaplain, wearing a large blue cloak and carrying a magnificently bound missal in his hand. No hostile demonstration occurred ; although on the following days he was hooted on several occasions and stones were thrown at his carriage. But his mind was made up, and amid all the feverish interruptions occasioned by the excitement among the Catholics, and by the necessity of instituting the new order created by the restoration of the Hierarchy, he was continuing rapidly the preparation of the manifesto in which he intended to appeal for fair play to the people of England. It ran to enormous length, but it was written with scarcely an erasure or an altered word. Dr. Whitty could only conclude that the idea had formed in his mind when he had received the first shock in Vienna, and that he had been thinking out his pamphlet closely during the journey home. Before the end of the week he had sent it to the printers, and on November 20th, five morning newspapers in London published it *in extenso*. By the end of the week some 30,000 copies had been sold in pamphlet form as well ; while its effect upon public opinion had been astonishing. To ensure that the *Times* would publish it in full had required ingenuity ; but the son of his host, Mr. Bagshawe, succeeded first in persuading four of the other dailies to publish it *in extenso*, and by so doing compelled the *Times* to decide, when they received it in the evening, to do the same. It appeared accordingly on the following morning and occupied six and a half columns of small, close type.

Both as a reply to his critics, and as a vindication of the decision to create a Catholic hierarchy in England, it was found to be a magnificent combination of straightforward argument and eloquence. Still more remarkable was his insight into the essential character of the people of England when he brought his attention to bear upon a direct appeal to them. He was convinced that they would never fail to respond to an earnest appeal for fair play, and that they would appreciate the courage of any man who faced opposition squarely. Reviewing the course of events since the Hierarchy had been announced, he protested that the

storm had burst with such ' absolute fury ' that ' the energies of all seemed concentrated upon one single point,
that of crushing if possible, or denouncing at least to
public execration, the new form of ecclesiastical government which Catholics regarded as a blessing and an
honour. For this purpose nothing was refused, however
unfounded, however personal, even by papers whose
ordinary tone is courteous, or at least well-bred. Anec-
dotes without a particle of truth, or what is worse, with
some particles of distorted truth in them, have been
copied from one into another, and most widely circulated.
Sarcasm, ridicule, satire of the broadest character
theological and legal reasonings of the most refined nature
bold and reckless declamation, earnest and artful argument
—nothing seemed to some amiss ; and every invocable
agency from the Attorney General to Guy Fawkes
from *præmunire* to a hustling, was summoned forth to
aid the cry, and administer to the vengeance of those who
raised it.'

In the general hue and cry, the young Cardinal protested, the Prime Minister—who could have mitigated
the storm by a few words, in view of his own knowledge
of the real truth—had joined shamelessly as a leader
Wiseman contrasted his attitude vigorously with that of
Peel when a similar outcry had arisen over the increased
grant to Maynooth College. Peel, he recalled, had
' nobly stemmed the tide, carried his measure with calm
dignity through the legislature, and yielded nought to
public outcry.' In the present crisis, on the other hand
when the Catholics of England had neither expected nor
asked for any co-operation from the Government, but
' had the right of every citizen to impartiality,' the Prime
Minister had not only failed to remain neutral but had
' astonished not this country alone, but all Europe, by

letter which leaves us but little hope that any appeal to the high authority which rules over the empire would be received, to say the least, with favour.' Against the disgraceful outburst by the Lord Chancellor he protested in the same dignified and vigorous strain, before declaring his own intention, to appeal, in the last resort, to the one tribunal in England before which he was confident that justice would never be disowned. 'While thus the avenues to public justice seem closed against us,' he went on ; 'while the Press has condemned us and raised our death-whoop, in spite of proffered explanations, deaf to every call for a fair hearing ; while we may consider that the door of the Treasury may be barred against us, if we knock to ask, not for pensions or funds, but for a reasonable hearing ; when the very highest judicial authority has prejudged and cut off all appeal from us ; what resource have we yet left ? What hope of justice ? One in which, after God's unfailing providence, we place unbounded confidence. There still remain the manly sense and honest heart of a generous people ; that love of honourable dealing and fair play which, in joke or in earnest, is equally the instinct of an Englishman ; that hatred of all mean advantage taken, of all base tricks and paltry clap-trap and party cries employed to hunt down even a rival or a foe. To this open-fronted and warm-hearted tribunal I make my appeal, and claim, on behalf of myself and my fellow-Catholics, a fair, free and impartial hearing. Fellow-subjects, Englishmen, be you at least just and equitable. You have been deceived—you have been misled, both as to facts and as to intentions.'

Having dealt in detail with the accusation that the Pope's establishment of a hierarchy infringed the prerogatives of the Crown, he argued, with quotations from

the highest legal authorities, that it was no crime for
a Catholic to maintain and defend the supremacy of
the Pope ; that the Dissenters were no less opposed
to the authority of the Crown in religious matters, and
that the whole question of religious toleration in England
was involved in the controversy. ' Believe me,' he wrote
' at this moment the danger to the religious and civil liber
ties of Englishmen is not from any infringement of them
by the Pope, in granting to English Catholics what I hope
to show you they had full right to obtain from him
but from those who are taking advantage of the occurrence
to go back a step, if they can, in the legislation of tolera
tion, and take away from a large body of Englishmen what
at present is lawful to them in regard to the free exercise
of their religion.' Again and again he quoted from
judgements delivered by Lord Chancellor Lyndhurst
to show that the Catholics were absolutely entitled to
exercise their religion, which was essentially episcopal in
character.

Then, turning to the real cause of the recent outcry
which was based upon a misrepresentation alleging that
the Catholic bishops contemplated some sort of tangible
authority within the territory allotted to them, he insisted
that ' the new Bishops will not have occasion to cross the
path of the prelates of the Anglican Establishment in
their sphere of duty ; they will find plenty to do beside
their official duties, in attending to the wants of their poor
spiritual children, especially the multitudes of poor Irish
whose peaceful and truly Catholic conduct, under the
whirlwind of contumely which has just assailed them
proved that they have not forgotten the teaching of their
Church—not to revile when reviled, and when they
suffer, not to threaten.' From Lord John Russell's own
speeches in Parliament he showed the gross absurdity

of suggesting that the Pope had claimed territorial sovereignty over any part of England. From the records of previous Governments he showed that precedents for the restoration of the English hierarchy had already been established in Australia and in Ireland without any objection being raised. But it was in the final passages he displayed most decisively his remarkable and unsuspected power of commanding popular sympathy at the expense of his traducers by a straightforward declaration of his own aims. In regard to his own appointment as Archbishop of Westminster, he had an opportunity to reply to the protests of the Chapter of Westminster Abbey who had issued an hysterical protest ' as though some practical attempt at jurisdiction within the Abbey was intended.'

' Then let me give them assurance on that point,' wrote the Cardinal, ' and let us come to a fair division and a good understanding. The diocese, indeed, of Westminster embraces a large district ; but Westminster proper consists of two very different parts. One comprises the stately Abbey, with its adjacent palaces, and its royal parks. To this portion the duties and occupation of the Dean and Chapter are mainly confined ; and they shall range there undisturbed. To the venerable old church I may repair, as I have been wont to do. But perhaps the Dean and Chapter are not aware that, were I disposed to claim more than the right to tread the Catholic pavement of that noble building and breathe its air of ancient consecration, another might step in with a prior claim. For successive generations there has existed ever, in the Benedictine Order, an Abbot of Westminster, the representative in religious dignity, of those who erected, and beautified, and governed that church and cloister. Have they ever been disturbed by this " titular " ?

Have they ever heard of any claim or protest on his part touching their temporalities ? Then let them fear no greater aggressions now. Like him, I may visit, as I have said, the old Abbey, and say my prayer by the shrine of good S. Edward, and meditate on the olden times, when the church filled without a coronation, and multitudes hourly worshipped without a service. But in their temporal rights, or their quiet possession of any dignity or title, they will not suffer. Whenever I go in, I will pay my entrance-fee like other liege subjects, and resign myself meekly to the guidance of the beadle, and listen without rebuke, when he points out to my admiration detestable monuments, or shows me a hole in the wall for a confessional.

'Yet this splendid monument, its treasures of art and its fitting endowments,' he went on, ' form not the part of Westminster which will concern me. For there is another part which stands in frightful contrast, though in immediate contact, with this magnificence. In ancient times, the existence of an abbey on any spot with a large staff of clergy and ample revenues, would have sufficed to create around it a little paradise of comfort cheerfulness and ease. This, however, is not now the case. Close under the Abbey of Westminster there lie concealed labyrinths of lanes and courts, and alleys and slums, nests of ignorance, vice, depravity, and crime, as well as of squalor, wretchedness and disease ; whose atmosphere is typhus, whose ventilation is cholera in which swarms a huge and almost countless population in great measure, nominally at least, Catholic ; haunts of filth, which no sewage committee can reach—dark corners which no lighting board can brighten. This is the part of Westminster which alone I covet, and which I shall be glad to claim and to visit, as a blessed pasture in which sheep of Holy Church are to be tended, in which a bishop's godly work has to be done, of consoling, converting and preserving. And if, as I humbly trust in God, it shall be seen that this special culture, arising from the establishment of our hierarchy, bears fruit of order, peacefulness, decency, religion, and virtue, it may be that the Holy See shall not be thought to have acted unwisely, when it bound up the very soul and salvation of a chief pastor with those of a city, whereof the name, indeed, is glorious, but the purlieus infamous—in which the very grandeur of its public edifices is as a shadow to screen from the public eye sin and misery the most appalling. If the wealth of the Abbey be stagnant and not diffusive, if it in no way rescues the neighbouring population from the depths in which it is sunk, let there be no jealousy of anyone, who, by whatever name, is ready to make the latter his care, without interfering with the former.'

Never before had Wiseman been called upon to conduct a controversy which demanded all the vigour of a vehement counter-attack. In the past he had relied always upon the power of gentle persuasion ; and he had proved many times that conversions could be won by gentleness where indignation or hostility had always failed. But the deplorable situation which he had to meet on his arrival in England as the first Cardinal Archbishop of Westminster required gifts which he had hitherto never displayed. His own blundering indiscretion, and his own extravagant rhetoric, in announcing the restoration of the Hierarchy in the manner he had adopted, were in fact very largely the cause of the fury that had been aroused. And for the first time also under the new conditions he, whose previous record had been so conciliatory and so mild in controversy, had to assume the full responsibility of speaking on behalf of the whole Catholic

body in England, with the Protestant people of England
as the tribunal which he now sought to appease. Not
even Newman, whose admiration for his learning and his
zeal and his high courage was naturally greater than that
of the old Catholics, had ever believed that he could rise
to the occasion as superbly as he had done. ' He is made
for the world,' was Newman's considered verdict in a
letter[1] to Sir George Bowyer in January, ' and he rises
with the occasion. Highly as I put his gifts, I was not
prepared for such a display of vigour, power, judgement
sustained energy as the last two months have brought
I heard a dear friend of his say before he had got to
England, that the news of the opposition would kill him
How has he been out. It is the event of the time. In my
own remembrance, there has been nothing like it.'

The effect of his Appeal to the English People had in
fact been astonishing. Almost the entire Press now
acknowledged the power and force of his pamphlet, though
they generally adopted the same attitude as did the
London News, in hinting broadly that the misunderstanding had been the fault of ' the blatant indiscretion of the
many over-sanguine priests of the Roman persuasion
who have tortured what, if we are to believe Cardinal
Wiseman, was a harmless domestic arrangement among
the Roman Catholics themselves, into an aggression
The *Times* sheltered itself, with its usual truculence, behind
a similar complaint that ' if we have pronounced an
opinion against the Pope and the Cardinal unheard, it has
not been from any wish to deny them fair play, but because
they did not condescend to give us any more tangible
explanation of their acts than was to be gathered from
empty gasconades and pompous manifestoes, the very

[1] *Life of Newman*, I, 256.

sweepings of a literary wardrobe now nearly worn out,
and never very tastefully selected.' 'We congratulate
Dr. Wiseman on his recovery of the use of the English
language,' it declared sarcastically. 'If the popular demonstrations with which the arrival of the new Cardinal,
who has come with a commission from Rome to govern
half a dozen of the dioceses of our Church, and some two
of the kingdoms of the Saxon Heptarchy, have not been
all that was agreeable in other respects, they have, at
any rate, as the Scotch say, brought him to his English.'
And the *Times*, which had led the fierce campaign
against the new Cardinal and the new hierarchy, would not
yet desist from its efforts to sustain the public indignation
even though it had to admit that the outcry had been
based upon a complete misunderstanding. 'In her
authorised documents,' it declared, in pursuance of its
former hostility towards the Catholic Church, ' whatever
is not within herself is treated as non-existent ; her
language, her logic, are all founded on this principle.
Whatever is not her own she absolutely ignores. The
Pope employs the same style in constituting an Archbishop of Westminster as in appointing a prelate of some
petty town in Latium. The existence of the crown, of
the prelates, of the mighty people of England, he cannot
acknowledge ; all he sees is the land, a few Roman
catholics scattered up and down it, and those bishops
among whom he divides it ; the rest to him is nothing.'
It had been a strange reception indeed for the young
cardinal who had anticipated a triumphal return to his
own country after receiving the highest honour that the
Pope could give, and after having been greeted with
most unprecedented joy by the Emperor of Austria and
the rulers of Northern Italy. But Wiseman threw all
his energies into the contest, and the result of his own

o

indiscretion was to arouse an enormously wider interest
in the Catholic Church in England than could ever have
been expected ; while, in so doing, he galvanised the
Catholic body itself into new life. His pastoral had
provoked even the Prime Minister and the Lord Chancellor into hysterical outbursts of rage, which affected
the High Church party in the Church of England as
directly as it affronted the Catholics. Gladstone and other
influential politicians with strong Tractarian sympathies
were driven to taking up the defence of their friends.
And the Liberal veteran, Mr. J. A. Roebuck, entered the
lists soon after Wiseman's Appeal had been published
with an open letter to Lord John Russell which denounced
in scathing terms his incitement to religious persecution
and his abandonment of the principles which his party
had for so long held sacred. ' The same sort of feeling
as that which, in 1780, roused the mobs of London against
Sir George Saville,' he wrote with unflinching candour
' and made that madman Lord George Gordon a hero,
the idol and leader of the people, is now exercising a fatal
influence upon the good sense of the English people.
This feeling you have most unfortunately countenanced ;
you have given dignity and importance to an antipathy
which you ought certainly to have allayed ; and, by your
ill-timed support, have done your utmost to keep alive
for years a detestable intolerance, of which in your heart
I believe you to be thoroughly ashamed.' ' To you, my
lord,' he concluded, ' posterity will refer as a man who,
just when the real difficulties were conquered, when, by
the united and continuous labours of our greatest states-
men, the law had become just, and peace and goodwill
were about to be established, took advantage of your great
position to rouse up the spirit of strife and hate among us,
to quicken into active life the demon of persecution, and

to rend asunder a great empire, which, but for your fatal interference, would soon have become firmly united, peaceful and prosperous. A melancholy distinction this, my lord, for one who all his life has styled himself the friend of religious as well as civil freedom. Your common sense must long since have been shocked at the wretched fanaticism which you have evoked, and which unfortunately, you will find a spirit beyond your power to lay.'

Lord John Russell's attitude had unquestionably played a direct part in inflaming the agitation which found expression in many acts of mob violence. Protests from the victims of the agitation began to pour in, and on the Sunday that the Liberal Mr. Roebuck addressed his stinging letter to the leader of the Whig Government, another letter of vehement expostulation also was addressed to the Prime Minister by the Anglican rector of the parish in which he resided. For a succession of Sundays the rector had found his church surrounded by infuriated mobs, while copies of Lord John Russell's letter to the Bishop of Durham were distributed among the crowd in the street. On the Sunday before Wiseman's return from abroad, Mr. Bennett's church had been the scene of such violent interruptions during his service that the church had to be closed. The police authorities had found it necessary to guard the church night and day afterwards ; and on the following Sunday, he complained, a force of one hundred constables was required to keep the mob from overt acts of violence ; notwithstanding the exertions of the police, much violence was committed and the leader of the rioters taken into custody.' At the afternoon service the mob had assembled again ; and on the following Sunday also there had been similar scenes, and the preacher had been interrupted during his sermon by outcries. Mr. Bennett's letter was a most remarkable document, and it resulted in an indignant correspondence between Mr. Bennett and the Bishop of London, who in the end compelled him to resign his living. But it rallied the Tractarians and their sympathies for the movement, though many of them before long found it impossible to preserve their allegiance to the Church of England.

Wiseman himself realised quickly how great an effect his own Appeal had produced. He carried his own campaign a stage further by immediately preparing a series of addresses which he delivered in S. George's Church at Southwark, and these attracted large and respectful audiences. His wholly unexpected success in mastering the situation gave new heart to the Catholic body, and they acclaimed him with indescribable gratitude as the first leader of genius and of national stature that had arisen among them since Bishop Milner's death. At the outset there had been several deplorable instances of cowardice in face of intimidation. Even on the day that Wiseman's Appeal was published, Lord Beaumont saw fit to write a letter[1] to the Earl of Zetland, in which he stated publicly that ' the late bold and clearly expressed edict of the Court of Rome cannot be received or accepted by English Roman Catholics without a violation of their duties as citizens ' and he even announced that Lord John Russell's conduct towards the establishment of the new hierarchy was ' that of a true friend of the British Constitution '. Still more deplorable was the action of the Duke of Norfolk whose anti-Roman bias was already evident in the Gallican attitude of his chaplain at Arundel, Mr. Tierney. On November 28th, he wrote formally to Lord Beaumont to express entire agreement with his protests against the new hierarchy, and announced that ' I should think that many must feel, as we do, that ultramontane opinions

[1] Ward, II, 15.

are totally incompatible with allegiance to our Sovereign
and with our Constitution.' To give final confirmation to
his protest, the Duke publicly accepted the sacrament
of the Church of England, and ceased thereafter to be a
Catholic until near the end of his life.

For Wiseman this scandalous defection of two of the
most important Catholic noblemen was a terrible blow.
But he could find consolation in the many demonstrations
of loyalty by other leading Catholic laymen, and particularly in the attitude of Lord Stourton, who wrote to
regret his inability to take part in the Catholic protest
meeting, which had sent a loyal address to Queen Victoria.
'I most fully concur in the religious principles and
opinions expressed by the Roman Catholics on that
occasion,' he wrote, ' and I trust that those same principles, for the support of which my ancestors have suffered
for so many generations . . . will be held sacred and
inviolate by me to my dying breath.' The Duke of
Norfolk's apostasy had been the worst public scandal
in the Catholic body for many years. But there were
observers less well informed than Wiseman who could
realise already how greatly the old paramount influence
of the Catholic nobility had diminished in recent years.
Wiseman himself, while paying all deference to their
loyalty and their constant sacrifices through many
generations, had been unconsciously undermining their
influence by introducing the Tractarian converts into
positions of large responsibility. And already even the
Guardian noted[1] that ' the strength of Romanism in
this country, even as a political power, is no longer confined to noblemen's castles.' It had become ' something
rougher, more energetic, more aggressive, less English
in its attachments and sympathies and less amenable to

[1] *Ibid.*, II, 16.

influences which may not uncharitably be supposed to
have some weight with the Premier Duke, Earl Marshal
and hereditary Marshal of England.'

Wiseman's own impressions of the campaign were
reported to Rome in a series of letters to Monsignor Talbot
which were never made public until Cardinal Gasquet
edited a selection from them in the *Dublin Review* after
the conclusion of the Great War. ' The first great effort
of the excitement,' he wrote[1] from London early in
December, ' through the Press, was to keep me out of
the country by frightening me. Many timid Catholics
were going to write to me, for God's sake not to come over
as my life was not safe.' He desired Talbot to impress
upon the Pope that he had travelled ' as quick as I possibly
could,' but he admitted that it had been just as well that
he was not in England for Guy Fawkes' Day. ' I believe
that had I been here that day, something very disagreeable
might have occurred, for the people were fearfully urged
on. The Protestant Association at Exeter Hall contributed, it is said £1,400 towards that day ; Hoare's house
gave £100, and so on. For several days, or evenings
groups of people, evidently sent, were about Golden
Square.' But he was quite satisfied that ' my arrival in
London, my going at once to S. George's, and doing everything calmly and without showing either fear or forward-
ness, had a most beneficial effect. The next trial was
my publicly officiating. While at S. George's I said Mass
every morning at eight in the Madonna Chapel, so there
was no concealment. But many people feared a *row* at
our first function. I did not, because, independently of
higher reasons, I had seen how orderly everything had
been at all our churches, notwithstanding the disturbance
in Bennett's church. On Friday it was thought better

---

[1] *Dublin Review*, January, 1919, p. 8.

to admit by ticket ; and, though no pains were taken to make the thing public we had a full church and about one hundred and fifty priests. I preached and assisted at Mass. Nothing could exceed the decorum and respect shown by all. On Sunday the church was open, and you may judge of the crowds when I tell you that the *take* was £94. I had received continual warnings that I should be shot or attacked that day ; but of course, I despised all that. I sang High Mass and preached as usual to an immense congregation. In the evening the church was crammed, and I gave my first of three lectures on the Hierarchy. Everyone seemed completely absorbed in the subject. Through the whole day there was not a disagreeable occurrence, crowd, pressure, or trouble at all.' 'You may now therefore consider all danger of tumult or commotion at an end,' he went on. 'As for myself, I have not experienced the slightest approach to an insult, or any other behaviour than the most re-spectful.'

One surprising consequence, Wiseman found already, had been a most remarkable increase in the number of conversions. He was able to convey to the Pope through Monsignor Talbot direct evidence of this unexpected result. At the Oratory Newman reported that there had never been so many applications from intending converts. And there were many similar symptoms in unlikely places. 'In the little dead city of Canterbury,' Wiseman wrote,[1] 'under the very nose of John Bird Cantuar, twelve persons have at one time put themselves under instruction, including a niece of Sir W. Scott (Miss Peat) and Miss Stephanoff, daughter of the artist. Archdeacon Manning and Dodsworth are considered certain, and most probably Bennett and Archdeacon Wilberforce. In a few days we

[1] *Dublin Review*, January, 1919, p. 10.

shall hear of Lord Dunraven and Mr. Monsell, M.P. ; Lord Norreys I consider very hopeful. I saw him in Belgium and he sees Lord Arundel and Surrey almost daily ; Lord Nelson likewise, and others. Mr. Rogers, Dr. Hook's curate, has been received by Oakeley. A declaration has been signed by at least twenty clergymen that the Church of England must ask reconciliation with the Holy See ; 1,800 have signed the declaration against the Royal Supremacy. The sale of Catholic books is unprecedented.' Well might he feel satisfied with the general outcome of what had happened, and he wrote confidently to Talbot : ' I do not see that anything ought to have been done otherwise than it has been. Without any personal feeling on the subject, I believe that, if I had not been sent back, there would have been serious difficulties in establishing the Hierarchy. I have borne the entire brunt of the excitement ; the other Bishops have escaped almost unnoticed ; and as I have broad shoulders and some public estimation and good friendship among the aristocracy, I could stand a great deal.'

At the very end of December he wrote[1] again to Talbot, declaring his own belief that ' the hubbub is nearly at an end. The papers are giving it up ; and people on all sides are getting heartily ashamed of it.' A significant symptom had been Cobden's speech at Leeds, expressing fears that the reaction in favour of the Catholics might go too far, and so lead to a triumph for Popery. Meanwhile the interest in the Hierarchy seemed to increase. His own lectures at S. George's had been more crowded than ever, and inside a week the whole edition of 30,000 copies of his third lecture had been entirely sold out. Converts had continued to pour in. Serjeant Bellasis had come to Wiseman for confirmation. Dodsworth also had come, reporting that Manning's conversion was now imminent. And with Manning there was every prospect that Gladstone would also come. ' I now begin to expect Gladstone to follow him, especially if James Hope does, which seems certain,' he was able to write enthusiastically to Rome. ' Assure the Holy Father,' he told Talbot, ' that every day convinces not only me, but all Catholics, more and more that religion has been pushed on inestimably by all that has happened.' The Catholic nobility had rallied unanimously ' except the delinquents,' and many signatures which had never before been collected had been attached to their address.

CHAPTER XII

THE SECOND SPRING (1851–52)

THE storm had risen so fast that the Government found it necessary at the outset to introduce some measure to appease the popular discontent, which the Prime Minister and Lord Chancellor had helped to inflame. In February the Ecclesiastical Titles Bill was introduced in Parliament. Cardinal Wiseman attended the debate. A majority of three to one carried it quickly through all its stages in spite of the dignified and eloquent resistance by Gladstone and others. But the Bill, which imposed a fine of £100 upon any Catholic bishop who assumed a See, was a dead letter from the first; and after twenty years Gladstone carried its repeal. And before it was yet introduced, Wiseman had received news which more than compensated for the bitter humiliations and disappointments he had endured since he was made Cardinal. In the spring, when he had no inkling as yet that the end of the year would find him a Cardinal, he had been thrilled by the crisis in the Church of England which the Gorham Judgement had introduced. Throughout the rest of the year, the effects of that Judgement, with its revelation of where the ultimate authority in the Church of England really lay, had left the Tractarian survivors in a state of agonised suspense. They had seen their own teaching concerning the supremacy of the Church in religious matters completely repudiated and disproved

by the decision of the Privy Council; and the fierce
controversy which it provoked had intensified still further
the Protestant reaction against the movement which had
inspired them with a new faith and zeal. And now, at the
end of the year, the Pope's action in restoring the Catholic
hierarchy, and still more, Cardinal Wiseman's imprudent
manner of announcing it, had aroused such a violent reaction towards Protestant principles within the Church of
England that they found themselves completely isolated
as members of a Church which professed doctrines that
were entirely contrary to their own beliefs.

For five years, since Newman's surrender, the majority
of Tractarians who had declined to follow him in submission to Rome had turned instinctively to Archdeacon
Manning of Chichester as a leader upon whom Newman's
mantle appeared to have fallen. Aloof from the general
movement in Oxford, and devoting himself primarily
to the work that came to his own hands in Sussex, he
had withstood the storm, and he could proclaim that
even Newman's exposition of his own progress towards
Rome had not carried the Catholic case forward by one
step at their expense. But the Gorham Judgement had
been a shattering blow to his security; and while others
had relied implicitly upon him to sustain their confidence,
his own faith in the Church of England had been irreparably shaken. And then suddenly, when he was already
overwhelmed with doubts, there had come the mad
popular outcry against the 'Papal Aggression.' Like
nearly every other ecclesiastic of equal rank, Manning was
bombarded with requisitions to convene a meeting of
protest against what the Pope had done. To comply,
in the existing circumstances, could only mean a deliberate
repudiation of the Universal Church towards which he
had been drawn of late with overpowering conviction.

But to refuse meant much more than a conflict with the rest of the clergy and with the Anglican bishops. It would raise the whole question of whether an Archdeacon holding views so strongly opposed to the episcopate of the Church of England, could honestly continue in his position of authority. Through a week of fierce agony of mind, the question clamoured for a decision ; and within few days of Wiseman's return to England, Manning had found himself compelled to explain formally to his bishop that he believed the Royal Supremacy to be contrary to Christ's law, and that it had severed the Church of England from the Universal Church ; that the Pope's action in constituting a rival hierarchy had been inevitable and justified, and that he personally could not oppose the Pope.

Only two alternatives courses had seemed possible : either to resign at once, or to convene the desired meeting and to announce at it his own dissent and his resignation. His bishop, in dismay, had advised the latter course. The meeting was duly convened, and Manning announced to it that he would never appear among them again. They discussed and carried their resolutions against the Papal Aggression, adopted a vote of gratitude to him for his long services amongst them ; and then with tears they parted for ever. His resignation spread consternation everywhere and provoked vehement appeals from his many friends ; from bishops, from Gladstone and others who had shared his anxiety over the Gorham Judgement, but not least from the few who had already made up their own minds and gone over without further hesitation to Rome. He had thoughts of escaping from the turmoil to the Continent ; but that, his friends urged upon him, was only to walk into still greater temptation. Already two of his sisters-in-law had become Catholics, and each week

CARDINAL MANNING

brought news of further secessions. In the first days of
January he learned that his own curate, Laprimaudaye,
had become a Catholic, and he wrote[1] with deep sympathy : ' the world will censure you for reckless haste.
I do not. I know the long, mature, and suffering preparation you have gone through ; the haste is only external.'
Before the end of the month, he too had decided to take
the same path. But the ' bonds of duty ' that still had to
be severed caused delay. Not until March did he legally
resign his position as Archdeacon, and soon after, going
in company with Gladstone to the little chapel off the
Buckingham Palace Road, he decided during the service
that he could stay no longer. Laying his hands on Gladstone's shoulder, he said simply : ' Come ' ; and as
Gladstone stayed, he went out into the wilderness
alone.

On April 6th, 1851, the former Archdeacon, together
with Mr. James Hope, Q.C., was received into the
Catholic Church at Farm Street, and on the following
Sunday was confirmed by Cardinal Wiseman. By Wiseman's express desire, he received the tonsure immediately
on the same day ; and the few weeks between Palm
Sunday and Whitsuntide were regarded by the Cardinal,
in the excitement of the moment, as sufficient time to
prepare him for the priesthood. It was a tremendous
precedent, which outraged all the older Catholics and
provoked passionate letters of entreaty and remonstrance
as soon as Wiseman's intention became known. But the
Cardinal's position was now incomparably stronger than
when he had amazed England by receiving the submission
of Newman and the Oxford leaders. And in the conversion of Manning he now saw what might yet be the beginning of a still greater movement towards Rome. ' I look

[1] Purcell, I, 596.

upon you as one of the first-fruits of the restoration of the
Hierarchy by our Holy Father, Pius IX,' he told[1] Manning
immediately after he had ordained him in June. ' Go
forth, my son, and bring your brethren and fellow-
countrymen by thousands and tens of thousands into the
one true fold of Christ.' But the haste and the absence
of preparation in Manning's admission to the priesthood
was more than the old Catholics could be expected to
accept without a protest, and the *Tablet* expressed their
feelings incisively when it declared that Mr. Manning
was now going to Rome ' for the purpose of commencing
his ecclesiastical studies.'

Ill-mannered and wounding though its criticisms of the
Cardinal were, the *Tablet's* rebuke concerning the hasty
admission of Manning to the priesthood scarcely went
beyond what many Catholics in England felt towards the
impetuous Cardinal Archbishop. The Duke of Norfolk
and Lord Beaumont had openly repudiated him and
courted popularity by throwing in their lot with the
leaders of the No Popery agitation. The Earl of Shrewsbury, Ambrose Phillips' colleague in many pious enterprises, and a generous donor for the building of Catholic
churches, became henceforward the leading Catholic
nobleman. And under the influence of Ambrose Phillips,
who had entered the lists with several slashing pamphlets
in defence of the Hierarchy, Lord Shrewsbury was for a
short time one of Wiseman's most enthusiastic supporters.
He had felt Lord John Russell's anti-Catholic outburst
almost as a personal affront ; and among other contributions to the controversy, he published a satirical
anonymous parody of Lord John's letter to the Bishop of
Durham, which purported to be the ' Original Version

[1] Purcell, I, 633.

of the Letter.' ' I hope the Catholics will show spirit on this occasion,' he wrote[1] to Ambrose Phillips, ' and show Lord John a bold front, for he has foully calumniated them.'

But the excitement had scarcely died down when even Lord Shrewsbury began to waver in his first enthusiasm. Even in Italy the adverse influences were able to damp his spirit, and in February he was writing to Phillips that common prudence ought to have prevented not only ' the pompous Pastoral from outside the Flaminian Gate,' but even the bringing of the Cardinal's hat to England. Already he had doubts as to the wisdom of restoring the Hierarchy. If it did not have the effect of giving their rights to the inferior clergy, he now said, it would have been a bad mistake. Besides,[2] ' why did they abolish the old Canon Law before they had another ready ? Or why was it abolished at all ? ' Complaints against the Cardinal began to increase on all sides. His introduction of Italian devotions was resented hotly by the older type of English Catholics who had no use for continental customs, and who regarded every Roman innovation as an attempt to infringe upon English traditions and liberties. They were deplored no less strongly by others who felt chiefly concerned to avoid giving any unnecessary offence to English Protestants. And while Wiseman was driven to relying more and more upon the superior abilities and zeal of the converts whom he had encouraged so constantly, even they began to cause him further trouble. Father Faber's excessive Roman zeal produced a definite revolt against the extreme tendencies which he introduced.

There had been a crisis over his convert zeal before he

[1] *Phillips de Lisle*, I, 321.
[2] *Ibid.*, I. 322.

had yet left Birmingham for London. Faber had initiated
a new series of popular Lives of the Saints, under his
own editorship, which gave him ample opportunities for
displaying the uncompromising spirit in which he had
absorbed the most extreme tendencies of continental
Catholicism. He deliberately selected lives which were
chiefly composed of extraordinary miracles and aus-
terities and supernatural visitations. ' English readers,'
he wrote in his preface to the *Life of S. Rose of Lima*, ' who
may not have been in the habit of reading the Lives of the
Saints and especially the authentic processes of the Con
gregation of Sacred Rites, may be a little startled with the
life of S. Rose. The visible intermingling of the natural and
supernatural worlds, which seem to increase as the Saint
approach, through the Grace of God, to their first inno
cence, may even offend where persons have been in the
habit of paring and bating down the " unearthly " in
order to evade objections and lighten the load of the
controversialist, rather than of meditating with awe and
thankfulness and deep self-abasement on the wonders of
God in the Saints, and mastering the principles and genera
laws which are discernible even in the supernatural
regions of hagiology.' And in a postscript to the bio
graphy, which provided an extreme instance of the super
natural manifestations accepted by Rome as authentic
in the process of canonisation, Faber added jubilantly
' Let us thank Almighty God in the fervent simplicity
of our faith for the seal His Church has set upon
these authentic wonders ; wonders not lost in dubious
antiquity but adequately proved in the face of modern
criticisms, so short a time ago ; and remembering
that this bold exhibition of the marvellous is by
no less an authority than the Catholic Church, pre
sented to our veneration and our love, let us take

t like awe-stricken children, as a page from the lost chronicles of Eden, and strive to unlearn that bold timidity with which we have too often been inclined to court favour where we shall never get it, and to avoid sneers which are to us as an heritage and vouchers of our truths, by smiling with the profane and doubting with the sceptical. For one of the faithful to look as like an unbeliever as he can, is a sight which never won a soul to Christ, or gained for the Church the esteem of an opponent.'

Wiseman himself could not have written in such a strain without provoking fury among the old Catholics whose traditional attitude was thus severely criticised. But when a very recent convert like Faber took upon himself to lecture the old Catholics upon their reluctance to believe miracles, and their tendency to cringe before Protestants, complaints were inevitable. They were forthcoming quickly in a review[1] of the Life of S. Rose in *Dolman's Magazine* for September, 1848, which protested vehemently that ' when the recorded actions of saints utterly oppose themselves to the natural end and being of man, they are worthy neither of admiration nor imitation, and had far better be consigned to respectful oblivion. They provoke cavil. They give wrong impressions of what true piety really consists in. They reduce religion to an unmeaning course of puerilities.' Alban Butler, the reviewer insisted—and Butler was one of the great modern figures among the English Catholics —' had doubtless read all this, and perhaps more. He wisely and prudently omitted it. Why resuscitate such more than charnel horrors ? ' And the review concluded with a solemn outburst against Faber and his convert

[1] *Life of Faber*, p. 347.

P

associates, that ' in the name of all those who know thei.
religion, in the name of all those who revere it in it:
innate and immaculate purity and truth, we protest mos·
solemnly against this and such-like publications. However painful to our feelings, we must not shrink from :
public and sacred duty in thus exposing the dangerou:
tendencies of this species of modern hagiology.'

So vigorous were the protests against Faber's *Lives o*
the Saints that Newman, as the Superior of the Oratory,
found it necessary to face the prohibition of their continuance. ' I have consulted the Fathers who are here
on the subject,' he wrote[1] to Faber in October, 1848,
' and we have come to the unanimous conclusion of advis-
ing you to suspend the series at present. It appears there
is a strong feeling against it on the part of a portion of
the Catholic community in England, on the ground
as we are given to understand, that the lives of foreign
saints, however edifying in their respective centres, are
unsuited to England, and unacceptable to Protestants.
To this feeling we consider it a duty, for the sake of peace,
to defer.' But Newman expressed his own attitude
defiantly by declaring that ' you know well how absolutely
I identify myself with you in this matter,' and that he had
' no sympathy at all with the feeling to which I have
alluded ' ; while he concluded by assuring Faber that
' in particular, no one can assail your name without striking at mine.' Both men were still new to the traditions
and the practice of a Catholic religious community, and
Newman's letter provoked a confidential communication
from Bishop Ullathorne which probably was the basis
of their long subsequent intimacy, but which at the time,
notwithstanding its immense charity and affection of tone,

[1] *Life of Faber*, p. 349.

must have hit Newman hard by its complaint that he had shown himself excessively sensitive and lacking in humility.

Not long afterwards the publication of the *Lives of the Saints* was resumed, and their temporary suppression did not mitigate the zeal with which Faber sought to arouse the English Catholics to a more active and public manifestation of their faith. Almost as soon as he took charge of the new London Oratory in 1849, Faber began boldly to introduce continental devotions, and formal complaints against him were soon lodged with Wiseman. Faber had introduced the daring habit of wearing religious dress on all occasions, and in the outcries against the 'Papal Aggression' the Oratory became accordingly a general target for denunciation. To the old Catholics Faber was little more than a reckless and highly emotional convert, whose uncontrollable zeal brought unnecessary odium upon the Church. And Wiseman's well-known personal affection for Faber, and his genuine sympathy with all the converts, involved him also in the intense unpopularity which Faber aroused among them.

But it was not only the old Catholics who kicked against the ultramontanism and the extravagant pieties which Faber thought it to be his special mission to popularise in England. Pugin had for long deplored the Roman, or as he called it, the Pagan taste of Wiseman, and he found that his old friends at Oxford, whom he had been partly instrumental in bringing into the Catholic Church, were even more obnoxious to his own ideals than Wiseman himself. And Ambrose Phillips, who shared completely Pugin's unrestrained enthusiasm for Gothic art, and regarded all Italian forms of decorative art or of music as scandalous perversions inherited from the Renaissance, was continually working with Pugin to stem the Romanising tendencies in regard to ceremonial and the arts. In 1848 the differences of opinion had gone to such lengths that Phillips solemnly informed[1] Faber, in a heated interview, that ' God for his pride had destroyed and brought to nought his first effort ' and that ' He will curse and destroy your order,' and ' it will perish if you go on thus.' Newman himself thought it necessary to intervene with a protest when this lurid language was reported to him by Faber ; and he reproached Phillips in a pained letter for having ' cursed the Oratory.' Phillips replied that he had done nothing of the kind, but he did formally accuse Newman, in reply,[2] of ' preaching a Crusade ' against Pugin and himself. Wiseman had invited Newman to transfer his Oratory at once from Birmingham to London, when he was himself transferred from Oscott to be pro-Vicar Apostolic in London ; but Newman had declined and instead sent Faber to open a new branch of the Oratory in King William Street, Strand. Its activities only deepened Pugin's disillusionment. ' The Oxford men, with some few exceptions,' he confided[3] in Phillips in his despair, ' have turned out the most disappointing people in the world. They were three times as Catholic in their ideas before they were reconciled to the Church. It is really quite lamentable. They have got the most disgusting place possible for the Oratory in London, and fitted up in a horrible manner, with a sort of Anglo-Roman altar. These things are very sad, and the mischief they do is inconceivable.' In Church music things were even worse ; for, as Pugin impressed upon Phillips repeatedly, ' a man may be

[1] *Phillips de Lisle*, II, 204.
[2] *Ibid.*, II, 206.
[3] *Ibid.*, II, 218.

judged by his feelings on Plain Chaunt. If he likes
Mozart, he is no chancel and screen man. By their music
you shall know them, and I lost all faith in the Oratorians when I found they were opposed to the old song.'

Harassed on all sides by such diverse criticisms and
controversies, and regarded with real distrust by the old
Catholics, both because of his Flaminian Gate Pastoral
and his Italian enthusiasms and because of his deferential
attitude towards the converts, Wiseman proceeded as
best he could with the enormous task of consolidating
the new regime introduced under the restored Hierarchy.
Among the older laity many even persisted in ignoring his
title as Cardinal and called him still Dr. Wiseman,
holding him responsible for having provoked a hostility
towards Catholics which had almost died down, until
the ' Papal Aggression.' But the proportions of the
Catholic body had been completely transformed by the
vast Irish immigration in the years immediately before
the Hierarchy was restored ; and the great inarticulate
mass of poor Irish Catholics rallied behind him as a
courageous leader who had upheld their faith publicly
in a Protestant country, where they had felt very friendless
since they came. And on all sides converts were still
flocking in. Wiseman's decision to ordain Archdeacon
Manning within so short an interval after his submission
had been quickly rewarded by the number of converts
whom he brought over, with what seemed to be an almost
hypnotic power, after his own conversion. He had gone
to Rome immediately, but even on his journey, his
company had been the cause of the poet Aubrey de Vere's
conversion at Avignon, and many others followed as the
months passed. Lord Shrewsbury, in his querulous way,
was complaining[1] to Ambrose Phillips that ' the public

[1] *Ibid.*, I, 336.

seem far more Protestant than ever, and our progress anything but great. Manning is certainly a great acquisition, and we must hope will influence others ; but it was the Gorham controversy that displaced him ; and this appears to be the case with all who have yet joined us.' Even the brief months of delay before they had surrendered seemed to Lord Shrewsbury evidence that the Hierarchy had retarded, rather than hastened, their conversions.

But Wiseman himself had never doubted, since the success of his own ' Appeal,' that the Hierarchy had given a tremendous impetus to the Catholic revival. And while many cautious men were dismayed by the favour he had shown to Manning, he had not the smallest misgiving as to what he had done. ' I knew how much Manning would feel the *ignominia sæcularis habitus*, the being an *Esquire*, after seventeen years of a devout ministry with a most clerical appearance and leading a most strict life,' he wrote[1] to Talbot in April. ' No conversion yet has produced the effect of his,' he wrote with absolute confidence, ' nor has caused such deep regret through all the " Divided House," as I call the Anglican Establishment. The Queen, it is said, is quite struck and moved ; one clergyman observed that the Church of England had only one great man left now (Dr. Pusey). Archdeacon Hare told Bowyer that he deplored the loss beyond anything ; and, as everyone says, Manning has never been reproved or called to account, but has kept the esteem of all to the last, and it is hard to say how many his conversion will influence. As to Hope, he is the most admired man at the Bar. He has the greatest Parliamentary practice in England ; is the inheritor and occupier of Abbotsford,

[1] *Dublin Review,* January, 1919, p. 14.

and bears the highest possible character. Manning said to me that if we had to pick out the most eminent layman in the Establishment, it would have been Hope.' The conversion of both Hope and Manning might, he felt, have enormous repercussions. Gladstone particularly had been their intimate ally for so long, and had been so stirred, together with them, by the scandal of the Gorham Judgement, that Wiseman still believed that he also would ultimately find his position as an Anglican untenable. ' I really hope much for Gladstone,' he told Talbot in the same letter ; ' he is quite altered in manner with Catholics, with his sister particularly.'

There were many other clear indications also that ' the unnatural effervescence caused by the Hierarchy, instead of impeding, is wonderfully forwarding the cause of religion.' S. George's at Southwark, as the centre of a great concentration of Irish Catholics, had been packed to overflowing on many occasions ; and as it was by far the largest Catholic church in the London district, Wiseman was full of apprehension at the prospect of losing it when it passed to the new See of Southwark. The position was complicated by the fact[1] that ' the worst anti-Roman clergy in England are in Southwark—Tierney, Costigan, Rock, North, etc.' Wiseman told Talbot plainly that he regarded them as ' either actively or passively opposed to all progress.' They were working hard to secure the appointment as bishop, of Dr. Cox, the president of S. Edmund's College—who had been the choice of the old school for the London District when Wiseman had been appointed Vicar Apostolic, to their dismay, in 1849. But he succeeded in frustrating their efforts, and Dr. Grant, who had succeeded him as Rector

[1] *Ibid.*, January, 1919, p. 13.

of the English College in Rome, came to Southwark instead. Even without S. George's, however, Wiseman had found immense congregations assembling in other parts of London to hear his own sermons and lectures. ' On leaving S. James's every evening,' he told Talbot, ' five hundred persons outside gave me three hearty cheers.' And by August he was able to report that ' the College is cleared of its terrible obstruction. Dr. Cox has *cheerfully* left, and accepted Southampton, the mission which he likes of all others. The whole system will be reformed, and a sound high-toned ecclesiastical spirit will be introduced ; Moorfields will be under my direction, Dr. Whitty will live there, with about five or six priests, and we propose getting it up equal to Islington or the Oratory and then making it the training school— every priest from College going there first and leaving the place as wanted.'

And amid all his preoccupations with converts, with sermons and lectures, and the machinery of the new regime, he could still report[1] that ' our work among the poor is progressing wonderfully. Orchard Place was one of the very worst in London—three or four thousand people about it—nearly two thousand in it habitually drunk, fighting and scandalous. Drs. Faa and Ferrara, assisted by the good Spanish Place clergy, opened a mission—almost everyone has been brought to his duty. On the first night Ferrara saw six young men in a corner smoking with their hats on, and paying no attention. After the sermon he went up to the first and took him by the ear, asking him what he was. " A Catholic." " I don't believe you ; you must be a Protestant." " No, I am a Catholic." " Then you are an Englishman." " No ;

[1] *Dublin Review,* January, 1919, pp. 22–4.

I am an Irishman." " It is impossible ; no Irish Catholic
would keep on his hat and smoke while a priest was
preaching. Why do you not come to confession at once ? "
He took him by both arms, and the youth followed him
like a lamb and went to confession, followed by all his
companions, who have been the most edifying of all the
people, coming almost every day to confession. The
Ragged School was soon closed, and the people became
most orderly.' Cardinal Wiseman had said that he would
himself go and conclude the mission, and his description
of the scene to Talbot gives a vivid picture. ' I found the
place crammed from end to end, all round and behind the
platform. Every window was filled with tiers of faces,
the whole line of roof covered with legs dangling over the
parapets—most with candles in their hands, and every
window illuminated, while against the walls were
illuminations with lamps ; so that altogether on coming
to the entrance and looking down, it had the appearance
of a street Madonna festival in Rome. On alighting I
went into the crowd, which made way, and our procession
formed. I was in my usual black dress, black cassock,
and red fariazolo, with biretta, cross, etc. On the platform
were the Bishop of Texas, Dr. Kirby, etc. After a hymn,
I addressed the people, who listened intensely. I preached
on perseverance, especially in sobriety, going to their
duties, peaceableness and not sending their children to
Protestant schools. They all with one voice promised
fidelity.' He had arranged, and announced to them,
that henceforward a priest would come every Saturday
' to hear confessions, say prayers, preach, and keep them
in order,' and that Mass would be said in a room, since
no church was yet even contemplated.

As he left that open air mission there had been remarkable scenes, for a part of London where no Catholic

church as yet existed. 'The cheering as we went along
to the carriage must have been heard for miles. I never
heard anything like it,' Wiseman wrote to Talbot. 'Every
one wanted to touch me, of course ; but there was no
disorder or confusion, and everyone who witnessed the
scene was amazed. Serjeant Bellasis was in the midst
of the crowd, and said he was now satisfied that I might
trust myself confidently to the people—he never knew
before what the Church can do.' A request had followed
soon after 'from the neighbouring nest of courts,
asking for a mission and saying " we are all drunkards,
come and reform us." ' In many parts of London
similar missions were being undertaken, and Wiseman
never spared himself in going personally to encourage
them with his own new prestige. The Little Sisters of the
Poor—then a recently founded community of nuns in
France, 'who support old people entirely out of the scraps
collected after dinners '—had been welcomed to London
by the Cardinal, and they too had begun to radiate an
increasing influence. 'And now that the Aggression
business is over we shall have leisure and quiet to improve
ourselves. I own I see such a revival and progress in
store for us, to which the past agitation has contributed,
that I hope all will see how much better God has known
and cared for His Church than man would have done if
left to himself.' His own personal courage had been
no less remarkable than his prodigious energy and organising powers. He had quickly realised what an effect
could be obtained by exploiting the curiosity and interest
in himself as the first English Cardinal in London ; and
his natural love of ceremonial had led him to introduce
Roman fashions in all his own public appearances. On
Easter Sunday he had gone to S. George's 'in full
robes, *just as I should have gone to the Capella* at S. Peter's.'

There had been delay in the preparations for his arrival, and a great crowd had collected as he waited outside, ' the police keeping the way open ; but there was not a word or a look that could be considered offensive.' He had even insisted at first—until the conservatism of his friends persuaded him to moderate his zealous display—that whenever he went out in the evenings to a private function his carriage must be met, as for any Cardinal in Rome, by torch-bearers. His first carriage had been extremely ornate in the traditional Roman style ; and even afterwards he always kept up a more elaborate style than English Catholics either thought advisable or liked.

Newman, at any rate, had fully appreciated the immense moral consequences of having a new Hierarchy ; though he had at first confided[1] in Capes that ' we are not ripe ourselves for a Hierarchy. Now they have one, they can't fill up the Sees, positively can't. We want seminaries far more than Sees.' He had been amazed by the virility and courage with which Wiseman had dominated the storm ; and as his own contribution to refuting Wiseman's enemies, he had delivered in Birmingham the most famous series of his public lectures, on ' The Present Position of Catholics in England,' in which he had for the first time deliberately played to the gallery with his inimitable command of invective and irony. The lectures produced an immense impression, and even before they began, public opinion in Birmingham had reacted so strongly against the No Popery campaign that a resolution condoning the Papal Aggression had been defeated by a substantial majority. Newman devoted a great part of his lectures to an analysis of the common accusations brought against Catholics, and to denouncing the ignorant

[1] *Life of Newman*, I, 260.

prejudice which made Protestants willing to listen to any anti-Catholic propagandist, however stupid or disreputable. As an extreme instance of this form of prejudice, Newman decided to deliver a public attack upon a notorious apostate priest from Italy, Father Achilli, who had recently been touring England, and meeting with distinguished receptions everywhere when he gave lectures denouncing the iniquities of the Catholic Church. Father Achilli had even been received with special favour by Lord Palmerston at the Foreign Office ; and the success of his scandalous lectures had determined Wiseman to expose his character publicly. A few months before the Hierarchy was restored, Wiseman had actually written an article in the *Dublin Review*, in which he challenged a libel action by producing the whole of Father Achilli's almost incredibly infamous record in various places in Italy, as a profligate seducer of women. Wiseman had taken pains to collect the facts, and the case against Achilli was so overwhelming that he did not dare to institute a prosecution.

Wiseman's article about Achilli had naturally produced a great sensation among Catholics, and Newman now decided to make full use of the facts which Wiseman had already published. In the fifth lecture of his series he accordingly delivered a merciless onslaught upon the profligate Italian apostate, denouncing him with a series of scathing accusations in detail which are astounding now to read as Newman's work. Only a profound conviction that it was his duty to make his appeal to the public of Birmingham as telling and effective as he could, induced him to deliver such an attack. He was well aware of the possibility of incurring a libel action, and to safeguard himself, he took legal advice beforehand from James Hope Scott, who was one of the foremost Queen's

Counsel of the day, and who had quite recently become a Catholic, at the same time as Manning. Hope Scott had said plainly that a libel action was a possibility ; but that in view of the publication of Wiseman's article in the previous summer, and in view of the evidence in Wiseman's possession, it was extremely improbable that Achilli would face his own inevitable exposure in court. So Newman had attacked him without mercy and without reserve. And even when his attack did force Achilli to institute proceedings, Newman accepted the prospect calmly, and almost with joy, at the certainty of winning his case and utterly discrediting the most notorious anti-Catholic propagandist in the country.

Only then did Newman obtain his first experience of the terrible disadvantages of Wiseman's temperamental weakness. He had frequently found in the past that Wiseman did not deal with his correspondence when his mind was full of other concerns. And since the creation of the new Hierarchy, Wiseman's affairs were in a hopeless state of confusion through overwork. Newman wrote urgently to say that a libel action was pending against him, and to ask for the immediate delivery of the *dossier* which gave the details of Achilli's innumerable offences in Italy. His letter was not answered, and when he wrote urgently again, there was still no reply. Newman, in growing anxiety, wrote to one of the London Oratorians, begging him to do what he could. But when Father Gordon waited upon the Cardinal, he found him in great agitation, having failed completely to discover the necessary papers. ' I dare not write to him,' the Cardinal said ; ' I have hunted in vain, and cannot find the documents.' And once again the huge figure went down on his knees to hunt through piles of accumulated papers, and he sought in vain while Father Gordon

watched in deepening gloom. Soon afterwards the proceedings were due to start ; and when Newman was
entirely unable to produce any evidence, the rule against
him was given in court. On the same day Wiseman
had searched again, but this time successfully ; and the
papers were brought at once to Newman on the very day
that his case had gone by default. There was no escape
then from a complete trial of the whole action ; and
Newman was now obliged to send some of the Oratorians
to Naples to obtain first-hand evidence on the spot. Once
again Wiseman let him down, by sending letters of introduction which were not sufficiently forcible to give access
to the police reports. When they arrived in Naples, Newman told W. G. Ward afterwards[1] ' they were told that
everything could have been done had the Cardinal been
more alive.' The result was enormous labour and expense
in collecting evidence, which eventually proved to be
quite inadequate. Newman had to face a trial in which
not only the jury but Lord Campbell, the judge, was
strongly prejudiced against him. The verdict against
him was a foregone conclusion, once it became apparent
that Newman would have to prove every one of the series
of accusations he had made. And when the jury duly
reported that they found the charges ' unproven,' Newman
was confronted with a seemingly certain prospect of
imprisonment, in addition to having to bear legal expenses
amounting to over £10,000.

The fact that even the *Times* protested against the
unfairness of Lord Campbell's conduct of the case, only
added to the bitter disappointments which Wiseman's
dilatory and unmethodical habits had caused. And
although subscriptions to defray Newman's legal expenses

---

[1] Ward, II, 40.

poured in from all parts of the world, in response to an appeal initiated by Cardinal Wiseman, until there was a handsome surplus which enabled Newman afterwards to build a beautiful chapel in Dublin in connection with his unsuccessful attempt to create a Catholic University there, Wiseman's part in the whole proceedings was lamentable. But he had had more work than he could possibly cope with in the organisation of the new Hierarchy, added to the enormous task of providing for the multitudes of poor Catholic immigrants who swarmed in the slums of London.

Newman's heroic endurance, through all the unending series of frustrations which defeated almost everything he undertook in his life as a Catholic, is one of the marvels of the Catholic revival. Even though the Cardinal was directly to blame, both for his own decision to attack Achilli without having the evidence at his disposal, and for the failure of his case through lack of sufficient evidence when it was tried, Newman's deep affection towards him never diminished, and they preserved their old feelings of mutual confidence and sympathy until Wiseman's death, even though Wiseman was in most cases unwittingly the immediate occasion of Newman's failures and disappointments. Newman had been so disheartened by the whole legal proceedings and so grieved at having become involved in a scandalous libel action, that, even after the *Times* had expressed its disgust at the unfairness of his trial, he refused absolutely to consent to an appeal. Only at the last moment did he yield, under direct instructions from Wiseman himself, and the appeal succeeded so far that he escaped imprisonment, and was punished only by a nominal fine. But the appeal had not yet been heard when Wiseman singled him out for the highest honour that he could bestow, in inviting him to preach the inaugural sermon at the first synod of the reconstituted Hierarchy. The court's decision had only a few weeks before found him guilty, and the menace of imprisonment was hanging over him when he preached on July 13th, 1852, what is probably the most famous sermon in the English language, on the ' Second Spring.'

There was a special appropriateness in having one of the leading converts to preach at the first synod ; and of all Wiseman's converts, Newman was still incomparably the most widely known. His recent trial and conviction for having attempted to expose the apostate Achilli had moreover won him universal sympathy. But neither his admirers nor his critics had anticipated anything like the superb composition in which, with incomparable restraint and eloquence, he gave expression to his own intense feelings, which reflected in so much more sensitive a form the thoughts that were in the minds of all. Taking as the main idea of his sermon the renovation of the natural world and the perennial disappointments of human achievement in contrast with the abiding life of the Church, he likened this new revival to a second spring. ' The same sun shines in heaven from first to last,' he said, developing his theme, ' and the blue firmament, the everlasting mountains, reflect his rays. But where is there upon earth the champion, the hero, the law-giver, the body politic, the sovereign race, which was great three hundred years ago, and is great now ? ' And looking back to the condition of the Church in England within his own recollection, when it was ' not a sect, not even an interest, as men conceived of it—not a body, however small, representative of the great communion abroad— but a mere handful of individuals '—' no longer the Catholic Church in the country ; nay, no longer, I may say, a Catholic community ; but a few adherents of the

Old Religion, moving silently and sorrowfully about, as memorials of what had been.' ' You have seen it on one side,' he said, ' and some of us on another ; but one and all of us can bear witness to the fact of the utter contempt into which Catholicism had fallen by the time that we were born.' He recalled, addressing the assembled bishops in the magnificent Cathedral which the convert Pugin had built in Birmingham, the memory of the great Bishop Milner, whom some of his hearers could still remember among them there ; and as his imagination ranged over the glorious history of the Church in England since Augustine first came from Rome to Christianise the country, his audience were swept by the intensity of his own austere emotion.

' The past has returned,' he cried, ' the dead lives. The English Church was, and the English Church was not, and the English Church is once again. This is the portent worthy of a cry. It is the coming in of a Second Spring.' ' A second temple rises,' he said, ' on the ruins of the old. Canterbury has gone its way, and York is gone, and Durham is gone, and Winchester is gone. It was sore to part with them. We clung to the vision of past greatness, and would not believe it could come to nought ; but the Church in England has died, and the Church lives again. Westminster and Nottingham, Beverley and Hexham, Northampton and Shrewsbury, if the world lasts, shall be names as musical to the ear, as stirring to the heart, as the glories we have lost ; and saints shall rise out of them, if God so will, and doctors once again shall give the law to Israel, and preachers call to penance and to justice, as at the beginning.' His voice broke, and he could scarcely continue as he neared the end, when, still under the intense strain of his own recent trial and conviction, and with the sentence still hanging over his head, he went

Q

on—' Yes, my fathers and brothers, and if it be God's blessed will, not saints alone, not doctors only, not preachers only, shall be ours—but martyrs, too, shall reconsecrate the soil to God.' ' Something, for what we know, remains to be undergone to complete the necessary sacrifice May God forbid it for this poor nation's sake ! But still could we be surprised, my fathers and my brothers, if the winter even now should not yet be quite over ? Have we any right to take it strange if, in this English land, the springtime of the Church should turn out to be an English spring : an uncertain, anxious time of hope and fear, of joy and suffering, of bright promise and budding hopes, yet withal of keen blasts, and cold showers, and sudden storms ? One thing alone I know, that according to our need so will be our strength.'

Bishop Ullathorne, who was by far the ablest figure among the old Catholics, and who treated the converts with the outspoken instinct of a Yorkshireman of old Catholic stock (who, by an accident of his early up-bringing, spoke without the use of his aitches all through his life) had dealt severely enough, though with infinite tenderness, with Newman in the first years of their association ; but they soon established such sympathetic relations that he became much the most intimate friend and confidant of Newman's life as a Catholic. Newman's sermon at the first Synod was not the least factor in cementing their intimate friendship ; and in his history of the Restoration of the Hierarchy, Ullathorne afterwards described[1] the extraordinary emotion which was aroused by Newman's sermon. ' There were assembled the thirteen bishops with their theologians, the delegates from the thirteen newly created Chapters, the heads of the religious Orders, the rectors of the ecclesiastical colleges, and the

[1] *Restoration of the Hierarchy,* 108.

officials of the council. The sentiments of that moment will never be forgotten ; for deep and soul-stirring as they were, they found their expression in Dr. Newman's exquisite discourse.' ' The bishops and clergy were nearly all in tears,' says Ullathorne. ' And when the preacher came out from the Synod, they crowded upon him, giving full flow to the ardent outpourings of their gratitude. It was an indescribable scene ; a scene so over-powering to the gentle preacher, that Dr. Manning rescued him from it, and quietly accompanied him to his room.' One of the Canons of the Birmingham Cathedral in which the sermon was delivered has left on record[1] how, when Newman described his own vision of the long procession of the English Saints assembled to watch the ' resurrection of the Church ' in England, ' all were weeping, most of us silently, but some audibly ; as to the big-hearted Cardinal, he fairly gave up the effort at dignity and self-control, and sobbed like a child.'

[1] *Life of Bishop Grant,* 103.

CHAPTER XIII

ARCHBISHOP ERRINGTON (1852–56)

ALTHOUGH he was still barely in his fiftieth year, the strain of the No Popery campaign and of the immense labour he had to undertake, had told cruelly upon Wiseman in the year before the Synod had assembled. Complaints against him had also been growing, as the new regime was found to disappoint many hopes which had been raised. Instead of giving a fuller scope to the parochial clergy, the new Hierarchy had strengthened the authority of the bishops ; and Wiseman himself, in the first years of transition, exercised an almost supreme control. His cordial, sympathetic temperament made him loved personally, but his Roman training, and his individual leanings towards the Ultramontane School, created many grounds for friction, which gradually became much more acute. At the first Synod, various grievances were keenly discussed. The parish clergy were still without any security of tenure, and they had not gained even any voice in the election of their bishops. Certain concessions were granted at the Synod, even though it was of necessity occupied chiefly with routine matters ; and Wiseman not only drafted nearly all its decrees himself, but infused such a spirit of harmony and goodwill into every controversial discussion that Bishop Ullathorne, who was one of his most vigorous critics on many subjects, declared afterwards[1] that ' the

[1] *Autobiography*, p. 258.

conducting of this Synod was the masterpiece of Cardinal Wiseman. He it was who drew up the decrees, excepting the constitutions for the Cathedral Chapters, which were committed to Bishop Grant and myself. The unity and harmony which pervaded that Synod is one of the most delightful reminiscences of my episcopal life. Certainly no one but Cardinal Wiseman, who concentrated his whole capacious mind upon it in one of his happiest moods, could have brought it to so successful an issue, or have given it so great an amount of ecclesiastical splendour.'

The Synod had been a triumph of Wiseman's personality, and it strengthened enormously his position of leadership among the hierarchy. But in his own diocese the task of providing priests, missions and schools for the immense poverty-ridden population in the slums was a problem which caused him more and more anxiety. ' At times I could despair at finding so little help, except the *auxilium de sancto*,' he confided[1] in Father Faber, a few months after the Synod was over, in a long letter imploring him to waive the Oratorian rules so as to assume some direct part in the work that remained to be done. ' When I first came to London,' he wrote, ' I saw that the neglected part was the poor, and to that I resolved to give immediate attention.' Experience had shown him almost immediately that the only possible way of developing the work with any rapidity was to invite various religious communities to come in. ' When I came to London,' he went on, ' there was not a single community of men.' There were two Jesuits *en garçon* in a house ; that was all. But though the Jesuits had increased, and already had ' a splendid church, a large house, several priests,' they had been unable to provide any priests for mission work.

[1] Purcell, II, 2–9.

Instead, their church was ' attracting and absorbing the wealth of two parishes but maintaining no schools, and contributing nothing towards the education of the poor at its very door.' Similarly the Redemptorists had already in practice become fixed in one district alone. Neither the Passionists nor the Marists had been able to fulfil his expectations. To the Oratorians he was now driven to appealing for at least some slight assistance in his general plans, while he had still in view the formation of a new religious congregation under the convert Manning.

' Now look at the position in which I am,' he wrote despairingly to Faber. ' Having believed, having preached, having assured Bishops and clergy, that in no great city could the salvation of multitudes be carried out by the limited parochial clergy, but that religious communities alone can and will undertake the huge work of converting and preserving the corrupted masses, I have acted on this conviction, I have introduced or greatly encouraged the establishment of five religious congregations in my diocese ; and I am just (for the great work) where I first began ! But what makes it to me more bitter still, from them comes often the cry that in London nothing is being done for the poor ! ' With the difficulties of the religious congregations he had every sympathy, and he had scrupulously refrained from asking them to depart from their own rules. Now, in a poignant appeal to the convert Father Faber, he asked imploringly whether some modification could not be made. ' Do you think,' he urged, ' that if he (S. Philip Neri) had ever contemplated a Bishop in a Protestant country, who, whatever his un-merited dignity, can hardly make ends meet ; whose whole court consists of one priest ; who, for his sins, if not for God's Church, is as much howled at, barked at, scoffed at, as any Bishop has ever been for a long time '—the appeal for special assistance would be made in vain ?

But these attempts to solve an immense problem by introducing religious communities from abroad, and founding new communities in England itself, only created more internal difficulties, as friction between them and the parochial clergy inevitably arose. Wiseman, ' with only one priest as his Court,' could only labour on alone, forcing his way through misunderstandings, and striving always most definitely to find means of employing the converts who had entered the Catholic priesthood since their conversion. He knew their boundless zeal and their special confidence in himself. For them the foundation of new religious communities provided new scope everywhere. Already the two Oratorian houses, in Birmingham under Newman and in London under Faber, had supplied work for many devout and zealous men who would otherwise have found great difficulty in obtaining anything to do. And, after having introduced five religious congregations into his own diocese within four years, he was now completing arrangements which were to provide a boundless field of Catholic activity for Manning and for others, who were only awaiting the first opportunity to serve in whatever capacity they might be allowed. But with Manning, though Wiseman never guessed it at the time, he was preparing to introduce new causes of still more intense conflict and distrust. With a new convert, a new religious congregation, new claims to intervention in the established system, and above all, a new personality of extraordinary dominating force, his own life was to be made intolerable with anxiety and controversy between zealous men. But while his own peace was to be irreparably broken, he had already discerned, among the converts from Anglicanism upon whom he had always built his hopes, the man who most fully shared his own ideals and his own dreams, and who within fifteen years of his conversion and hurried ordination to the priesthood, was to become Wiseman's own successor as the second Archbishop of Westminster.

For the administrative details of a great diocese, Wiseman himself had in fact neither inclination nor aptitude. As Rector of the English College in Rome, he had been able to leave all the details of routine to his Vice-Rector, Dr. George Errington. When he had come to Oscott, Errington had joined him there again, and Wiseman had regarded himself as being virtually free from administrative responsibilities, in view of his other work as coadjutor to the Vicar Apostolic. Now, as the organiser of the new Hierarchy, his larger national responsibilities made it almost impossible for him to attend to diocesan routine ; while the public controversies aroused by the new Hierarchy had strengthened his own natural inclination to labour as a propagandist rather than as an administrator. Even while he was deploring to Father Faber that ' nothing is being done for the poor,' and while he was striving to introduce new religious communities to undertake special work, he was already accepting invitations to give lectures on many platforms, even outside his own diocese.

In Bath a local divine had been spreading stories about alleged scandals in Catholic convents, and Wiseman took up the challenge by going down to Bath to give a public lecture in the Catholic chapel for a Protestant audience. It was packed long before he arrived, and his appearance in his scarlet robes and skull cap produced an immense impression, while his lecture, lasting for more than two hours, was heard with profound interest. The police had been asked to provide protection in case of disorder, and this precaution, added to the fact that a fee of half a crown was required for admission to the chapel, provoked angry criticisms ; though Wiseman's personality and gifts as a lecturer made a great and undeniable impression. 'The manner in which Cardinal Wiseman has forced himself upon the notice of the Protestant inhabitants of this city is strikingly characteristic of the Romish Church,' wrote[1] the *Bath Chronicle*. 'To challenge their attention for a secular and semi-political lecture on a Sabbath evening exhibits the arrogance which requires that everything shall bow to its convenience ; to fix upon a place of worship, and to summon the police, are signs of that timidity which shrinks from discussion ; to levy blackmail upon Protestants for Popish objects because the opportunity offers, is an exemplification of its mischievous rule of " doing evil that good may come ! " ' And it warned its readers against being misled by this ' cunning address ' in which the ' crafty Cardinal ' had laid ' a trap to catch the generosity of men and the sentiment of women, and thereby to stifle reason,' by his insistence upon the goodness and the modesty of ' weak and defenceless women ' in the convents which he had championed.

The success of his own persuasiveness on such occasions and the vigorous propaganda which was being conducted everywhere to discredit the Catholic Church, made Wiseman more than ever anxious to devote himself chiefly to propaganda and to the wider questions of organisation. In 1853 and the following years, his public lectures became more and more numerous. He was the most picturesque public figure in England, and one of the most successful platform speakers. Invitations for lectures poured in before long from all sorts of institutions and

[1] Ward, II, 49.

societies, especially in London, and his versatility made him in demand for all manner of subjects. As an anti-quarian, an expert on Italian painting and music and architecture, as an Oriental scholar, an expert on modern science, he had original views and wide experience, and his charm as a public speaker drew crowds every-where. In the Crimean War he could speak with special knowledge of Miss Nightingale's work and of the devoted nuns who had gone out there with her to nurse the wounded ; besides having vastly more knowledge of foreign politics than most Englishmen. His natural taste for public speaking made him all the more anxious to come before the public as a distinguished and popular figure, and it would be difficult to exaggerate the enormous influence of his public lectures and writings, in making Englishmen familiar with the growing importance and activity of Catholics in the country's life.

Not the least important factor in his growing prestige was the immediate and phenomenal popularity of his romance *Fabiola*. It was Wiseman himself who had suggested, when the idea of the ' Popular Catholic Library' was proposed, that[1] ' a series of tales illustrative of the condition of the Church in different periods of her past existence ' should be included. His own idea was to have stories written around ' the Church of the Cata-combs,' ' the Church of the Basilicas,' ' the Church of the Cloister,' ' the Church of the Schools.' The notion appealed to him so much that he offered to write the story of the Catacombs himself ; and in *Fabiola* he proceeded to set down the results of his own years of exploration and devout enthusiasm among the relics of early Christian Rome. By 1854 the book was completed, and in the following year it ran through edition after edition. Nearly

[1] *Fabiola*, Preface.

all Wiseman's work, even as a young man when he was writing abstruse and scholarly treatises, was soon translated into other languages ; but *Fabiola* had no less than seven translations in Italian alone, and it was translated also[1] into French, Spanish, Portuguese, Hungarian, German, Danish, Polish, Slavonian and Dutch. From many countries requests poured in, frequently signed by Cardinals and Archbishops, that he should himself complete the series of tales suggested in his preface.

It was no wonder that while Wiseman devoted so much of his energies and time to propagandist enterprises, the affairs of his own new Archdiocese suffered from neglect, and complaints against him began to multiply at Rome. Ill-health reduced still further the time that he could devote to diocesan affairs ; and his practice of always turning to religious congregations for assistance in undertaking new schemes, while the ordinary routine work was being neglected, provoked constant resentment among the parochial clergy. His predecessor in London, Bishop Griffiths, had shared the old English prejudice against religious congregations, and Wiseman had reversed his policy to an extent which exasperated and alarmed the older Catholics. Their conflict of views was intensified by the fact that the converts generally desired to enter religious Orders, being inspired by the austere ideals of the monastic life ; and Wiseman's introduction of new religious communities invariably meant that converts were given wide commissions. Faber and Newman were both conducting a zealous propaganda of Roman ideals in their respective Oratories ; and when Wiseman persuaded Manning to form the congregation of Oblates in Bayswater, to undertake almost undefined activities on an ambitious scale, the friction between

[1] Ward, II, 101.

old and new Catholics grew much more severe. It was
not lessened by Wiseman's appointment of the convert
Oakeley as a Canon of Westminster, or by his having
persuaded the Pope to adopt the convert Monsignor
Talbot as his special confidant in Rome and adviser upon
English Catholic affairs.

At the end of 1853 Wiseman went to Rome, to discuss
many matters, and also to recuperate from an illness which
had incapacitated him for several months. Already the
friction between him and his colleagues had reached an
acute stage. Bishop Grant, who had succeeded Wiseman
as Rector of the English College in Rome, had been
nominated, on Wiseman's own recommendation, as the
first Bishop of Southwark, to whom he would delegate
part of the work of his own archdiocese. But Grant had,
almost at once after his arrival in England, joined forces
with the older Catholics against Wiseman, and he had
already taken the extreme step of lodging an appeal
against the Cardinal to Rome. Wiseman had been terribly
stricken by this development. ' The very idea of a suf-
fragan of the new Hierarchy, almost within a year, going
off to Rome to carry thither a cause against his Metropolitan,' he wrote[1] to Monsignor Talbot, ' and that that
one should be Dr. Grant, *homo pacis meae*, put at Southwark because he was my friend, is fraught with scandal.
But I regret to say it, after the first few weeks that he was
in England, he became estranged, kept aloof, and made
those men his counsellors who had always favoured and
headed the old party against me before he came.' His
early apprehensions had been tragically fulfilled. ' There
has been no cordiality, no sympathy ; months pass
without his calling on me, and every little complaint,
every discontent has gone to him.' The appeal to Rome

[1] Purcell, II, 56.

MONSIGNOR TALBOT
(*From a portrait at the English College, Rome*)

had arisen over the question of dividing property and funds in the London District between the two Sees ; and Bishop Grant was in fact claiming no more than his rights. The quarrel grieved Wiseman sorely, and he begged Talbot to insist that Grant's complaints must be reduced to writing, so that he could himself reply to it, and then Rome might decide between them. But Grant, like most of the old Catholics, had begun to regard Wiseman with such strong antipathy that the quarrel could not be composed easily ; and for seven years it dragged on in Rome.

Wiseman's own temperament contributed largely to the troubles and conflicts which developed rapidly in the following years. His incapacity for detail, and his habits of procrastination and lack of method went naturally enough with his immense enthusiasm and generosity, which he expected others to share. He would welcome and encourage every new idea that appealed to him, and then forget it when he had been seized with enthusiasm for some other project. And when his impulsiveness was aroused he would never consider the possibility of causing offence by interfering in the province of his colleagues. Thus, when he was in Rome in the early part of 1854, he took occasion to ask the Pope as a personal favour to appoint Newman to a titular bishopric, to strengthen his hands in the delicate work he had undertaken as Rector of the Catholic University in Dublin which he was then about to open. Pius IX was delighted to grant his request, and gladly recognised Wiseman's desire to assist and encourage the leader of the Oxford converts. Wiseman wrote[1] to tell Newman of the interview, concluding

I have only one thing to add—that I request the consolation and honour of conferring on you the proposed

[1] *Life of Newman*, I, 330.

dignity when the proper time shall come.' Newman, who had been for so long exposed to criticism and suspicion, and found that his own devoted work for the newly founded University was being hampered by lack of sufficient authority, replied with infinite gratitude. Letters of congratulation poured in upon Newman from important ecclesiastics who had heard of the intention ; and Newman replied to those of the Bishop of Southwark[1] that ' I never could have fancied the circumstances would exist such as to lead me to be glad to be made a Bishop, but that so it was.' He had been paralysed for several years in his preliminary work upon forming the University, by the opposition and distrust his name aroused in Ireland. As he recorded afterwards, he anticipated now that he could ' come back from Rome with a prestige, as if I had a blunderbuss in my pocket.' But the expected summons to Rome never followed ; and after a lapse of many months it dawned upon Newman that Wiseman's plan had miscarried, and that he had probably even forgotten all about it. ' The Cardinal never wrote to me a single word,' Newman records[2] in his Notes, ' or sent any sort of message to me, in explanation of the change of intention about me, till the day of his death.' The fact was that Wiseman's impulsive request to Pius IX had been resented by the Irish Hierarchy, on the very reasonable ground that if the rector of the new University in Dublin was to be made a bishop, the suggestion ought to come from them and not from Westminster.

The incident was typical of many similar misunderstandings ; and Wiseman's particular enthusiasms for Roman ideas and for encouraging the converts had aroused a general attitude of suspicion towards him in the English Hierarchy which was greatly aggravated when he

---

[1] *Life of Newman,* I, 331.   [2] *Ibid.,* I, 357.

made mistakes in tact. Their attitude was moreover strengthened by the fact that Wiseman, as the first resident Cardinal in England since the Reformation, was inclined to take his own position of leadership very much for granted. The other bishops would in any case have felt obliged to assert their own rights as against him on many matters, even if the special antipathy towards his point of view had not existed. So many general questions arose in the first few years of the Hierarchy that Wiseman himself saw the necessity, in 1855, of petitioning Rome for a coadjutor who should relieve him of most of his diocesan work. He was already at loggerheads with Bishop Grant in Southwark, and the hostility of the old Catholics was a constant anxiety to him. To overcome their distrust, and also to obtain as his assistant an old Catholic who had been his most intimate colleague since their school days together at Ushaw, Wiseman decided boldly to request that George Errington should become his coadjutor. There were obvious difficulties about such an arrangement. Errington had himself become Bishop of Plymouth when the Hierarchy was established, and to become coadjutor would consequently involve his accepting a subordinate position. But Wiseman's affectionate nature relied so implicitly upon the long years of their association in Rome and at Oscott, that he waved all objections aside. He insisted that Errington should not only be made a titular Archbishop, with the right of succession to Westminster, but that he was to consider himself as Wiseman's equal rather than as his lieutenant. Errington himself had the strongest misgivings as to the scheme, but Wiseman would not hear of refusal. Errington was accordingly brought to London as titular Archbishop of Trebizond, on the clear understanding that his responsibilities in London would be even larger than those he had exercised as Bishop of Plymouth. Even a special dispensation had been obtained by Wiseman, in order to conciliate his critics, by which the Chapter of Westminster was allowed to submit a *terna* of names as their own recommendation for the successorship to the See. And Errington's appointment consequently had all the appearance of being a direct choice of the clergy.

For a few brief months of 1855 the new arrangement brought increased activity into every department of the archdiocese, and Wiseman could now regard himself as free to carry on the ambitious planning and the bold Catholic propaganda for which he was pre-eminently suited. But the acute conflict of views between the two Archbishops was very soon apparent. Wiseman had counted on restoring confidence among the old Catholics by bringing Errington to London and choosing him as his own successor. But Errington's uncompromising and resolute temperament provoked crisis after crisis. When Wiseman asked him to undertake a canonical visitation of the diocese, Errington stipulated plainly that there must be no appeal from any of his decisions. The affectionate intimacy of the two men had lasted for years, and Wiseman agreed without hesitation. But Errington not only shared fully the objections of the older Catholics to many of Wiseman's innovations, but insisted that what he regarded as scandals must be ended. W. G. Ward's appointment, although a layman and a married man, as professor of theology at St. Edmund's College was perhaps the most glaring instance; and on his first visitation to the College, Errington conveyed his own feelings in the matter by placing such restrictions upon Ward's teaching of theology that he resigned his chair. Ward very generously told the Cardinal that he wished to assist Errington in every way, and that his own resignation seemed the obvious course. But Wiseman's selection of Ward for the position had been one of his most deliberately significant actions. He had hoped that Errington's visit to St. Edmund's would convince him of the value of Ward's work, and he now found that Errington was not open to conviction. Already his promise that Errington's decisions should be final had been frequently broken ; and while Errington, as a strict disciplinarian, was exasperated by such undermining of his own authority through Wiseman's habitual readiness to yield to emotional appeals, he now treated the question of Ward's professorship as a test case. Errington was quite right in believing that authority could not be maintained under such conditions, and his own straightforward nature had no sympathy with Wiseman's temperamental unwillingness to face internal controversies.

Conditions had become so impossible within the first six months of the new arrangement that in August, 1855, Errington wrote formally to Monsignor Talbot in Rome, telling him[1] that ' I have serious thoughts of begging the Holy See to remove me from my present position to any occupation, place, or country the Holy Father may think fit, where I might do good, instead of harm ; but I am delaying for the purpose of taking more time and counsel before adopting this step.' In the meantime he suggested that he should be detached temporarily from Westminster to take charge of the vacant See of Clifton. But he concluded by saying quite definitely ' If you think it still better, you can offer at once to the Holy Father my resignation, and readiness for such other work as may seem to him more proper.' A more self-sacrificing letter could not have been imagined, from a man who had

[1] Ward, II, 261.

R

earned respect on all sides by his energy and capacity and unfailing loyalty to his superior. It was the tragic irony of Wiseman's closing years that in almost every case when his colleagues appealed to Rome against him, Wiseman had put himself in the wrong on small matters, either by a disregard of English sentiment or by an excessive assumption of authority or by laxity in enforcing discipline ; whereas on the main issues he continued to stand for a more active and enterprising policy than they were generally willing to support. And while the earlier evidence published concerning his protracted duel with Errington left the impression that Errington was an impossible obstructionist, the more recent account by Canon Rymer, published by Abbot Butler in his *Life of Ullathorne*, makes it clear that even in the beginnings of the quarrel, Rome exerted very active pressure to restrain Wiseman from antagonising his zealous, loyal, and transparently honest coadjutor.

Monsignor Talbot, after receiving Errington's letter suggesting his own resignation, reported the matter to the Pope, and his reply[1] to Errington showed a very real sympathy. ' By this very post,' he wrote, ' I am writing to His Eminence, beseeching him to place on your shoulders all the labour, the odium, and the responsibility of the diocese, and to content himself with the direction of the higher and more important affairs of the Church in England.' ' It was for this very purpose,' Talbot insisted, ' you were nominated coadjutor, in consequence of there being many appeals made to Rome regarding the details of the administration of the diocese of Westminster.' And in the letter to Cardinal Wiseman despatched on the same day, the convert Talbot expressed himself with a courageous outspokenness which shows him to have

[1] *Life of Ullathorne*, I, 280.

been a very different person to the officious, tractable, wire-puller which he has so generally been thought. Informing the Cardinal—to whom his own recent position as the Pope's confidant on English affairs was directly due—that he had received Errington's intimation of a desire to resign, Talbot impressed upon Wiseman without the least circumlocution that ' it is hardly necessary for me to say that this would cause a great scandal and be the source of great displeasure to the Holy Father himself, as well as to all those who have had to act in his name.' Dr. Errington's nomination as coadjutor, he reminded the Cardinal, ' was in order to relieve you from all the details of government, which were a constant source of annoyance to you, and from the neglect of which constant complaints were being made to the Holy See. Now I hold it for certain that if a rupture were to take place between you and the Archbishop, it would cause a great scandal, and it would be openly proclaimed in Rome that it is impossible to satisfy you. Already it is thought a pity that Dr. Grant of Southwark should have been your nominee, and I know not what will be said if the Archbishop of Trebizond cannot agree with you.' ' If I were your Eminence,' this remarkably frank epistle continued, ' I would cast upon him all the responsibility, all the labour, and all the odium of the visitation and not mix myself up with it in any way whatever ; otherwise I am sure he will not undertake it, and he will be quite in the right.'

Talbot's courageous plain speaking and his tact in Rome itself succeeded in restoring the situation. Errington's suggestion, that he should go temporarily to Clifton until a new Bishop was appointed, was acted upon, and a truce was established. But during Errington's absence a new power began to make itself felt throughout the diocese, and the rapid increase of Manning's masterful influence aroused the old prejudices against the converts and against Wiseman's encouragement of them and of their Romanising zeal, to a greater intensity than ever. The contrast between Wiseman and his new ally could scarcely have been more remarkable. Ill-health, and the habit of receiving extreme deference to all his desires, had gradually sapped the magnificent vitality of Wiseman. After the appointment of his coadjutor, he no longer felt any personal responsibility for matters of diocesan routine ; and his imagination ranged more freely over the dreams that were still so far from being fulfilled. In Manning, with his volcanic energy, and his ascetic attitude towards life, he had discovered a born administrator whose experience as an Anglican had trained him for great responsibilities ; and Manning's convert zeal made him more eager even than Wiseman himself to strengthen the ties between the Church in England and Rome. All the qualities of energy, loyalty, dependability and practical ability, which had made Errington his most indispensable ally in the past, were now available in this austere, dynamic convert who could command such extraordinary personal influence, and who, instead of regarding the Catholic Church in England as a small and struggling section of the people, shared all Wiseman's own dreams of the conversion of England and only begged for opportunities to serve.

In Errington's absence at Clifton, Manning's plans for the formation of the Oblates materialised swiftly. The Cardinal, whose health was already failing, had appealed in vain to one religious congregation after another to undertake the work of organising missions and a general forward movement, and in Manning he had at last found a new leader capable of attracting the ablest and most zealous of the younger priests. And Wiseman was now completing his arrangements for entrusting to him the widest enterprises, on the understanding that Manning was to be the Superior of a new militant community of secular priests in London, who would undertake the active work that neither Newman nor Faber had been able to attempt. Manning went to Rome in 1856 to complete his final arrangements and there met Errington, whose sympathy he immediately sought to enlist. But in spite of all efforts at appeasement, Errington's natural distrust towards the converts was undiminished, and he saw at once that a greater menace than ever to the traditions of the parochial clergy was about to be introduced. More even than Newman or Faber, it was obvious that Manning would gather around him the most ardent of the younger clergy, and would have them under his own control, while his very success must tend to lower the standard of education and ability among those who did not enlist for service with these restless, innovating convert leaders. Still more alarming was the fact that Manning had not only gained the complete confidence of the Pope's convert adviser, Monsignor Talbot, but was treated with very special favour and consideration by the Pope himself. And then Errington learned to his dismay that the Pope himself had just decided to appoint Manning as Provost of the Cathedral Chapter of Westminster.

CHAPTER XIV

MONSIGNOR MANNING (1856–62)

ARCHBISHOP ERRINGTON had already promised to return to Westminster when he learned this staggering news. Talbot, realising how much he dreaded the prospect of returning to the former situation with Wiseman, had offered him the position of Archbishop of Trinidad, and Errington had begged to be allowed to accept that permanent exile from his old friends and his own people, rather than resume the duties which he knew could only lead to bitter conflict. But Wiseman had insisted so strongly upon his return to London that he had once more yielded, and he came home to face with unflinching courage and a stern sense of duty his thankless and heart-breaking task. Wiseman had appealed to their old and unbroken friendship since they had been school-boys together, and had promised him free scope and full authority. But the Cardinal's nerve was already failing, as he suffered more and more from the diabetes which had gained hold upon him ; and Errington was to find almost at once that Wiseman was more accessible than ever to appeals against the decisions which he made himself, in his own stern insistence upon the letter of every law.

Once again W. G. Ward became the centre of a heated controversy. Errington had assumed that Ward's retirement from the professorship at St. Edmund's

seminary was to be regarded as one of the guarantees that
Wiseman would take no more liberties with ecclesiastical
custom. But Wiseman's own faith in Ward was unshaken,
and Ward had been so gratified at finding that he still
retained the Cardinal's confidence that he had withdrawn
his resignation. Wiseman had been overjoyed but had
not dared to reopen the old question with his coadjutor ;
and even when he accompanied Errington to the station,
on his way to conduct a second visitation at the College,
it was not until the train was actually in motion that
Wiseman broke it to him by saying[1] casually ' By the
bye, I have arranged with Mr. Ward that he is to continue
in the Chair of Dogma.' Thereafter, mutual confidence
became impossible, and Errington could only persevere
in a hopeless struggle which he had desired to avoid even
by exile to Trinidad, as a desperate means of escape.
But the quarrels over W. G. Ward were only the prelude
to a protracted and increasingly acute conflict over the
position of the convert Manning. The Pope himself,
who shared all Wiseman's enthusiasm for encouraging
the new converts, had appointed Manning as Provost
of the Chapter ; but Manning now combined this position
of great influence with undivided control over the new
Congregation of Oblates, whose primary purpose was
to serve the Cardinal's plans, but who were responsible
directly to Manning himself.

Not until Whit-Monday, 1857, were the Oblates for-
mally installed at Bayswater ; but already most of the
Cathedral Chapter, including particularly the Cardinal's
Secretary, Monsignor Searle, and his Vicar General
Dr. Maguire, were profoundly apprehensive at the
powers which the new congregation would give to the

[1] Ward, II, 263.

newly appointed Provost. To Errington at Westminster, and to Bishop Grant in Southwark, every conceivable rumour or cause of complaint against the Cardinal and his convert Provost were now immediately reported ; and before the Oblate community was yet started, Errington had drawn up a long and elaborate protest against its rules. Again he returned to the attack early in 1858, and Wiseman was forced to insist upon certain modifications. But with the main principles of the new institute—both in its efforts to introduce the practices of a Roman seminary, and above all, in its intention to galvanise Catholic activities throughout London—Wiseman was in complete sympathy. It was the manner, much more than the principle, of his methods that, as the years advanced, surrounded Wiseman with a deepening cloud of mistrust. Determined to encourage Manning in the execution of plans which he had himself cherished for years, Wiseman gave him guarantees and facilities which the Chapter resented as an encroachment upon the rights of the clergy. At S. Edmund's, where Errington as much as Wiseman had for so many years wished to raise the standard of teaching and of discipline, since their early association in Rome, there was a rooted traditional antipathy towards Roman or continental ways. And the problem soon became much more complicated when, in fulfilment of Errington's fears concerning Manning, several of the ablest of its members, including the young Vice-President Fr. Herbert Vaughan, enrolled as Oblates under Manning's jurisdiction.

Another crisis had been precipitated, and the Chapter now met to confront Manning with the Canon Law, which the rules of his community were alleged to infringe. The Cardinal himself became directly involved when the Chapter were able to produce rules which he had drawn up for them and had since forgotten. A sense of persecution and of being surrounded by enemies on all sides grew upon him, causing him infinite pain and depression of spirits, and throwing him more and more into intimate association with Manning and the other converts, who shared his own ideals and who were free from the traditional prejudice among the old English Catholics against Roman customs. When the Chapter, feeling that they must assert their rights once and for all, or else allow the creation of disastrous precedents, pressed the matter vigorously against Manning with a view to breaking his alliance with the Cardinal, Wiseman at last took the law into his own hands and simply annulled its proceedings. The result was to mobilise Archbishop Errington on their side in open revolt against the Cardinal. A clear case for dispute in the Canon Law had arisen over the control of S. Edmund's, and Errington now came forward as the champion of the Chapter in their appeal to Rome against the Cardinal. After two years of smouldering antagonism the position had become entirely intolerable, and the coadjutor was now appealing openly to Rome against the Cardinal Archbishop who had begged for his appointment.

Only extreme provocation and a real sense that great issues were at stake could have led the whole Chapter to support Errington, or even have led Errington himself to oppose his oldest friend in this almost unprecedented way. Wiseman, thrown completely off his balance and distraught by the misery and loneliness of his own position, asserted himself with lamentable lack of judgement by dismissing his Vicar General Dr. Maguire, and replacing him with a plainly incompetent successor. Not only Errington but Searle, his secretary—who had also been his intimate friend since their student days in

Rome, and again at Oscott—now sided openly with the Chapter in their revolt. It was no wonder that even Manning's masterful diplomacy failed to convince Rome that the Chapter must be overridden. The question was referred back to England, and every effort was made to produce a peaceful settlement. But while Wiseman had obviously committed grave blunders and had mismanaged a difficult situation, Errington's position had still more obviously become quite impossible. Twice within ten years of the restoration of the Hierarchy, English bishops had now appealed to Rome in personal quarrels with the Cardinal who was not only their chief, but the author of the Hierarchy itself. Rome might well be dismayed by the uncompromising quarrelsomeness of these English prelates to whom such relatively small matters seemed to raise enormously important issues.

Only the inflexible and fanatical conscientiousness of Errington could account for his extraordinary behaviour in the sequel. He felt quite naturally that, having been begged to become coadjutor to Wiseman against his own wishes, and then having been recalled, after their first estrangement, in spite of his own warnings and entreaties, real issues of far-reaching importance to the Catholics of England were at stake. Even Wiseman's affectionate feelings towards him could not withstand this latest departure, when his own Coadjutor, who should have been his inseparable right-hand, was not only leading the party that opposed his whole policy but was conducting the onslaught upon him in the Eternal City. He wrote mournfully to Talbot to ask whether some alternative See could not be found for Errington, intimating that in any case some means of forcing Errington's resignation must be found. But the trouble with Errington had by this time assumed an entirely different character to their earlier estrangement over the position of W. G. Ward as a seminary professor. The intervention of Manning had made Errington regard himself as the champion of English traditions against the innovations of an ambitious convert, who was notoriously out of sympathy with the traditions of the old English Catholics and who was by nature inclined to use every possible means to gain his ends. Two years before, Errington had begged to be spared the difficulties and trials of a position in which he believed he could do no good. But the intrusion of Manning had made him feel now that a new duty was laid upon him of saving the Church in England from the tendencies which Manning personified.

Had Manning not been appointed Provost of Westminster, the whole trouble could have been surmounted easily enough. But it was Wiseman's fate to have brought together as his principal assistants two men who each represented the opposing forces that it had been his own aim to amalgamate, and who were both equally inflexible and uncompromising in insistence upon their own ideals. And Wiseman himself, who at no time had been gifted with the capacity for firm decisions in settling disputes, had for several years been losing his old vitality with the encroaching infirmity of his fatal disease. In body he had grown enormously corpulent and lethargic ; and diabetes gave him an insatiable craving for food and drink which was all the more pitiful in a man who had always continued to be strictly abstemious in his tastes. Frequent heart attacks added to his infirmity, and there were many occasions when his life seemed to hang by a thread. 'I dare say that often I am found irritable and worried,' he wrote[1] in confidence

[1] *Dublin Review*, October, 1921, p. 176.

to Manning, ' I ought to check it, and with God's help I often do, with great effort and after pain. When some eight or nine years ago I was the first to tell Mr. Hawkins that I feared diabetes had come upon me, he had no idea of it, and asked by what symptoms I judged. After mentioning others, as thirst, I added that what convinced me most was irritability of temper. For though when young, I was very hot, and perhaps passionate, my years of quiet study, and higher means, had brought me into a state of habitual peace, which had not been broken ever by much to plague and provoke me. Yet suddenly there had come upon me a fretfulness about trifles which perhaps even showed itself in my manner, which I knew from observation in others was a symptom of that complaint (dependent mainly on overwork of brain) as much as gentleness and softness is in consumption. I trust, therefore, that at least before God this may form some excuse for what man may not have so easily overlooked.'

Lonely and isolated, surrounded by perpetual warfare in his own house, he relied more and more upon the austere, ascetic Provost whose energy sustained his own flagging vitality, and whose efforts were directed towards the purposes that had inspired his whole life in England. Complaints became more and more general that[1] he now ' governed the diocese through Manning and saw everything through his eyes.' It was no question of personal jealousy, but of the opposing principles of two schools ; and Manning, with a conviction that Wiseman's whole life work was at stake, prepared grimly to fight to the last ditch. ' All my own affairs are of little importance to me compared to the trial in which your Eminence stands for a moment,' he had written[2] to the

[1] Ward, II, 361.   [2] *Dublin Review*, January, 1923, pp. 109-10.

Cardinal at the end of 1858, when the storm over the Oblates was raging furiously. ' I say for a moment, because I believe it to be a crisis permitted to put an end for ever to an unsound state, full of future dangers of a graver kind. I am as calmly and firmly convinced that all this is for the solid good of the Diocese and of the Seminary, for the final rooting of the Congregation, and the ascendancy of a Roman over every other kind of spirit, as I can be of anything which rests on the acts of men. I go to this Chapter with a light heart and with a feeling that nothing can give me pain, for I have felt that all the pain has come upon your Eminence. I wish I knew how I could lighten it. I can only renew what I have said. Your judgement and will shall guide us in everything. The work is yours. We will do all the labour with our whole heart and strength, and you shall direct. And it shall be seen who has at heart the *jura episcopi*. Our very existence, our Charter of privileges, are all the grant of the Bishop for his own service and we wish to be in your hand.'

And Manning, with his bolder conceptions of the new tasks that lay ahead of the English clergy, had gained the confidence and support not only of Monsignor Talbot in Rome but of the Pope. ' It seems to me,' he wrote[1] to Talbot in June, 1859, ' that the work of the Church in England has so rapidly become both so much larger and so much more exacting, that men are needed now who, twenty or even ten years ago, were comparatively not required. The first thing I see is that the Church has begun to touch upon the English people at every point, and that entirely new demands are made upon it. Before the Emancipation, and even until the Hierarchy, the

[1] Purcell, II, 139–41.

work of the Church consisted (1) In ministering to the old Catholic households and missions on family estates : and (2) In ministering to the Irish settlers driven over by poverty, or drawn by industry, into our large towns, etc. Now, for these two works the English priests were eminently fit, from their great goodness, devotion, and detachment from the world. But since the Church has re-entered into the public and private life and order of the English people, entirely new kinds of work are demanded. (1) First the contact, and sometimes conflict with English society in all its classes, from the lowest to the highest—the most educated, intellectual, and cultivated—requires a new race of men as teachers, directors, and companions. (2) Next, the whole work of the Church in relation to the Government, in all the public services, civil and military, at home and in the colonies, needs a class of men of whom we possess very few. (3) Thirdly, the Catholic laity, including Catholics by birth, are beginning to be dissatisfied with the standard of education both in themselves and in their priests. The close contact with the educated classes of English society forces this on them. (4) Again, a large number of our laity, chiefly converts, are highly educated, and our priests are, except individuals, not a match for them. (5) This touches on a large subject, which I can only put in few words. The educated laymen, in London at least, are passing out of the spiritual direction of the secular clergy of the diocese. They find their spiritual and intellectual wants insufficiently met and they go to the religious bodies. I think this a very serious matter for the diocese and for all its active works ; and I see no hope of redressing it, unless Spanish Place, Chelsea, and Warwick Street can be made vigorously efficient, both spiritually and intellectually, before five years are out.'

With much of this Errington himself would have entirely agreed. But it was the autocratic methods, the provocative insinuations, and the special enthusiasms of Manning that aroused fierce hostility. To Talbot in the same letter he explained that he could see no hope of remedying the existing state except by ' raising the standard of the future secular clergy, the first step to which is Council of Trent seminaries, of which we have not yet got one. And I do not believe that seminaries will ever be what they ought to be in England unless they are directed by secular priests who have learned to live by rule and who can act with unity of mind and purpose.' If any better means of attaining that result than his own Oblates could be found, he would be immediately willing to give place to it. But ' at least such a body as ours,' he told Talbot plainly, ' is better than the discordant and shifting set of men who are looking to go out upon missions. These changes are the ruin of all stability of discipline and spirit.' He was not yet prepared, even if it were offered, to assume charge of the seminary at S. Edmund's. But already Errington and the Cathedral Chapter were appealing formally against him to the Holy See ; and in the winter of 1859 Wiseman himself went to Rome to urge definitely that Errington must be deposed. Already the Cardinal had become convinced that, if Errington were to retain his right to succession at Westminster, his own life's work would be largely undone and the old regime would be reinstated. Yet it was he himself who had not only chosen Errington but had insisted upon his having the right of succession.

Early in 1860 he summoned Manning to join him in Rome, to defend himself ; and in a long memorandum[1]

[1] Ward, II, 354–65.

for Cardinal Barnabò Wiseman committed to paper such a tribute to the work and apostolic zeal of Manning as few prelates have ever earned. ' I do not hesitate to say,' wrote Wiseman, after a long summary of the many fruitful activities which Manning had initiated and carried through, ' that in all England there is not another priest who in double the time has done what Dr. Manning has for the advantage of the Catholic Church. Let your Eminence ask any who are hostile to him, is there any church or convent or school which they, I will not say have founded, but even suggested, if they have ever converted even one learned man, such as Dr. Manning has many. If the activity of the one be contrasted with the inertness of the other, it will be easy to see which merits more to be encouraged in the Church of God ; this generous activity which acts and gives without any limit, or the easy part of criticising and defaming works and words.' Was such a man, he asked in a passionate outburst, ' to be despised and treated as a man merely ambitious, cunning, dishonest, seeking nothing but his own interests and to gain influence ? ' In regard to Manning's private life, Wiseman declared that ' no one would dare to speak of his personal character without reverence.' As a preacher he ' ranks in my opinion as the first in England without any exception.' Besides, he had ' in a special way the gift of converting others, so that the noble and learned and Protestant ministers as a rule go to him to declare their doubts and abjure their heresy.' In regard to the poor, he declared that Manning had been almost alone in volunteering to assist the Cardinal in every undertaking. Yet the personal antipathy of Errington had estranged one after another of his principal advisers and assistants. His direct interference had even prevailed upon Wiseman's own young nephew, whom he had educated and treated almost as a son, to leave the Oblates after joining them. And Wiseman recorded with poignant sorrow the exact words that Errington had used to another bishop, who had appealed to him not to cause so much friction in the diocese. ' The lion is asleep,' Errington had said. ' In order to awake him it is necessary to bring every possible external pressure to bear upon him. One day he will awake, he will put out his paw, and then he will drive them all away '—meaning the Oblates.

Even yet Errington might have been willing to relinquish his self-imposed task of wrecking Manning's influence, which he sincerely regarded as the bane of the Cardinal's rule—if Talbot had not spurred him to a last stand by accusing him of disloyalty to the Holy See. Errington, declining to answer Talbot's letters, had replied with dignity to Cardinal Barnabò that he himself had done all in his power to refuse the position in which he had been placed. But now, he wrote, ' as I have been accused by Monsignor Talbot (and others who think as he does, repeat it here) of anti-Romanism, Anglo-Gallicanism, and other failings which, if they really existed, would be incompatible with the faithful fulfilment of the episcopal duties, and as these accusations are given as reasons why I should not remain here, it does not seem to me that I can of myself take any step for my own removal, since such a step would confirm these erroneous assertions and accusations, and hence would bring much damage not only on myself and my future work, but also on the credit of those (not a few) who are said expressly, or supposed by the same accusers, to think as I think, instead of viewing our affairs with the same eyes with which Monsignor Talbot and others see them.' Talbot, he complained, had in Cardinal Barnabò's name threatened him openly that if he did not resign, he must expect to be deprived of his position. He appealed, therefore, for the right to defend himself ; and in face of Talbot's injudicious accusations it had indeed become all but impossible that he should resign. Again the Archbishopric of Trinidad had become vacant, and was now offered to him, but he refused to take any step which would apparently imply that he admitted the charges with which he had been accused. In the last resort Pius IX appealed to him personally to resign, and in a heated interview Errington told the Pope to his face, even taking down a verbatim report[1] of their words in the Pope's own presence, that he would not resign unless by the Pope's express command. The command was eventually given, after a committee of three Cardinals had reported against him, and Errington retired forever from the scene, to end his life as a humble parish priest in the Isle of Man, refraining, with the gallant and self-sacrificing devotion to duty which he had always shown, from any word or action that might tend to revive old quarrels.

So the long feud was closed, and Manning now reigned with greater authority over a hostile Chapter, who could not forgive him for the humiliation and disgrace and sacrifice that he had brought upon Errington, whom everybody loved for his straightforward fearlessness, and for his spotless integrity. Wiseman's policy and his had triumphed with Errington's removal ; but the victory had been fraught with much bitterness. At one stage of the proceedings in Rome Wiseman had had a heart seizure which looked for a time as though he would not live ; and the reversion of the See would then have gone automatically to Errington, against whom the only formal complaint considered by the Holy See was his incompatibility with Wiseman. The Cardinal's health declined

[1] Leslie's *Life of Manning*, p. 133.

continually while he struggled on, lonely and disconsolate, in his conviction that the future of the Church in England required the new blood and the new methods which, twenty years earlier, he had proclaimed to be indispensable. But the interval had brought many new causes of division ; and the dismissal of Errington made the other bishops more determined than ever to resist any infringement upon their own individual or collective jurisdictions ; while their hostility made Wiseman himself more highhanded and more suspicious of opposition for any cause. Not the least tragedy of the years that followed was the conflict of views between Manning and Newman, who had become the devoted disciple of Bishop Ullathorne in Birmingham, and who had, in the long interval since his conversion, evolved views that were more in sympathy with the traditions of the Church in England than they had been in his first fervour for Rome. No less than Wiseman and Manning, Newman was specially anxious to improve the standard of education among the Catholic laity, and he had given every encouragement and support in his power to several literary reviews which were founded for the discussion of Catholic affairs. The arrival from Germany of young Sir John Acton, a disciple of Wiseman's old friend Döllinger, who gave promise of extraordinary eminence as a historical scholar, might well seem a portent of great advance. But Acton's connection with the *Rambler* soon led to his being associated with open criticisms of the bishops, and to highly speculative excursions in lay theology which provoked Manning's stern disapproval. The prejudices against Rome began to find expression in print with an appearance of academic authority which had never been shown before, and Talbot and Manning, and Cardinal Wiseman himself as their principal patron, became the target for many attacks or insinuations. Capes, the editor of the *Rambler*, had a tendency to bishop-baiting which even W. G. Ward in his Anglican days scarcely surpassed ; and the publication of highly provocative articles, raising doubts as to the soundness of various beliefs which were generally regarded as of faith, soon led to such a crisis that its suppression was inevitable. Wiseman, with his unfailing desire to avoid open conflict, appealed desperately to Newman to undertake the editorship of the review, in order to save it from condemnation ; and Newman with infinite reluctance undertook one more ungrateful task which within a few months only brought suspicion of unorthodoxy upon his own head.

Troubles seemed to multiply without number as Wiseman's health and courage went to pieces. Ullathorne, whose zeal and ability was equalled only by that of Wiseman in his prime, had shared with Newman the dream of founding at Oxford a college of some kind where Catholic laymen could obtain a University education. At Ullathorne's request, Newman had actually bought land in Oxford with the object of founding a branch of the Oratory there. Manning had heard of this with alarm, and immediately set to work to persuade Wiseman of his own view that the Catholics would have no influence whatever upon the life of Oxford itself, but that their own faith and loyalty would be jeopardised by an education among anti-Catholic surroundings. The controversy inflamed all the suspicious side of Manning's nature, and before long Newman, like Errington, was being accused in Rome of Gallicanism and anti-Romanism. When certain injudicious writings of Newman's appeared he was even accused of unorthodoxy as well, and formally delated to Rome.

Manning's persistent denunciations gained such a

paramount influence upon Wiseman that the other bishops
began to take counsel among themselves without reference
to him.   This new development caused Wiseman acute
distress, and it never occurred to him, while he was subject
to Manning's dominating influence, that his own attitude
might be at fault.   He was so isolated that he received
no confidences from those who differed from him ;
and his ill-health made him a tragic figure indeed.
' I pass nights awake and my old worst symptoms are
hovering about my chest,' he told Manning[1] in February,
1862.   In the long sleepless nights he was driven to
composing light Latin verses, which he would send to
Manning, for lack of any more appreciative friend.
' Let Herbert (Vaughan) give me a few lines occasionally,'
he wrote pathetically.   ' You know how little sympathy
I find about me, and I really want a little.'   Wiseman
learned with dismay that the bishops had been holding
private meetings of their own without including him.
' The policy is now evidently to carry by *majorities*,
not by weight of arguments,' he wrote plaintively[2] to
Manning.   ' It was so at Synod (1859), it was so last
summer, and so it is again.   Eight against one or two,
such is to be our mode of carrying on affairs.   In reality
it is two or three against two or three, the rest being dead
weight thrown into the scale.'   It was not surprising,
when Wiseman felt thus towards decisions by majorities,
that the other bishops preferred to discuss things among
themselves without his presence, when they would be
expected to bow to his own decisions.   In March, 1862,
he wrote[3] of Ullathorne to Manning that ' I fancy the
episcopate is roused to exhibition of its true colours.
They have hauled down the Tiara and Keys and displayed

[1] *Dublin Review*, October, 1921, p. 177.
[2] *Ibid.*, p. 180.
[3] Leslie's *Life of Manning*, 511.

their " Confederate " flag, the Gallic cock that crowed against S. Peter. However I have given up troubling myself much on the matter but calmly await the decision of the Holy See.' His own expressions were only a feeble echo of the language used in confidence by Manning and Herbert Vaughan, who were now almost alone in sharing his confidence. Ullathorne became known among them as ' Monsignor Ego Solus,' and Herbert Vaughan was writing[1] of him to Manning as having 'come out in his true colours, Anglican and Gallican in the strongest way.'

Wiseman made fitful efforts to restore more harmonious relations from time to time, but the estrangements had gone too far and he was never able to recover from the isolation into which he had fallen. ' I think you should enter a protest,' Wiseman wrote[2] to Manning in the beginning of 1862, ' against the bishops holding meetings apart as if they formed a body corporate without the Metropolitan to discuss or concert affairs of the Province apart.' Some of these recent meetings he deplored as ' most pernicious, injurious to peace and scandalous,' and he had decided once and for all that he ' must make good the rights of my See.' ' God grant us peace ; for I shall not much longer stand this pelting on all sides. And I believe I can better stand stones than mud,' he wrote[3] to Manning towards the end of March. ' But we have many consolations. Besides Hendon and Fitzroy, I trust we shall have new missions started this year at Hounslow, Southend and Dovercourt (Harwich), perhaps another in Essex. The country is thus being opened. I told Bentley he must be the first baptised in his beautiful font, and by me, and he is under instruction for it. Many other good symptoms present themselves to prove that

[1] Leslie's *Life of Manning*, 491.
[2] *Ibid.*, 511.
[3] *Dublin Review*, October, 1921, p. 180.

in spite of me and my many miseries, God has not abandoned this poor Diocese, and surely when a better comes in my place it will flourish with greater prosperity.'

Misunderstandings only deepened as Wiseman felt it his duty to assert himself. When the annual Low Week meeting of the Hierarchy was due to be held that year, most of the bishops on one pretext or another begged to be excused from accepting his invitation. Their attitude not only intensified Wiseman's sense of being opposed on all sides, but drove him to further assertions of his authority. ' I think it is not too much to consider these two letters as conspired and deliberate insults to the head of the Hierarchy,' he told Manning in his Easter letter[1] to him, ' and you had better put the matter as another phase before Cardinal Barnabò. Circumstances, of course, may be created, but if such an excuse be admitted, every one may stay away when he likes from anything. It is indecorous in the last degree, and surely will not be tolerated.' The situation was fast becoming intolerable. It was not made easier by the fact that Pius IX was entirely on Wiseman's side. It was to Cardinal Barnabò, as Prefect of Propaganda, the bishops turned for protection of their rights ; and his influence gradually averted what to Roman eyes looked like the possibility of an open schism. Manning in a letter[2] to Talbot summarised the views of Barnabò, which showed an extremely clear appreciation of the difficulties that had arisen. He saw that the conflict was between two contrary systems and points of view, and that the friction had been greatly intensified by Wiseman's own temperamental mistakes. 'The bishops feel the superiority of the Cardinal,' was Barnabò's diagnosis of these repeated references and appeals to

---

[1] *Ibid.,* January, 1923, p. 127.
[2] Purcell, II, 117.

Rome. Most of the bishops, he knew, had been Wiseman's pupils at the English College in Rome in the past, and the Cardinal probably failed to treat them with sufficient deference on that account. 'Perhaps his superiority may be made more sensible than it need by manner,' was another accurate diagnosis ; and, in general, Barnabò believed that Wiseman was probably no more free than anyone else from the infirmities of human nature.

The main trouble had been the inability of Wiseman to allow for English ways and prejudices ; and the procedure of Rome, in delaying a decision indefinitely upon each appeal, only aggravated their discontent and their sense of being unfairly treated. At last the climax was reached when practically the whole English episcopate assembled in Rome on the occasion of the canonisation of the Japanese martyrs. Pius IX took the opportunity to deliver himself straight to them all in Wiseman's presence. Talking to them as though they were schoolboys, when they had been brought together standing around him, the Pope told them that he was not surprised that differences should have arisen, as they had arisen even between S. Peter and S. Paul. But he told them at once that he wished to hear no more of their continual disputes and that they must henceforward find means of agreeing among themselves. His wish, wrote[1] Wiseman to Manning in June, ' —and he added later this must be considered a command—was that we should take the highest and largest mountain in the Alps and put it over all past questions and dissensions and without any tunnel through to get at them. They were never to be referred to again or brought up under any circumstances. So end the six months' attacks, personalities, etc.' Not a word

[1] *Dublin Review*, October, 1921, p. 182.

Ward. Doug goss work into devils way

was spoken at the audience except by Wiseman and the Pope; and the Bishops all filed out, as Wiseman recorded the interview, ' blank and speechless. In the ante-room, where many bishops had come, I hunted each one out, asked him if he was going next day, and shook hands, wishing a pleasant journey. Not a· hand was kindly held out. I had almost to lift some up dead from the side. They went into S. Peter's, where a person who saw them wondered what had come over them. Talbot called on them at dinner and found them very low and prostrate. Such,' he concluded, ' is the grand total of this unhappy attempt to make void the Hierarchy and return to Vicarial regimen.' ' So I trust is ended the great campaign of 1861–2,' he wrote in a later letter. ' God grant that it may never have to be renewed.'

But although Wiseman felt that he had gained his point, and hoped that no more would be heard of their many differences, the bishops had in fact gained the main substance of their appeal. It was decided that attendance at the Low Week meetings must be obligatory henceforward; but the agenda of the episcopal meeting must now be circulated in advance, and in the discussions, decisions must be taken either by a majority of votes or else by direct reference of any disputed question to the Holy See itself. Rome had spoken, and in ending a long quarrel, had not only asserted the authority of the Cardinal but had imposed clear restrictions upon the supremacy which in the first stage of the new Hierarchy, Wiseman had assumed to be his own right. And the two remaining assemblies of the bishops in Low Week were marked by a pacific and friendly tone. ' All is really gone off well and quickly,' Wiseman wrote after the meeting of 1863, and a very marked improvement in their relations was already apparent. Twelve bishops had taken part on the following day at the opening of the new Italian Church, and although Bishops Ullathorne and Grant were still unable to overcome their old differences with the Cardinal sufficiently to meet him publicly in social intercourse, he had brought all the rest of the Bishops with him after the ceremony to his country house at Leyton, 'where they all seemed to enjoy themselves immensely and dined very cheerfully.' And in the following year, during the proceedings at the last of the Low Week meetings over which Wiseman presided, conditions were still more amicable, and Wiseman was able to report[1] to Manning that ' nothing could have been more pacific and friendly than our meeting.'

[1] *Dublin Review*, October, 1921, p. 199.

Errington (Old Catholic – Eng.)

Archbishop of Trebizond

D Gynn was a good turn for Talbot.

CARDINAL WISEMAN AND FATHER HERBERT (CARDINAL)
VAUGHAN
(*From a photograph kindly lent by V. Rev. Herbert Vaughan, D.D.*)

of men, and 34 hospitals or charitable institutions, had
all come into existence since 1826.

Montalembert's two lectures at Malines, on the ' Free
Church in a Free State ' and on ' Liberty of Conscience,'
gave great offence to the Ultramontanes in England ;
and W. G. Ward, with his usual lack of restraint, not only
denounced them in an attack which he was prevented from
publishing in the *Dublin Review*, but attempted to have
Montalembert's addresses condemned by Rome. His
efforts were unavailing, and the Pope even instructed his
Nuncio in Paris to inform Montalembert that there was
no intention of censuring his views. But Ward's attack
was made the basis of suggestions that Wiseman had
prompted it, and Ambrose Phillips was requested to discover privately whether the suggestion was well founded.
Once again Ward's uncontrollable temperament had produced misunderstandings, and Wiseman hastened to
reassure his old ally in the Catholic revival on the Continent that he did not even know that Ward had written
any such pamphlet, and that, however he might disagree
with Montalembert's political principles, it had ' never
entered his mind to denounce it to the Index, or to ask
to have it even reproved, still less condemned.' The
years had already taken heavy toll of the pioneers of that
religious revival which had inspired Wiseman's youth and
had led him to petition for his own removal from Rome
to England ; and it grieved Wiseman that any misunderstanding should arise between himself and one of
the few survivors of their early co-operation.

The autumn of 1863 had been passed in another long
illness. ' My appetite completely left me again,' he wrote[1]
to Manning in October. ' I had been reduced to great

[1] Purcell, II, 177.

T

weakness, and only to-day, in spite of dreadful weather, I have felt the first symptoms of rallying. But I am far from being myself, and I have a sort of languid despondency which makes me feel as if I never shall be so again. Of course I am lonely, and have no means of keeping my thoughts out of the two extremes of over-activity or self-devouring, except inward efforts and control which feels like riding a very hard-mouthed horse along the top of a cliff by way of recreation. However, I must bear my cross as it is shaped for me ; but only God knows what I suffer inwardly at times—I could not write it.' In November he had regained sufficient energy to write to his old friend, Dr. Russell of Maynooth, telling him[1] that after months of prostration he was now at 'a charming villa facing the sea, with a nice flower-garden round it, in which I can walk sheltered and unoverlooked.' Months had passed before his working powers returned sufficiently even to revise his Malines lecture. Only a few matters which appealed to him particularly could now be attended to. At the end of October he had been well enough to write an affectionate letter to Father Vaughan from Broadstairs, where he was convalescing, to encourage him in his plans for the Missionary College at Mill Hill. ' I have no news to tell you, except about myself,' he wrote,[2] ' as I am here living for myself, and almost by myself. I am better, much in body, a little in spirits and vigour. But the beautiful situation, the fine weather, and the rest which I am enjoying will, please God, restore me.' He had made a pilgrimage on the previous day to Canterbury Cathedral, ' where S. Augustine, S. Winifred, S. Anselm, etc., yet repose, and S. Thomas once received the worship of thousands.' But what

[1] Ward, II, 462.
[2] *Ibid.*, II, 464.

delighted him most was the thought, as he stood beside Cardinal Pole's tomb, that he was himself ' the first Cardinal that ever entered the splendid cathedral, since he was in it, alive or dead.' It was his first walk beyond the garden since his illness, and he managed to slip in between the services, escaping recognition even by the vergers, so that he could see the whole building in peace.

Just before Christmas he wrote again[1] to Herbert Vaughan, who was about to start on his begging tour in America to raise funds for his Missionary College. Only now, he wrote, did he ' realise the greatness of your devotedness and self-sacrifice, in separating yourself from home and friends ' ; and while he was himself immersed ' in so much darkness and depression about himself,' the feeling of ' inexorable confidence in the powers and goodness of God shines brighter and seems given to me to compensate for my past and actual sufferings.' To Dr. Russell he wrote at the beginning of 1864 that ' I enter on this new year in fair health and spirits, welcoming it as a new gift from God,' though even still ' I have more cloud than sunshine over me.' His energy had failed so far that only on special occasions could he rouse himself to any public activity. But in the spring of 1864 he was so outraged by the ecstatic reception given to Garibaldi on his visit to England that he dealt with the matter in his pastoral, which provoked a public controversy in the *Times*.

Wiseman had quoted from a violent letter in which Garibaldi had protested against the reaction in France since the glorious days when she had in 1793 ' given to the world the Goddess Reason, levelled tyranny to the dust,

[1] Ward, II, 465.

and consecrated brotherhood between nations. After almost a century, she is reduced to combat the liberty of nations, to protect tyranny and to direct her only efforts to steady on the ruins of the Temple of Reason that hideous and immoral monstrosity the Papacy.' In his pastoral, Wiseman had protested vigorously against the deplorable demonstrations of honour shown to a man capable of making such statements, and had appealed to his people to co-operate so as ' to multiply the number of our churches and schools, into which the spirit of irreligion will never creep, nor any tampering be allowed with the faith of our fathers.' His protest quickly provoked one of the usual outbursts[1] of truculence in the *Times*, which now accused him of having misquoted what Garibaldi wrote in order to attack those who had received him with honour. ' He inserts a word or two to make it suit his purpose,' sneered the *Times*, ' and then feigns a transport of pious horror at our impiety in doing honour to such a reprobate.' It accused Wiseman openly of having ' invented such profanities ' to ' damage a political enemy,' and declared that such conduct was ' quite as shocking as the honest utterance of them.' But the *Times* had misjudged its opponent, forgetting that he had been trained in the most fastidious school of scholarship in Rome. To tamper with any quotation would have been unthinkable to him, and to do so in attacking any opponent whatsoever would have outraged all the generous impulses of his nature. He replied indignantly at once that his quotation was actually copied from the translation of Garibaldi's letter published in the *Times* itself ; and within a week the *Times* had to apologise publicly.

[1] The *Times*, May 25th, 1864.

But though Wiseman had won a victory which encouraged all Catholics, his vitality was already almost gone,
and in the few remaining actions of his life he intervened
to oppose and not to initiate. Ambrose Phillips had
committed himself deeply to the programme of the
Association for Promoting the Union of Christian
Churches ; and his willingness to meet the High Church
Anglicans on level terms provoked Manning particularly
into efforts to obtain a formal censure from Rome.
Wiseman himself sent in a long report[1] in which he complained that, although Phillips repudiated the charge
that he encouraged Protestants to refrain from becoming
Catholics ' with the false idea that they could serve it
better by staying in Protestantism,' yet ' it is certain that
all his writings tend to strengthen the Anglicans in their
intrenchments, and to make them more confident of the
validity of their order, and to encourage them to look for
the conversion of their whole body, rather than for that
of individuals.' He felt obliged to explain at considerable
length the difference between the attitude of Phillips—
to whose zeal and generosity he paid full tribute—and
his own famous ' Letter to the Earl of Shrewsbury '
on the question of reunion in 1841. The result was the
formal condemnation of the A.P.U.C. by the Congregation of the Index, in an uncompromising letter addressed
to all the English bishops issued in September, 1864.
But Wiseman's old affection for this convert knight-
errant who had been one of the first to turn his own
attentions to Apostolic work in England, never failed.
And in his last illness he still greeted Ambrose Phillips
with a cordial welcome in his house at Leyton, and received long letters[2] from him which revealed his old

[1] Ward, II, 483.
[2] *Phillips de Lisle*, I, 394–6.

enthusiasm, undaunted by the blow that had fallen upon his hopes.

Only in one other controversy did Wiseman engage before the end ; and once again under the influence of Manning. In the first years of his work in England, when Newman's ascendancy at Oxford was still so strong, Wiseman had dreamed of a Catholic college there in which Newman would, after his conversion, revive and carry still further the moral and intellectual influence he had formally exercised. But the intervening years had brought many changes. Ullathorne, as Newman's bishop in Birmingham, was now encouraging Newman to take steps to found an Oratory there ; but all Ullathorne's activities were now regarded with instinctive antipathy at Westminster after so many years of smouldering conflict ; and Newman's recent attitude towards the Temporal Power, concerning which both Wiseman and Provost Manning held uncompromising ultramontane views, had aroused a new hostility. The question of the Temporal Power had begun to loom large, as the Nationalist aspirations in Italy rose higher, and the future of the Papal States became always more precarious. In 1861 Wiseman had founded, chiefly through Manning's efforts, the ' Academia of the Catholic Religion,' and in the preceding weeks had committed himself to extreme opinions in regard to the Temporal Power. Newman's sensitive mind had perceived possibilities of future conflict at once, and in June, 1861, he had thought it necessary to forestall possible complications by writing a confidential letter[1] to Manning in which, while disclaiming any intention of ' writing anything in the shape of a threat,' he had made his own position quite clear. ' I

[1] *Life of Newman,* I, 525.

ought then to say what I am resolved on,' he wrote,
' but this is for you, not for the Cardinal. Should His
Eminence put out any matter bearing on the same question
in the same way in *his Inaugural Address of the 29th*,
I certainly will not remain a member of the Academia.'
The letter was signed ' ever yours affectionately,' and
Manning replied to it in a friendly manner. But Manning's attitude towards the Temporal Power before the
catastrophe of 1870 was so fanatically intolerant that
Newman's cautious attitude was to Manning almost a
confession of heresy. And now, three years later, when
he learned that Newman had bought land in Oxford at
Ullathorne's suggestion with a view to encouraging
Catholics to enter the University, Manning's hostility
had been confirmed by the recent publication of Pius
IX's famous *Syllabus Errorum*, which was regarded as
virtually a declaration of war upon the modern world.

In the *Dublin Review*, which Wiseman had by this time
placed unreservedly in Manning's hands, the dangers
of sending Catholic young men to Oxford was immediately
urged in the strongest terms ; and Manning mobilised
all the influence he could exert through the unhesitating
co-operation of Monsignor Talbot in Rome. But Cardinal Barnabò, as usual, declined to take either Manning's
or Wiseman's view as unprejudiced. With an appreciation of national rights and of local influences for which
Rome seldom receives credit, the whole question, as
on various other occasions, was referred back to the
decision of the English bishops. The decision was a
further blow to Talbot and to Manning, who were convinced that Barnabò lacked courage, and was afraid
to assert the rights of Rome lest the bishops in England
should be offended. But Wiseman, in the solitude of his
last years, had mitigated his own assumption of authority,

and he received the news without dismay. A circular letter was issued to consult the opinions of the leading clergy and laity, before the bishops' meeting was to take place, but Newman was deliberately excluded from the consultation. When the bishops met, the general verdict was strongly against encouraging Newman's plans, and Newman himself bowed at once to their decision when he learned that they had sent a letter to Rome recommending that English Catholics should be sternly discouraged from attending the old Universities. But the decision was one more blow to the many hopes in which Newman had been disappointed time after time. The bishops' meeting was the last at which Cardinal Wiseman was to preside, before death claimed him a few months later. And Newman wrote mournfully[1] after his death to a friend ' The Cardinal has done a great work. Alas ! I wish he had not done his last act. He lived just long enough to put an extinguisher on the Oxford scheme— quite inconsistently too with what he had wished and said in former years.'

Only the question of who should replace him as Arch-bishop of Westminster remained unsettled ; but in spite of all the efforts of Manning and Talbot to persuade him to nominate his own successor in 1863, the Cardinal had refused absolutely to face the problem. It was too late now to expect that he could be aroused to a final effort. In Rome itself the desirability of appointing a coadjutor was clearly seen ; but after the disappointment of Errington's co-operation, it was scarcely to be hoped that Wiseman could be prevailed upon to nominate another. Talbot had written[2] to Manning in June, 1863, declaring that only by the selection of his own successor

---

[1] Ward, II, 477.
[2] Purcell, II, 175.

could Wiseman avert ' a great scandal in England at his death.' He foresaw already that ' all the bishops in England would write to recommend Dr. Errington for Westminster, not from liking the man, but from an English feeling of triumphing over Cardinal Wiseman and gaining a victory over the Holy See.' Manning had reported to Talbot that Cardinal Wiseman ' would be relieved if the Holy See would decide for him. He is timid and wishes to end his days without any more troubles.' But Wiseman's aggravated illness during the summer and autumn had made any development impossible. In December, Manning broached the subject again in a letter from Rome, but without evoking any response. At last, under strong pressure from Cardinal Barnabò in Rome, Manning himself suggested a coadjutor, in a private audience with the Pope. Believing that the suggestion would not only win over a formidable critic but would give[1] to the Chapter of Westminster ' neither victory nor defeat but a master,' Manning had daringly suggested the nomination of Ullathorne, with immediate right of succession. In a report to Wiseman, Manning had said[2] plainly that ' I think him beyond all compare the fittest man to come after you.' But Ullathorne had for years been the leader of the English party as against Wiseman's own ultramontane tendencies. Manning's report had grieved him deeply, and when Manning returned Wiseman told him sorrowfully that, on receiving it ' I felt as if my last friend had left me.' He wrote at once to Rome protesting vehemently against the proposal. But by February Manning had been driven to give up the attempt, and he had written from Rome to say[3] that

[1] *Ibid.*, II, 185.
[2] *Ibid.*, II, 183.
[3] *Ibid.*, II, 187.

' you may consider the coadjutor question as ended, and in your own hands. I believe also that, though many painful things have happened in the course of it, yet what has passed has done good, and brought out much that will be of use. I feel sure that the Holy Father is as much alive as ever to the fact that your work in England is a whole, and that it has been a counteraction against an old spirit, and I must say an old party, who at any moment might, in your absence, wreck or retard a great deal of your work since the Hierarchy, and through the Hierarchy.' But the infirm and suffering Cardinal had already made up his mind, that he would leave the choice of his own successor to the unfettered discretion of the Chapter of Westminster.

His decision had ensured at least peace of mind in the protracted agonies and melancholy of his long fatal illness. The gravity of his condition had aroused widespread sympathy with him among all classes. He was unable to attend to the business of his own diocese, which involved constant attention to detail from day to day, but the long months of his last years were alleviated by many expressions of public esteem and by a continual succession of invitations to deliver public lectures on important occasions. It pleased him greatly when the Astronomer Royal invited him as his guest, to sit at his right hand and to receive the principal toast, at the dinner of the Royal Astronomical Society. But the last great consolation of his public life was the invitation to join the National Committee organised to celebrate the Shakespeare Tercentenary, and to deliver a public address. In a temporary return of his old enthusiasm, he himself proposed the publication of a great illustrated edition of Shakespeare's plays in honour of the tercentenary; and the proposal brought him enthusiastic letters, and even hopes of the patronage of the Prince of Wales, from the Queen's librarian at Windsor Castle. The original National Committee came to nothing, but a still more welcome honour came to the Cardinal when he received from the Working Men's Shakespeare Committee— which represented more than two million members— a formal request to deliver his lecture under their auspices, ' at S. James's Hall, or any other place agreeable to your Eminence, they undertaking to make all arrangements connected therewith, and to announce it, in a manner worthy of the object and the lecturer.' A still more flattering letter[1] had preceded it to ask ' whether it would be more agreeable to his Eminence to receive a requisition to give an address from members of the Shakespeare National Committee, or that a deputation of the Trades Unions of London who have associated themselves with the movement should wait upon his Eminence.' Wiseman had decided at once to accept the invitation. ' One would hardly have expected this a few years ago,' he wrote to Canon Walker. And to Dr. Russell of Maynooth he wrote[2] that ' I have considered it quite a matter of religious importance to accept, as it has a good influence to see such a national subject thrown into Catholic hierarchical hands.'

The lecture was to have taken place at the end of January, and for months beforehand his mind was occupied with its preparation. But his strength was already failing fast. A hurried trip to Bruges had seemed to revive his health while he was there, and he had been immensely encouraged by the great demonstrations of public welcome that had greeted him. But he relapsed quickly after his return, and a sore in his foot

---

[1] Ward, II, 499.
[2] *Ibid.*, II, 503.

showed symptoms of mortifying. For weeks he could scarcely leave his sofa. By way of relaxation he would write little plays and stories for a few children who had gained his special affection : the small daughters of the Count de Torre-Diaz, of whom one was afterwards to become the mother of Cardinal Merry del Val. His last effort was to preside at the bishops' meeting which decided against Newman's scheme for a Catholic hostel at Oxford. Returning to his sofa at Leyton, he devoted all his remaining energies to an enthusiastic study of Shakespeare, dictating parts of his lecture in the hopes of having it ready for publication before it was due to be delivered. But a fortnight before the appointed date, on January 15th, he had a sudden onset of illness which made it necessary for him to receive the Last Sacraments. His strength rallied two days later, and for a month more his life dragged on. ' He was quietness itself, and his patience and obedience were perfect,' wrote[1] Canon Morris afterwards. ' He had not said a querulous word during the three weeks he had been so ill, and he was ever ready with gentle thanks for any little service. He passed whole days in silence, uttering only a few sentences ; but all the while he was quite collected and himself. . . . We never once saw him dejected or in low spirits.'

In the days that passed in waiting for the end, he would utter occasional fragments of conversations which revealed the trend of his thoughts. ' I have never cared for anything but the Church,' he murmured one day. ' My sole delight has been in everything connected with her. As people in the world go to a ball for their recreation, so I have enjoyed a great function.' He saw already that his own funeral, as the first Cardinal Archbishop to

---

[1] Ward, II, 510.

be buried in England since the Reformation, was to be the most impressive and magnificent function of all. In a letter from Bruges in the previous autumn he had confided in Dr. Russell that ' somehow I feel more at home abroad than at home.' So now, his thoughts kept on turning back to Italy, to Rome, and above all to Monte Porzio. ' I can see the colour of the chestnut trees,' he said, ' and Camaldoli, and the top of Tusculum. What a beautiful view it is from our Refectory window ! A newcomer does not value Monte Porzio properly. It takes a hard year's work in Rome to enable you to appreciate it. I loved it dearly. I keep a picture of it in my bedroom, both here and at Leyton. They have kept the Rector's chair in the place where I used to sit. I got that gold chair for Pope Leo's reception, and I always used it afterwards. I used to sit there writing for hours after everyone was in bed, and then I would refresh myself by a look out of the open window into the moonlight night.'

Manning was in Italy now, while his beloved master lay upon his death-bed ; and he was waiting in tense anxiety for news as to whether his own return was yet urgent, wondering whether he ought to have gone at all. At Genoa he had received news of Wiseman's last rally of strength, and he had decided that duty called him on to Rome. He too was thinking[1] of ' those old days in Rome which I shall never forget '—of ' dear S. Agnes and her lambs ' and of the first day that Wiseman had brought Manning to see them blessed on her feast day, when they had both been young men full of hope, though a chasm still divided them. ' I trust, my dear Lord Cardinal,' he wrote, ' that you will still be over us for many years, and see the maturity of many more of your

[1] Purcell, II, 191.

works. These last twelve years have been a great time and full of a great future. I said very little of what I think in the article on your sermons. What we owe to you in the rooting and development of the Hierarchy, and in raising the Catholic spirit and practice of England towards the level of Rome will be known only hereafter. But it is not only on public grounds that I pray in every Mass for your restoration to health and prolonged life. In talking with you I am always restrained, partly by something on your part, and partly by something on my own, from saying how much I prize the friendship to which you have so kindly admitted me. In these thirteen years, and above all, in the last seven years, it has been my chief support in very hard times and very hard trials. To do anything to lessen your burdens has been among my chief desires.' But on the day this last letter in their so long and intimate correspondence reached its destination, a telegram was despatched to Manning in Rome telling him to return immediately.

CHAPTER XVI

RETROSPECT (1865)

ALL hope of recovery had gone, yet in the last days one strangely dramatic consolation had been brought to the dying Cardinal. Sibthorpe, the first of his converts from the Oxford Movement, whose reversion to Anglicanism during the Tractarian days had been so often and so cruelly thrown against Wiseman as proof of the reckless folly of his own policy, had after twenty years been reconciled to the Catholic Church again. The news reached Wiseman as he lay dying in his house, and there was unbounded joy over the prodigal's return. Wiseman insisted[1] that Sibthorpe must say his first Mass, on the feast of S. Paul's Conversion, in his own private chapel. And then the end approached more quickly. On February 2nd he insisted upon having his bed carried downstairs to the drawing-room, knowing that the end had come, and in preparation for the final scenes. 'I shall look to you and Patterson,' he said to Canon Morris, 'for the ceremonial. See that everything is done quite right. Do not let a rubric be broken.'

He asked that no one should read to him as he was dying, as he would rather be left to his own meditations. But he desired that the Litany for a Departing Soul should be recited; 'I want to have everything the Church

[1] Ward, II, 511.

gives me, down to the Holy Water. Do not leave out anything. I want everything.' So, on the 5th, when Manning had already been summoned back from Rome, he lay in his bed robed in the full vestments prescribed for a Cardinal Archbishop's dying profession of faith. The Canons filed in, in their correct order, and stood around while the author of the Hierarchy lovingly recited the solemn words in their presence, and then asked to receive Extreme Unction at their hands. Only Manning, the Provost, was absent from the Chapter ; but on the walls of the drawing-room there hung the large life-like portrait of Pius IX who, Canon Morris noted, ' looked down upon us, and seemed to form part of the group, who were engaged in one of the most solemn acts the Church has devised.' When the recital was ended, the familiar voice rose feebly among them for the last time, speaking to them of his own successor and reminding them that the appointment lay with the Holy See, and that the method of election which he had established since the Hierarchy would be applied. ' I have one word to say,' he spoke with his final solemn injunction, ' and it is to beg you to cherish peace, and charity, and unity, even though it may be at the price of our occasionally having to give up our own individual opinions for the sake of peace. And if in the past there has been anything that has made against charity and unity, in God's name let it pass into oblivion ; let us put aside all jealousies, and let us forgive one another and love one another.' Then, having given them all the Pontifical blessing, and received from each Canon the ' kiss of peace,' he settled down to await the call of death. For a whole week he lived on, though his consciousness was ebbing fast ; and when Manning arrived on the 12th, he did not seem to recognise him. He could only whisper ' I thank him, I thank him,' when Manning told him that the Pope had sent his special blessing. Three days later, in the morning, when Manning and Monsignor Thompson had just finished saying their daily Masses for his happy death, the watching Sisters announced that the end had come.

By the last wishes of the dead Cardinal, the task of preaching his panegyric in the pro-Cathedral at Moorfields had, unknown to him, been reserved for Monsignor Manning. The Provost's own hopes of ensuring the continuance of his work had been sorely broken by the Cardinal's refusal to choose his own successor ; and he too was now to feel the agonies of encroaching loneliness and despondency, as he contemplated the prospect of his defeat as soon as Wiseman's successor should be chosen. Little did he dream that Wiseman's decision that Manning should preach his panegyric was to give a symbolical character to the event ; that it was to bring before the whole brilliant gathering of Catholics and of non-Catholics at the funeral, the man who in a few months' time was to be directly appointed by the Pope as the Cardinal's successor. Only ' the command of authority,' he stated at the outset of his sermon, would have led him to face his task. ' It is beyond the power of any of us to speak as we ought of the great Pastor and Prince of the Church who lies here in the midst of us. It is altogether beyond mine. I have, moreover, a further hindrance— the private sorrow for the loss of the truest of friends, the last in this kind I can ever have in life.' But no man was so qualified to express before a mixed and unique congregation the guiding principles and inspiration of the dead Cardinal's life. He took for his text ' *Let Nehemias be a long time remembered, who raised up for us our walls that were cast down, and set up the gates and the bars, who rebuilt our houses* ' ; and with only a momentary hesitation,

U

he had entered upon the most remarkable sermon of his long ecclesiastical life. He recalled the words spoken by the Pope himself, when he had seen Manning before he hastened back to Rome in answer to the Cardinal's dying summons, that ' this and the loss of the Archbishop of Cologne are two heavy blows to me. The Archbishop for Prussia, and the Cardinal for England, at this moment were of inestimable worth. But the will of the Lord be done.'

' We are all poorer by this loss,' the clear incisive voice, so charged with sadness, went on, while the austere preacher broke into gestures which scarcely anyone had seen him use before, as he was swept by the intense emotions of his own bereavement ; ' the voice which had taught, cheered, elevated, and strengthened tens of thousands in every land, will be heard no more on earth. Henceforth it is mingled with the voices which are eternal. The name Nicholas Wiseman is a panegyric in itself,' Wiseman's beloved disciple proclaimed—still overborne by the darkness of the future which seemed to forebode a frustration of all his own efforts, and the triumph of those who had found it impossible hitherto to work in harmony with him. ' The life which is before you in all its completeness, its unity, its expanding powers, its multiplying honours, its exuberant works, its calm tranquil sunset—all this, which you already know, sets before you a noble and stately picture of a great character, a chief Pastor of the flock, a prince over the Church of God.' Giving full rein to his own dreams and aspirations, which the dead Cardinal had taught him and had shared so fully to the very end, he reviewed the extraordinary growth of Catholicism in England from the days when ' the change of our policy in 1828, 1829, let loose a flood upon this country. It had been ice-bound for generations.

But the thaw had set in. After the frost comes the flow, and as in the floods which inundate the land, all things are lifted, the fruits of the earth, the trees of the forest, the dwellings of men ; so it was in England when the old tradition of three centuries gave way before the larger spirit of modern legislation.' A crisis had come, ' and as the crisis had been preparing for him, so he had been prepared to meet it.' Twenty years of study and life in Rome had trained him for the great mission of his later years, and his contact with the reviving vitality of the Church at its fountain-head had enabled him to see what others could not yet discern. ' Many good and prudent men looked at the same horizon, and saw no signs, no harbinger of the morrow. They treated the Bishop of Melipotamus as sanguine and visionary, one whom hope had distempered. They saw nothing in England but the hard surface of the earth seared by the old storms of religious controversy which had furrowed the land. He saw beneath the surface, and discerned the delicate and vivid lines of new habits of thought, new aspirations after an inheritance which had been forfeited.' And the sudden climax of the Oxford Movement within a few years after his coming to live and work in England had confounded the unbelievers, even though its results had fallen far short of the great hopes that had been raised.

' In these last days,' Monsignor Manning went on, ' I have read again and again such words as these : " Great beginnings, doomed to a great disappointment. Lofty undertakings, and, it must be confessed, closed by a signal failure." Not so fast, men of this world ; not so lordly and confident, wise and prudent of the earth. The ploughing of December may be drenched with the rains of January and the February snows hide all things from the eyes of men. But the sweat of the ploughman and of the sower is not in vain. . . . The conversion of England ! Do men think that we expect the twenty millions of Englishmen to lie down Protestants at night and to wake up Catholics in the morning ? Do they so little know the calm wisdom of the illustrious dead who lies here, the centre of our veneration and of our love, as to think he was such a dreamer of day-dreams, so unreal and fantastic in his hopes ? He was a believer like one who for a hundred and twenty years built the ark ; and a hoper like him who all alone entered imperial Rome, a simple fisherman, but the Vicar of the Son of God. Such were his expectations ; and when he closed his eyes upon England, he had already seen the work he had begun, expanding everywhere, and the traditions of three hundred years everywhere dissolving before it.'

Years had passed since those amazing days when Wiseman, in the restless ardour of his prime, had watched for the happening of miracles, and they had taken place. Of late he had been very little among his people, in the feebleness of his advancing age. But it was as ' a friend, a father, and a pastor, whose memory will be with us while life lasts,' that Manning recalled him now. ' We have all lost somewhat which was our support, our strength, our guidance, our pattern, and our pride. We have lost him who, in the face of this great people, worthily presented the greatness and the majesty of the Universal Church.' In a series of swift, vivid pictures he brought back the memory of that great and varied life in its different stages. ' Some of you remember him, as the companion of your boyhood, upon the bare hills of Durham ; some, in the early morning of his life, in the sanctuaries of Rome ; some see before them now his slender, stooping form, on a bright winter's day, walking to the festival of S. Agnes out of the walls ; some again, drawn up to the full stature of his manhood, rising above the storm, and contending with the calm, commanding voice of reason against the momentary unreason of the people of England ; some, again, can see him vested and arrayed as a Prince of the Church, with the twelve suffragans of England, closing the long procession which, after the silence of three hundred years, opened the first Provincial Synod of Westminster. Some will picture him in the great hall of a Roman palace surrounded by half the Bishops of the world, of every language and of every land, chosen by them as their chief to fashion their words in declaring to the Sovereign Pontiff their filial obedience to the spiritual and temporal power with which God has invested the Vicar of his Son. Some will see him feeble in death, but strong in faith, arrayed as a Pontiff, surrounded by the Chapter of the Church, by word and deed verifying the Apostle's testimony, " I have fought a good fight, I have finished my course, I have kept the faith." And some will cherish, above all these visions of greatness and of glory, the calm and sweet countenance of their best and fastest friend and father, lying in the dim light of his chamber—not of death, but of transit to his crown.'

Five years before his death, when illness had brought him to death's door, Wiseman had composed his own epitaph, simple yet eloquent, dignified in its unaffected humility. He had chosen, too, the place for his own grave, at the centre of the place where his clergy would be buried. The grave-diggers had already done their work, and the grave was waiting as Manning reached the conclusion of his panegyric. ' Bear him forth, right reverend fathers and dear brethren in Jesus Christ,' he said ; ' bear him forth to the green burial ground on the outskirts of this busy wilderness of men. It was his desire to die and to be buried, not amid the glories of Rome, but in the midst of his flock, the first Archbishop of Westminster. Lay him in the midst of that earth, as a shepherd in the midst of his sheep, near to the Holy Cross, the symbol of his life, work and hope ; where the pastors he has ordained will be buried one by one, resting in a circle round about him in death, as they laboured round about him in life. He will be among us still ; his name, his form, his words, his patience, his love of souls, will be our law, our rebuke, our consolation. And yet not so ; it is but the body of this death which you bear forth with tears of loving veneration. He is not here ; he will not be there. He is already where the Great Shepherd of the sheep is numbering his elect, and those who led them to the fold of eternal life. And the hands which have so often blessed you, which anointed you for the altar, fed you with the Bread of Life, are already lifted up in prayer, unceasing day and night, for us one by one, for England, for the Church in all the world.'

The ex-Archdeacon had finished his message, and in leaving the pulpit he had expressed his farewell in public not only to the friend who had given new life to his own activities, but to the prospects of their continuance with the same encouragement as in the past. But his words carried farther than to the hearts of that varied audience who listened in awed silence ; and before many months had passed, he, of whom the dead Cardinal had written[1] to his favourite nephew ' if God gives me strength to undertake a great wrestling match with infidelity, I shall owe it to him,' was to be appointed by the personal decision of the Pope to carry on the work of the master

[1] Ward, II, 183.

whom he had loved and served. But for the present all thoughts of the future were drowned in sorrow as the long procession formed up outside the church, as the hearse started on its way preceded by a carriage which bore the Cardinal's hat and the robes of his principal orders.

' I think a good many will be sorry for me—Protestants, I mean. I don't think they will always think me such a monster,' had been one of the last things Cardinal Wiseman had said[1] as he lay on his death-bed. And as he lay dying, many, including Gladstone, had come to pay their respectful homage at his house. And as the body had lain in state after his death, such crowds had come that only personal friends could be admitted. But the scenes as the funeral procession made its way along the seven miles from Moorfields to Kensal Green were beyond all expectations of sympathetic mourning. ' Not since the State funeral of the Duke of Wellington,' wrote the *Times* in a report[2] filling three columns on the following day, ' has the same interest been evinced to behold what it was thought would be the superb religious pageant of yesterday. Since the death of Cardinal Wolsey, we believe no English Cardinal has been buried in this country, and the funeral obsequies were looked forward to as likely to afford a splendid ceremonial of the most impressive kind. Those indeed who were present in the pro-Cathedral of Moorfields were not disappointed in this expectation. In the streets, however, the procession was remarkable only for its enormous length. It soon, too, got broken and disarranged and mixed up with vehicles of all kinds, and this made the whole outdoor portion of the ceremonial ineffective, except as regards

[1] Ward, II, 515.
[2] The *Times*, February 24th, 1865.

the immense crowds it attracted along the whole seven miles of road it had to traverse from Moorfields to the cemetery. Everywhere, however, the *cortège* was received with marks of profound respect. At least three-fourths of the shops along the line of route were closed—the streets were lined with spectators and every window and balcony was thronged.'

Changed indeed were the days since the same newspaper had led the reckless campaign inciting to public violence against the Cardinal, in anticipation of his return when the Pope had restored the English Hierarchy fifteen years before. ' Altogether the feeling among the public seemed deeper than one of mere curiosity—a wish, perhaps, to forget old differences with the Cardinal and render respect to his memory as an eminent Englishman, and one of the most learned men of his time.' Scarcely less significant than this suggestion of remorse on the part of the *Times* was the fact that among the distinguished congregation which filled the pro-Cathedral to overflowing, was Lord Campbell, whose father had, as Lord Chancellor, delivered the most inflammatory speech against the ' Papal Aggression ' when at the Mansion House he had declared that England would ' trample underfoot the Cardinal's hat.' The whole educated world in London had been profoundly moved by Wiseman's death, and gave expression to its sincere regret. But while the country as a whole awoke for the first time to a realisation of Wiseman's greatness, both as a man and as a Prince of the Catholic Church which he had raised to new life and vigour in England, it was among the Catholic body themselves that the full measure of his moral character and courage and zeal were now appreciated for the first time at their proper worth.

Great reputation as a scholar had come to him at an

extraordinarily early age ; and, as a public lecturer and preacher, he had become famous in England as well as in Rome while he was still in his early thirties. As an administrator at Oscott, and later as a bishop, it had soon been discovered that he had no aptitude or capacity for ordinary routine. But he had the rare and invaluable gift of being able to inspire others, and his whole life had shown a wonderful combination of enthusiasm with profound scholarship, and of courageous leadership with the tenderest human sympathy. Only through having been trained for a long period outside England could he have approached the task of his life with that freshness of idealism, which could not possibly have developed adequately in the restricted conditions of England during his own youth. He came back free from the old prejudices that inevitably dominated Catholics who had only just secured their political emancipation ; and at the same time inspired by a sense of the great Catholic revival in Europe which was an unknown factor to the small remnant of English Catholics. Free from their prejudices towards all Protestants, however well-meaning, who desired a better understanding with Rome ; and free from the fears of renewed persecution which prevented them from even contemplating any missionary activity in England, he had arrived at the very time when a coincidence of accidents had left the ground ready for an immediate advance. And it was the very fact of his Roman training that had made him welcome with open arms both the earnest converts to Catholicism from the Oxford Movement and the swarms of destitute Catholic refugees from the Irish famine.

Only a man who was capable of unlimited sympathy with both these new forces could have welded them into a coherent body, and assisted their rapid assimilation under conditions which had previously made the Church in England almost the personal possession of a small and exclusive class. Wiseman succeeded not only in restoring the Hierarchy but in establishing it securely on a basis of cordial co-operation within a few years. And when, in his last years, he could look with satisfaction upon a Church that was growing continually more coherent and harmonious, while it expanded with extraordinary rapidity in size and in the scope of its activities, he could feel at last that there was one man at least, discovered and fostered and promoted by himself, until in due time he became his own successor—whose conversation[1] he had found so often ' to touch a chord which renews old vibrations or recalls and evokes unevoked sympathies ' and who realised as no other realised, that the leader of the restored Hierarchy must be more concerned for the needs of the poor than of the rich among his flock, that he must never fail in encouragement either to the converts who had still to find their moorings or to the old Catholics who had lost the energy of freemen ; and that upon his shoulders must fall the enormous task of guiding each different group by its own special path in the persistent progress towards winning back England to her allegiance to the Catholic Church.

[1] Ward, II, 183.

Nil sapientiae odiosismus acumine nimio

Nil sapientiae odiosismus acumine nimio

BIBLIOGRAPHY

THE following are the principal sources of information which have been consulted :

WORKS BY CARDINAL WISEMAN

Recollections of the Last Four Popes (popular edition).
Appeal to the English People.
Lectures on the Catholic Church (1836).
Fabiola.
Essays on Various Subjects (edited with biographical introduction by Rev. J. Murphy).

Life of Cardinal Wiseman, by Wilfrid Ward.
Life of Cardinal Newman, by Wilfrid Ward.
W. G. Ward and the Catholic Revival, by Wilfrid Ward.
Letters of Cardinal Newman.
Life of Cardinal Manning, by E. S. Purcell.
Life of Ambrose Phillips de Lisle, by E. S. Purcell.
Cardinal Manning, by Shane Leslie.
Life of Father Faber, by Bowden.
Recollections of Augustus Welby Pugin.
Life of Bishop Ullathorne, by Abbot Butler.
Apologia pro Vita Sua, by Cardinal Newman.
Life and Letters of Lord Macaulay, by Sir G. O. Trevelyan.
Life of Bishop Grant, by Grace Ramsay.
The Sequel to Catholic Emancipation, by Bishop Bernard Ward.
The Dublin Review.

INDEX